D1383562

They
Led
by
Teaching

Kappa Delta Pi Biennial
2002–2004

They Led by Teaching reflects the Society's commitment to study issues and practices relating to the biennial theme. This volume is among the books that the Society commissions each biennium to explore critical issues in education in ways that develop new knowledge and new understandings.

Kappa Delta Pi, International Honor Society in Education, was founded in 1911 and is dedicated to scholarship and excellence in education. The Society promotes among its intergenerational membership of educators the development and dissemination of worthy educational ideas and practices, enhances the continuous growth and leadership of its diverse membership, fosters inquiry and reflection of significant educational issues, and maintains a high degree of professional fellowship.

They
Led
by
Teaching

Edited by Sherry L. Field
and Michael J. Berson

Foreword by Michael P. Wolfe

KAPPA DELTA PI

International Honor Society in Education
Indianapolis, Indiana

© 2003 by Kappa Delta Pi, International Honor Society in Education

All rights reserved. No part of this book may be reproduced or utilized in any form or by any means, electronic or mechanical, including photocopying, recording, or by any information storage and retrieval system, without permission in writing from the publisher.

Printed in the United States of America
03 04 05 06 07   5 4 3 2 1

Direct all inquiries to the Director of Publications, Kappa Delta Pi, 3707 Woodview Trace, Indianapolis, IN 46268-1158.

Executive Director
Michael P. Wolfe

Director of Publications
Kathie-Jo Arnoff

Editors
Karen L. Allen
Helen McCarthy
Grant E. Mabie

Cover Design
Chuck Jarrell

Interior Design and Layout
Katherine J. Jarrell

To order, call Kappa Delta Pi Headquarters (800-284-3167) or visit KDP online (*www.kdp.org*). Quantity discounts for more than 20 copies.
KDP Order Code 535

Library of Congress Cataloging-in-Publication Data

They led by teaching / edited by Sherry L. Field and Michael J. Berson ; foreword by Michael P. Wolfe.
       p. cm.
Includes bibliographical references.
   ISBN 0-912099-41-0 (pbk.)
   1. Teachers—United States—Biography. 2. Educators—United States—Biography. I. Field, Sherry L. II. Berson, Michael J. III. Kappa Delta Pi (Honor society)

   LA2311.T52 2003
   370'.92'2—dc22   2003020191

Contents

Part One
Educational Leadership and Reflection 5

Part Two
Teaching Young Children 47

Part Three
Forging New Cultural and Social Ground 101

Foreword

Kappa Delta Pi, International Honor Society in Education, was founded in 1911, based on high standards of scholarship among men and women, on faculty supervision and participation, and on the broad principles of democracy, without any racial, religious, or other restrictions not affecting the member's standing as an educator (Hall-Quest 1938, 44). From its inception, Kappa Delta Pi established and maintained high standards of professional scholarship. The founders made provisions for united efforts through the fellowship of minds engaged in the study of problems basic to education as a science and a profession (Hall-Quest 1938, 14).

During the past 83 years, the Society has published scholarly journals, research studies, lectures, and books that address issues, practices, and important people affecting the field of education. The Kappa Delta Pi legacy in publications includes authors whose influence continues to shape programs and practices in schools today. Educators such as John Dewey, Jean Piaget, Ernest Boyer, Florence Stratemeyer, and Margaret Mead from the distant past were prominent authors. Present-day authors include Howard Gardner, Maxine Greene, John Goodlad, Linda Darling-Hammond, and Nel Noddings. These eminent scholars and members of Kappa Delta Pi's Laureate Chapter are a few examples of the Society's commitment to scholarship, teaching, and research.

Also part of Kappa Delta Pi's legacy is paying tribute to educators who have made a lasting impression on education. *They Led by Teaching* captures—through biographical scholarship—the lives of important educators who are part of the legacy of excellence in teaching. This collection of biographies is another example of professional scholarship. It is a timeless contribution to professional literature, in that the stories of nine teacher leaders have been forever captured in biographical form. The authors pay tribute to educators who influenced the lives of students through their teaching prowess and, in turn, affected the education profession.

Kappa Delta Pi is pleased to present *They Led by Teaching* to the educational community. As a leader in helping teachers, administrators, and professors prepare for the future, Kappa Delta Pi is dedicated to providing high-quality scholarship that preserves the best of the past and present to invent the future. The Society's efforts in publications continue to be a source of insight and knowledge that will assist educators to discover meaning in their work.

This book presents chapters by Kappa Delta Pi scholars noted for their work in critical areas of education. Reactions to clusters of chapters by eminent Kappa Delta Pi Laureates makes *They Led by Teaching* a valuable contribution to educational literature and an extension of the Kappa Delta Pi legacy.

Reference

Hall-Quest, A. L. 1938. *Kappa Delta Pi, 1911–1936.* New York: MacMillian.

Michael P. Wolfe
Executive Director
Kappa Delta Pi

Acknowledgments

The editors and publisher would like to thank the following education professionals, all leaders in Kappa Delta Pi, for reading and critically analyzing early drafts of the chapters.

Barbara Day
University of North Carolina
Chapel Hill, North Carolina

Barbara S. Stern
James Madison University
Harrisburg, Virginia

Billie J. Enz
Arizona State University
Tempe, Arizona

F. Morgan Simpson
Auburn University at Montgomery
Montgomery, Alabama

Geneva Gay
University of Washington
Seattle, Washington

Harold D. Drummond
University of New Mexico
Albuquerque, New Mexico

Ronald W. Wilhelm
University of North Texas
Denton, Texas

Susan Brown
University of Portland
Portland, Oregon

Vincent R. McGrath
Mississippi State University
Mississippi State, Mississippi

The authors would like to thank Michael P. Wolfe, Kathie-Jo Arnoff, Karen L. Allen, Helen McCarthy, and Grant E. Mabie for their tremendous contribution in supporting this book from its inception through to its final production. Their skill, patience, and thoughtful insight embodied the essence of commitment and quality, which are reflected thoughout the text.

Introduction

by Sherry L. Field and Michael J. Berson

They Led by Teaching was conceived a few years ago as we discussed prominent figures whose insight and vision contributed to education and who had made an impact on the field. We asked our colleagues and students who they would like to know more about, who they had questions about, and who they would most like to interview if given the opportunity. A list of several dozen educators was produced. We sought to prepare a collection of educational biographies, diverse in nature, but with an overarching theme. The theme, that of significant contributions to pedagogic and content knowledge in the field of teaching, was revisited time and again as we selected key educational figures to be included in the volume. Five women and four men were finally chosen.

At first glance, the subjects found within *They Led by Teaching* may seem an unusual mix. Their career and research emphases, areas of specialization, theoretical underpinnings, and political stances are disparate. Closer inspection reveals, however, several commonalities. Each subject lived and worked in a time of extraordinary scientific and educational change. Each subject devoted lifelong careers to the promotion of scientifically based education, development of curriculum, research on pedagogy and content, and improvement of teaching and learning. Each subject impressively worked within the larger milieu of social change.

Biography and Education

Educational historian Barbara Finkelstein (1998, 4) stated, "Biography is to history what a telescope is to the stars." Interest in educational biography has grown substantially over the past two decades. According to Carter and Doyle (1996, 123), "there has been a rapidly expanding interest within the teaching and teacher education community in narrative and story as forms of both inquiry and pedagogy." Kridel (1998, 3) suggested that this development "has promise as a way of bridging critical relationships," while Rollyson (1992, 1) asserted that "scholars from many disciplines have been attracted to biography as a way of dealing with social, political, cultural, and psychological issues and of reaching [a larger] audience." Recognizing the possibilities of educational biography to establish "discourse among the varied, often polarized communities of our era" (Kridel 1998, 11), "provoke comparison" (Rose 1983, 5), and "consider the universal in a single human life" (Kridel 1998, 11), this volume places educational biography prominently into the realm of teachers and teacher education.

For both teachers and teacher educators, educational biography serves multiple purposes. First, biographies may reveal important, often overlooked historical background about the subject and the times in which the subject lived and worked. Second, biographies present opportunities for perspective taking—and increased personal practical knowledge. Connelly and Clandinin (1990, 2), who conducted research emphasizing narrative perspective and inquiry, concluded, "the study of the ways humans experience the world" enhances a teacher's ability to integrate personal practical knowledge into the larger world of education, which they see as "the construction and reconstruction of personal and social stories." Finally, the study of biographies may help provoke deep reflection on the improvement of teaching. By reading and reflecting upon an educator's life story, considerations toward refinement and restructuring of the teaching process are possible.

Organization of the Book

Although authors were not asked to follow a specific format, each chapter does include biographical information related to the subject's life and career. Within this open-ended format, chapters feature the following:

- key biographical information about the subject;
- educational background and philosophy about teaching;
- lasting effects upon education; and
- contemporary relationship to teaching and teacher education.

The chapters are organized into three sections, each followed by insightful commentary from a Kappa Delta Pi Laureate. The first part, "Educational Leadership and Reflection," features biographies of William Chandler Bagley, Hollis Leland Caswell, and Ralph Tyler, three educators who recognized that teacher education and knowledge about the curriculum were central to schooling. In this part, J. Wesley Null writes about Bagley's contributions, especially in the field of teacher education. Bagley represented a balanced perspective of education and strongly advocated for high quality professional training of teachers to prepare educators for engaging students in learning and fostering a well-educated society. Lynn Matthew Burlbaw's chapter reveals the history of Caswell's school studies and how the implications drawn from them impacted educational and policy decisions for the next several decades. By collecting, analyzing, and reporting data from hundreds of schools across the nation, Caswell painted a revealing portrait of the status of education in the 1930s. Daniel W. Stuckart and Michael J. Berson's biography analyzes the forces that shaped Tyler's life. Importantly, Tyler's stance toward curriculum provided a helpful framework for countless curriculum workers in the 20th century.

Kappa Delta Pi Laureate O. L. Davis, Jr. draws upon his life's work of research and writing in curriculum history and foundations of education to synthesize the biographies in Part One. He reports the effects on education of the contributions of Bagley, Caswell, and Tyler.

"Teaching Young Children," the second part of this volume, illuminates the lives of three women—Patty Smith Hill, Alice Miel, and Maycie Southall—whose lives centered on early childhood and elementary education. Despite following what might be considered a "traditional" path, each portrayed resilience and fierce independence in her work. Hill's illustrious career in kindergarten education is reported by Rose A. Rudnitski. In this chapter, Hill's lasting contributions to the whole of kindergarten education, including curriculum, child needs, classroom structure, and teacher preparation, are reported. The life of Alice Miel and her commitment to elementary school civic education are recounted by Elizabeth Anne Yeager. Emphasizing the preparation of children for active citizenship, Miel helped thousands of pre- and in-service teachers think about how democracy would play out in their classrooms. Sherry L. Field highlights the productive career of Southall, whose impact on both southern teachers and international educators was profound. The mosaic of interests enhancing Southall's work included supervision, local curriculum development, and mentoring.

Laureate Bettye M. Caldwell's expertise in early childhood frames her commentary on the biographies of Hill, Miel, and Southall in Part Two. She notes that each woman made powerful contributions to education in spite of the marginalization of the work of many early childhood workers in the 20th century.

Finally, the third part, "Forging New Cultural and Social Ground," includes the biographies of W. E. B. Du Bois, Hilda Taba, and Myra Sadker. Derrick P. Alridge's chapter about Du Bois contextualizes his research, writing, and activism. Alridge provides a practical snapshot into Du Bois' educational thought. The philosophical complexities of Hilda Taba are captured by Mark Isham. Her ideas about the inquiry process, and the part that she played in making inquiry relevant to children's lives, are revealed. David M. Sadker's personal tribute to Myra Sadker reveals insights into her early life and their life and work together. Battling gender bias and engagement in the "invisible" civil rights struggle were at the heart of Sadker's memorable contributions to education.

William Ayers, also a Kappa Delta Pi Laureate, responds to the political and social climates encircling the professional lives of Du Bois, Taba, and Sadker. His essay highlights significant educational reform that can be attributed to the work of this trio of educators.

Each of the profiled educators has created a legacy that not only defines the past of education, but also seeds the potential for continual reflection and renewal. The lessons captured in their life stories are timeless and have enduring relevancy in our continually changing world.

References

Carter, K., and W. Doyle. 1996. Personal narrative and life history in learning to teach. In *Handbook of research on teacher education: A project of the Association of Teacher Educators*, 2d ed., ed. J. Sikula, T. J. Buttery, and E. Guyton, 120–42. New York: Macmillan Library Reference.

Connelly, F. M., and D. J. Clandinin. 1990. Stories of experience and narrative inquiry. *Educational Researcher* 19(5): 2–14.

Finkelstein, B. 1998. Revealing human agency: The uses of biography in the study of educational history. In *Writing educational biography: Explorations in qualitative research*, ed. C. Kridel, 45–60. New York: Garland Publishing.

Kridel, C., ed. 1998. *Writing educational biography: Explorations in qualitative research*. New York: Garland Publishing.

Rollyson, C. E. 1992. *Biography: An annotated bibliography*. Pasadena, Calif.: Salem Press.

Rose, P. 1983. *Parallel lives: Five Victorian marriages*. New York: Knopf.

Part One
Educational Leadership and Reflection

Chapter 1
William C. Bagley: Scholar, Gentleman, and Committed Educator of Teachers
J. Wesley Null

Chapter 2
Hollis Leland Caswell: Teacher, Principal, Professor, Dean, President, Mentor, and Friend
Lynn Matthew Burlbaw

Chapter 3
Ralph Tyler: A 20th-Century Innovator
Daniel W. Stuckart and Michael J. Berson

Laureate Commentary on Part One
By Their Leadership, They Taught
O. L. Davis, Jr.

Chapter 1

William C. Bagley: Scholar, Gentleman, and Committed Educator of Teachers

by J. Wesley Null

William Chandler Bagley (1874–1946), an impressively active scholar who dedicated his life to the betterment of the teaching profession, founded, critiqued, or participated in every significant academic issue that arose during the first half of the 20th century. His 50-year professional career spanned numerous highly influential intellectual movements—child study, developmentalism, social behaviorism, eugenics, scientific management, Progressive education, intelligence testing, Essentialism, and many others. Though he lived and worked through times of great change, he remained faithful to several fundamental principles of scholarship, scientific investigation, and teacher education. He authored or coauthored more than 25 books; published hundreds of articles in dozens of journals; founded and edited the *Intermountain Educator* and the *Journal of Educational Psychology* (among other publications); and taught on the faculties of Montana State Normal College, Oswego Normal School, the University of Illinois at Urbana-Champaign, and, finally, Teachers College of Columbia University. With all of his work, Bagley worked relentlessly to improve the fields of educational psychology, teacher education, history of education, and curriculum. From the time he received his Ph.D. from Cornell in 1900 to the year of his death, when he was still serving as editor of *School and Society*, Bagley contributed as much as any other American educator to the improvement of the teaching profession and the formation of schools dedicated specifically to the preparation of teachers for public school service (Null 2001a).

Educators distinguish Bagley primarily for two positions he took during the last half of his professional career. The first of these two positions, his critique of educational determinism and what he viewed as the inappropriate application of intelligence testing to the practical work of schooling, was largely ignored by leading developers of intelligence tests and other individuals eager to apply these new and incompletely formed theories to educational practice (Bagley 1925). A second position, most often associated with Bagley's "An Essentialist's Platform for the Advancement of American Education" (1938a), has been narrowly viewed as conservative or reactionary. Those who have made this assumption have paid little or no attention to Bagley's lifelong respect and admiration for John Dewey, his participation in previous Progressive pedagogical movements such as Herbartianism at the turn of the century, and his cautious acceptance of some Progressive ideas, for example the "project method," albeit in moderation (Bagley 1933). A limited categorization of Bagley as merely an "Essentialist" or one whose main contribution was a critique of intelligence testing ignores the majority of his professional career and ultimately obfuscates more than it clarifies. An inspection of Bagley's life, with a particular focus on his years as a student, his depiction of several "master teachers," and his early career, should illuminate an important period in the development of education in the United States and begin to reclaim a lost educator's valuable contributions to educational thought, practice, and teacher education (Ravitch 2001).

Bagley's Childhood and Public School Education

The first 20 years of Bagley's life provided few clues that he would go on to pursue teaching as a lifelong career. Little is known about his parents, William Chase Bagley and Ruth Walker Bagley, except for his father's occupation as a hospital superintendent in Detroit. However, evidence does reveal that his father's genealogical line stretched back to Orlando Bagley, who emigrated from Ipswich, England, to Boston in 1658 (Bagley Family Origins Genealogy n.d.). William Chandler Bagley was born on 15 March 1874 in Detroit, Michigan. After his early youth, the family apparently relocated to Weymouth, Massachusetts. The town bordered Quincy on the east, where Bagley attended elementary school (Bagley 1938c). As an elementary student, Bagley was educated in an environment that he later described as "Progressive" in a style fashioned after Francis W. Parker, who had worked to improve the Quincy public school system (Bagley 1938c). As a child, he was particularly impressed with his principal and first male teacher, William H. Bartlett. Bagley (1936, 427–37) later described Bartlett, a graduate of West Point and a Union Army Officer during the Civil War, as a "man of portly proportions" who moved with an "easy, graceful carriage" and was always "well groomed and clean-shaven." Bagley also was impressed with his elementary principal's emphasis on teaching in addition to his administrative duties, his ability to teach with a well-controlled and articulate voice, and his impressive mastery of subject matter. In his description of the instruction he received in Mr. Bartlett's school, Bagley, nearly 60 years later, recalled the school's garden and "projects" that were planned and cared for by the students, the "visual instruction" that he and other students received with stereopticon slides projected by lantern light, and the general attitude of teachers who saw their pupils as individuals and took account of their interests and needs. Teachers referred to all of these techniques, Bagley (1938c) remembered, as "Quincy methods."

By the time Bagley attended high school, his family had moved back to Detroit. He attended a selective public high school that offered Latin and other more traditional subjects. As with his elementary school experience, his principal affected him significantly as a "refined and scholarly gentleman" whose place in public education ended soon after Bagley's high school graduation. Bagley (1936) favorably described his high school principal, whom he could not recall by name 45 years later, as a "scholarly gentleman of the intellectually aristocratic type" whose tenure as principal ended with the transition of American public education from a selective institution to one that emphasized mass public instruction for "all of the children of all of the people."

From Michigan Agricultural College to Rural Michigan One-Room School

After graduation from high school in the spring of 1891, Bagley entered Michigan Agricultural College (MAC, later Michigan State University) with 130 other young men, most of whom were from the back-country farms of Michigan. At MAC, Bagley studied the application of the natural sciences to farming. He was particularly influenced by Roscoe C. Kedzie, his septuagenarian professor of chemistry. Similar to Bartlett, Kedzie impressed Bagley (1936, 429) with his ability to lecture in a "clear well-organized discourse" that Bagley never heard surpassed in all of his years around college and university professors. Significant to Bagley's graduate study at MAC was his experience with "experiments" or "projects" that the students conducted in their daily work on the farms around East Lansing. For one "project," Kedzie's colleague, Perry G. Holden, assigned Bagley an experiment in which he was to plant two adjoining plots of potatoes, one in which the potatoes were planted deep and the other shallow. At the end of the growing season, Bagley was to compare the growth of the two rows of potatoes to determine whether deep or shallow planting produced better results. After a determination that shallow planting was optimal, Bagley (1936) published his first article in the official bulletin of the Agricultural Experiment Station.

A second professor at Michigan Agricultural College, Howard Edwards, also impacted Bagley's thinking for the rest of his career. Edwards, an English professor and later a president of Rhode Island State College, impressed Bagley (1930, 713–14) as a "gentleman in the finest sense of the word—a man who gracefully and instinctively did the right thing in the right way" and who, with his high-minded integrity, "hated pose and cant and smugness and hypocrisy with a righteous hatred." In addition to his personal characteristics, Edwards's teaching style captured Bagley. Providing the young college student with his first experience with masterpieces of literature, Edwards, according to Bagley (1930), possessed the ability to open the world of literature in a creative style, to make pieces of literature such as Hamlet, Macbeth, and King Lear "tingle with life," and to weave the magic of artistry in the classroom that Bagley believed every student should experience sometime in his life. Of particular importance to Bagley's (1930) remembrance of Edwards was his tradition of inviting all of the graduating students to his house just prior to graduation and entertaining them with an elaborate banquet that included poetry written specifically for each of the students by their beloved English professor.

Upon graduation from MAC in the spring of 1895, Bagley was unable to locate any type of employment for which the agricultural college had prepared him. No doubt influenced by the depression of the mid-1890s, Bagley made a decision that would significantly influence the rest of his life. He chose to accept a teaching position in a rural one-room school near Garth, Michigan, a sawmill village of Delta County in the upper peninsula of the state. In this small setting, Bagley began to think of the possibilities for the application of scientific thought to the improvement of education. As someone with scientific training, he began to read all the available evidence on the science of teaching and was subsequently unimpressed. In fact, Bagley (1944) later recalled that, when he began to read the science of education literature, scientists had more well-established facts and laws to guide them in the raising of pigs than they had in the raising of children.

Bagley accepted this first teaching position with no intention whatsoever of it being anything more than a stop-gap assignment, yet he found the practical work with students so interesting, challenging, and enjoyable that he decided to look more closely into graduate schools of psychology and the application of science to the study of education. Bagley (1944) was delighted to learn of the serious movements that had begun in those years toward the study of the mind and its mental growth from a modern, scientific perspective. Desiring to find laboratory methods similar to those he had experienced at MAC, Bagley enrolled for a summer term at the University of Chicago on 30 June 1896. Bagley received his first experience with psychology and earned three "B's," one "C," and two "Pass" grades in courses that included introductory psychology (then called philosophy of modern science), laboratory psychology, psychology of childhood, early history of education, and the physiology of nerves and muscles (University of Chicago 1896).

Bagley's Study of Psychology at the University of Wisconsin at Madison and Cornell

After his one semester at the University of Chicago, Bagley returned to his same rural teaching position in Delta County, Michigan. After another year, he moved on to the University of Wisconsin at Madison, where he continued his study of psychology. In Madison, Bagley worked closely with Polish psychologist Joseph Jastrow and pedagogy professor Michael Vincent O'Shea. Jastrow introduced Bagley to the functional, practical side of psychology that was attempting to solve "real-world problems" directly related to the improvement of education. O'Shea was an encouraging and ambitious teacher whom Bagley (1936, 434–35) later remembered as "a strikingly handsome man," who was "always immaculately groomed," and who was "the most nearly perfect gentleman" that Bagley had ever known.

Though O'Shea's work in child study and developmentalism interested Bagley somewhat, he directed his efforts more toward Jastrow's psychology and the attempted establishment of educational decisions on sound, psychological principles. Jastrow had been a fellow student with John Dewey and James McKeen Cattell under G. Stanley Hall at The Johns Hopkins University (Boring 1950). He introduced Bagley to a different type of psychology than he later would study with E. B. Titchener at Cornell. With Jastrow, Bagley obviously was interested enough in the study of individual differences to complete a master's thesis related to this topic. Bagley's (1898) "A Study in the Correlation of Mental and Motor Ability in School Children" reported measurements of school children at the Fifth Ward School in Madison. A commonly held belief was that physical attributes, such as head size, grip strength, reaction time to stimulus, and the steadiness of hand, were somehow related to mental ability (Flugel 1933). Though he exhibited early interest in functionalist psychology, perhaps by institutional necessity, Bagley studied only one year in Wisconsin and earned the master's degree in 1898. Though he completed his degree, the extent to which Bagley's Wisconsin year affected his thinking on psychology was minimal compared to his later studies at Cornell.

In the fall of 1898, 24-year-old Bagley began his doctoral studies in psychology under E. B. Titchener at Cornell. The decision to attend Cornell and work with Titchener firmly placed Bagley's doctoral work in the "structuralist" category that Titchener advocated. For someone such as Bagley, who held interest in the application of psychology to education, Cornell was not the school to attend (Boring 1950). During his time with Titchener, Bagley was encouraged, and required, to conduct psychological studies that differed in important ways from the rest of the nation's psychologists, the functionalists, who also could be referred to as pragmatists (Bagley n.d.). Titchener chose not to concern himself with the practical applications of his science, and Bagley was quickly indoctrinated into Titchener's view of "pure" science. As did other students in Titchener's laboratory, Bagley (1936, 435–36) began to refer to philosophers who wrote about the nature of the mind as "arm-chair" psychologists rather than real "laboratory men" or "dyed-in-the-world" scientists. As both a student and (upon graduation) an assistant in Titchener's laboratory, Bagley received a clear notion of the scientific method, an understanding of the meaning of scholarship in any field, lessons on the importance of drawing conclusions from incomplete data, and instruction on the necessity for keeping personal prejudice out of research.

Bagley (1900) graduated from Cornell with his Ph.D. after completing his dissertation, "The Apperception of the Spoken Sentence: A Study in the Psychology of Language." With this study, Bagley sought to uncover how the adult, human consciousness perceived words differently when they were read individually as opposed to within the context of complete sentences. Interestingly, and in keeping with Titchener's brand of psychology, nowhere in the entire dissertation did Bagley refer to students, schools, or teachers. Nevertheless, Bagley likely appreciated the applications that his study might have to the improvement of the teaching profession, an aim that would occupy his attention for the remainder of his life. After earning his doctorate, Bagley remained in Titchener's laboratory for one more year, primarily because he was unable to find employment in the "public school service." On 14 August 1901, Bagley married fellow doctoral student Florence Maclean Winger, and the two of them quickly relocated to St. Louis, Missouri, where Bagley served as principal of Merrimac Elementary School beginning in September.

Bagley's First Collegiate Appointment in Dillon, Montana

After only a year in St. Louis, Florence Bagley's respiratory difficulties necessitated a move to a more hospitable climate. Therefore, the couple moved to Dillon, Montana, in August 1902, where Bagley accepted a position at that state's first teacher-training institution, Montana State Normal School (MSNS). Bagley assumed the responsibilities of professor of psychology and pedagogy and director of the Teacher Training School. As a typical normal school, MSNS professors divided instruction into the normal and training departments. Teachers in the normal department formed the general education equivalent and instructed students in courses such as physiology, English, history, physics, biology, German, and calculus. After students completed approximately two years of general coursework, Bagley directed them toward the more advanced topics of psychology and its relation to teaching. When students had a firm foundation in psychology, Bagley arranged for them to conduct their practice teaching in the Dillon Public Schools. As one of the first psychologists to begin making such changes in Montana's teacher-training system, Bagley was viewed almost instantly as a scientific expert on educational decision-making and prospects for improvement.

Bagley (1902a; 1902b; 1902c) worked toward the improvement of education for both his normal school students and the students of the Dillon Public Schools. In an interesting twist of fate, school board members released the superintendent of the Dillon Public Schools, and, after a good deal of controversy, Bagley accepted the superintendency on 21 January 1903. In its coverage of the former superintendent's release, *The Dillon Examiner* (1903a) reported that the school board "wished the position for another." This "other" was not specified, but Bagley was likely the desired candidate. In fact, he accepted the position, without newspaper reports of any other candidates, only 10 days following the previous superintendent's resignation (*Dillon Tribune* 1903a). This appointment to superintendent permitted Bagley to assume what many Dillonites viewed as a revolutionary position. He now occupied the twin roles of Director of the MSNS Training School and primary decision-maker for the entire school district. From this vantage, he assured that all normal school teachers-in-preparation could work closely with Dillon's teachers and students. Also, Dillon's students benefited from more intense instruction and a significant number of additional teachers. To many Dillon residents, however, the most laudable aspect of Bagley's new dual position was his refusal to accept any sort of payment for his role as superintendent. Every mention of Bagley as the new superintendent, in both papers, proudly emphasized that he worked "without pay" (*Dillon Examiner* 1903b; *Dillon Tribune* 1903b).

Science on the Frontier and the Growth to College Status

After their completion of normal school requirements and a foundation in psychology, students at MSNS then entered the classroom to begin their observations with "critic teachers," or, in contemporary terms, "cooperating teachers." Critic teachers created the link between the normal school and the public school classroom. Not all residents, however, reacted positively to Bagley's ideas for change. Some of them initially criticized his emphasis on experimentation with children. They viewed him as a "foreigner" who targeted Dillon's students as "guinea pigs." Nonetheless, Bagley quickly earned the admiration of Dillon's residents and became highly regarded throughout the community (Spiegle 1958).

In spring 1903, after Bagley's first full year on the faculty, the normal school adjusted its curriculum profoundly. Offering bachelor's and master's of pedagogy degrees, the school extended the curriculum and changed its name to Montana State Normal College (MSNC 1903). Faculty meeting minutes from this period indicate Bagley's heavy involvement with the changes in curriculum; his presence on campus no doubt aided the school in its ability to enlarge its curriculum offerings (Western Montana College 1903). This expansion to college status corresponded with yearly increases in student enrollment. From a graduating class of 3 in 1901 to a class of 21 in 1903 and 24 in 1906, news regarding the college and its efforts to improve Montana education was overwhelmingly positive (Western Montana College n.d.). In the spring of 1904, Bagley accepted the position of vice president for the upcoming 1904–05 school year and retained his director of training and professor of psychology and pedagogy appointments. Thus, since his arrival in August 1902, Bagley had quickly assumed the roles of superintendent, director of the state's only teacher-training school, and vice president of the Montana State Normal College.

Bagley's Work with Montana's Teachers in County Teachers' Institutes

In addition to these three important roles, Bagley traveled throughout the state to extend the teachings of the MSNC. College administrators required each professor of psychology and pedagogy to instruct, throughout the year, at various county teachers' institutes. Additionally, the state superintendent of public instruction required each county superintendent, usually in fall or summer, to host a teachers' institute. During his five years in Dillon, Bagley instructed at no fewer than 23 of these institutes and became well known by teachers and administrators throughout the state (*Intermountain Educator* 1906).

Naturally, Bagley's lessons for Montana's teachers corresponded closely with the classes he taught at MSNC. Specifically interested in, but somewhat skeptical of, psychology's application to education, Bagley's initial lectures at each of these institutes consisted of his definition of psychology as "a collection of facts about consciousness." Bagley (1903a) also emphasized those aspects of psychology that perhaps could be applied to education. Importantly, Bagley (1903a, 1) also stressed that "the utility of formal psychology to the practical work of teaching has probably been overrated." As he pondered the relevance of psychology to education, Bagley (1903a, 2) prioritized several important attributes of good teachers: "The teacher needs (1) common sense, (2) sympathy with childlife, (3) knowledge of subject matter to be taught, (4) cleverness at devices—and then formal psychology. The last named cannot, in itself, compensate for deficiencies in the others."

Though acutely aware of the limitations of psychology, Bagley held firm to the conviction that science and psychology provided the best available insight into the improvement of instruction. Other lectures that Bagley (1903b) delivered at the county teachers' institutes included:

- "The Function of the Mind," in which he spoke on life as the adjustment to future situations by the collection of experiences;
- "Attention," which he defined as a state or pattern of consciousness;
- "Habit and Fatigue," in which he distinguished between automatic and reflex actions and spoke on the pedagogical importance of understanding mental fatigue; and
- "Memory and Language," in which he discussed the importance of language and its role in educational advancement.

As has been seen, the possibility, or impossibility, of psychology's application to education occupied Bagley's thinking considerably during this period. Obviously eager to improve teaching through the application of science, Bagley attempted to discover the underlying principles behind the teaching process. Through the discovery and then teaching of these underlying principles to future teachers, he hoped that the educative process could be made more efficient. However, Bagley's mentally disciplined manner led him to hold doubts about the importance to education of experimental psychology in general and functionalist (practical) psychology in particular. As Bagley (1903b, 6) noted, "Works on educational psychology are of two kinds: (1) books written by psychologists who have little or no practical knowledge of the elementary school and its requirements; (2) books written by school men who have an inadequate knowledge of psychology. Of these two types the former possesses, probably, the greater value." Indicative of his views toward what he would later term "the much-abused cult of 'Child-Study'," Bagley (1905, 185; 1903b, 6) also wrote that the "standard works on child psychology are, however, numerous enough."

As he continued his study of psychology and its application to education, Bagley (1905) eventually concluded four years of reading and writing with the publication of his first major work, *The Educative Process*. As an impressively comprehensive study of an early "science of education," *The Educative Process* became a popular text for introductory educational psychology courses throughout the country and was reprinted at least 20 times over the next two decades (Null 2000). The book pioneered this century's emerging field of educational psychology and contained a reference to one of the first transfer-of-training experiments in the country, a study conducted by Bagley's MSNC colleague Carrie B. Squires. Before leaving Dillon, Bagley also founded the *Intermountain Educator*, which was the first publication in the Rocky Mountain region dedicated specifically to education (Null 2001a). In June 1906, after he had established considerable success with the publication of *The Educative Process*, Bagley accepted the position of Director of Teacher Training at the well-known school of Herbartian pedagogy in Oswego, New York.

The 'Fountainhead of Teacher Education' and an Overview of Bagley's Efforts at the University of Illinois

At the turn of the century, Oswego Normal School, which has been referred to as the "Fountainhead of Teacher Education," was well known throughout the country as one of the best teacher-preparation institutions in the nation. In a significant step forward in his career, Bagley served as superintendent of the practice school from fall of 1906 to spring of 1908 (Rogers 1961). At Oswego, Bagley apparently impressed the staff and students with his dynamic personality, his demanding attitude, and his ability always to "know what his students were doing and how much they knew" (Rogers 1961, 112). After two school years in Oswego, Bagley accepted a position related directly to the education of teachers, this time at the University of Illinois at Urbana-Champaign.

In the fall of 1908, Bagley began work in a position at the University of Illinois that would earn him national recognition in the field of teacher education. After only one full semester, he secured approval from school officials to begin a practice school in what was previously known as the University Academy (Johnson and Johanningmeier 1972). During his nine-year stay at the University of Illinois, Bagley brought significantly favorable publicity to the university, served as a cofounder and coeditor of the *Journal of Educational Psychology*, worked tirelessly to promote the necessity for professional teacher-preparation institutions, provided "boundless energy and a large vision" to the university's school of education, and founded the well-known honor society Kappa Delta Pi (Johnson and Johanningmeier 1972; Johanningmeier 1967; Hall-Quest 1938).

In 1914, Bagley's participation in a debate drew the attention of a dean at the best-known teachers' college in the nation, if not the world. In St. Paul, Minnesota, at the 52nd annual meeting of the National Education Association, Bagley (1914) debated David Snedden (1914) over the "Fundamental Distinctions between Liberal and Vocational Education." At that meeting, Dean James Earl Russell of Teachers College, Columbia University, observed Bagley as he critiqued Snedden's emphasis on vocational education. Dean Russell later remarked that anyone who had the speaking abilities of Bagley should speak in such debates as a member of the Teachers College faculty. In three short years, Dean Russell would get his wish; Bagley accepted an appointment to create the first university department that focused specifically on normal school administration and curricula (Teachers College n.d.).

The Formation of a New Department at Teachers College, a Critique of Determinism, and the Founding of Essentialism

From his earliest days as a rural schoolteacher near Garth, Michigan, to one of the premier teacher educators in the nation, Bagley had crafted himself into a position that allowed him to impart all of his experience and knowledge from the previous 20 years. Though, later in his life, he may have questioned the importance of a particular type of psychology to the practical work of schooling, Bagley never wavered from his fundamental belief in scientific investigation that he had learned as a young student in E. B. Titchener's laboratory (Null 2001b). As arguably the nation's leading educator of teachers for more than 20 years, Bagley continued to stress to his students the necessity for careful consideration of all available facts before rendering a decision on any issue (Proctor n.d.). Also at Teachers College, Bagley taught some of the nation's earliest courses with titles such as "Practicum in Normal School Administration," "The Technique of Teaching," "Normal School Curricula," "The Preparation of Rural Teachers," "School Management," and "A Research Course in the Professional Preparation of Teachers" (Teachers College n.d.; Proctor n.d.).

Bagley remained at Teachers College for the duration of his teaching career until his retirement in the summer of 1939. During this second half of his career, he remained highly active as a lecturer, writer, and professor who taught on numerous subjects such as curriculum, school administration, and teacher education. Bagley's boundless faith in education and his insistence upon the teacher's role as "social servant," however, led him to critique several prominent educational theories that exerted significant influence during his tenure at Teachers College. The first of these critiques, his attack on intelligence testing, educational determinism, and "Pro-Nordic Propaganda," began as early as 1918, when Bagley (1924; 1925) foresaw the dangers behind the practical application of Army Alpha testing to the nation's public schools in the name of "efficiency." As a relentless advocate of "the human race," which, for Bagley, meant every person regardless of race, color, or gender, Bagley never faltered from the fundamental conviction that education could improve the intelligence of any human being regardless of his or her mental ability, a belief that was in direct opposition to the "determinists" (Wolfe 2000).

In a second major critique for which Bagley (1938a) gained national prominence, a distinction he did not necessarily seek, he served as the intellectual and spiritual heart of the "Essentialist's Platform for the Advancement of American Education." During the fall of 1937 and spring of 1938, Bagley and a group of other like-minded educators began to correspond in hopes of forming an organization that could counteract some of the most extreme strains of Progressivism that they believed needed to be challenged (Shaw 1937a; Bagley 1937; Shaw 1937b). Bagley and the Essentialists met in Atlantic City during late February and early March to solidify their ideas in a platform that was soon published in *Educational Administration and Supervision*. As one who never fully accepted pragmatic philosophy, Bagley, along with Detroit Country Day School Headmaster F. Alden Shaw, led the Essentialists in a call for an increased emphasis on rigorous standards of scholastic achievement, an acknowledgement of the importance of sequence in learning materials, a recognition of the importance of and limits to "activity curriculum," a firmer establishment of the "exact and exacting studies" in high school curricula, and a system of schooling that accepted some limited aspects of progressive education yet recognized that an effective democracy demanded a community of culture consistent with the founding principles of democracy in the United States (Bagley 1938b).

Not forgetting the needs of children and society, Bagley and the Essentialists stressed the importance of subject matter and the necessity for teachers to be held partially responsible for passing down knowledge to students. Put simply, the Essentialists contended that students should learn . . . *something*. Notably, Bagley resisted the notoriety that followed the national movement toward Essentialism and instead pointed toward Shaw as the leader of the group. He did so primarily because Bagley wanted to emphasize the importance of and the necessity for a close connection to the practical application of educational theories. Furthermore, as the intellectual and spiritual heart of Essentialism, Bagley advanced a progressive position that he believed corresponded in many ways with the later positions of John Dewey; hence, Bagley's Essentialist's speech was timed to correspond with the publication of Dewey's (1938) *Experience and Education* (Bagley 1935; 1938b).

Unfortunately, some commentators reacted negatively to the Essentialist movement and referred to it as a mere "conservative" call for a return to "traditional" teaching methods. As any full reading of Bagley's works indicates, however, Bagley's philosophy was anything but a simplistic call for a return to 19th-century schooling. One such individual who reacted negatively to Essentialism, William Heard

Kilpatrick, derided Bagley and the Essentialists by stating that their movement was "so small" and on the whole came from "such inconspicuous people" (Wahlquist 1942; Beineke 1998). Unfortunately, Kilpatrick failed to recognize that Bagley began to work toward the replacement of "traditional" teaching methods with progressive ideas 11 years prior to Kilpatrick's completion of his dissertation. Bagley, however, resisted the temptation to respond to Kilpatrick in kind; instead, he chose to reserve his comments to personal communication with his closest friends (Hoover Institution Archives n.d.).

Bagley's 'Master Teacher' and His Challenge to Higher Education

Bagley bid farewell to his final class at Teachers College on 10 August 1939, ending a teaching career that spanned 44 years. During this time, he no doubt impacted countless students across the country. Throughout his impressive career, his complex understanding of the Master Teacher remained consistent on certain points, yet Bagley adjusted it with the times when a powerful idea was put forth. Bagley's Master Teacher had a firm foundation in the subject matter that he or she taught and a sympathetic understanding of child life. The Master Teacher also exercised common sense, had a deep understanding of pedagogy and all of its richness, understood the importance of humor in effective instruction, prepared carefully for every lesson, spoke with an articulate and engaging voice, demanded nothing short of excellence from every pupil, recognized individuality and allowed for students to follow their interests when appropriate, accepted the social responsibility of bettering the human race, took pride in the profession of teaching, modeled a zeal for knowledge and a respect for wisdom, strove to eliminate personal prejudice or bias on all issues, and demonstrated as a model to all students that the only road to true intellectual freedom was through rigorous self-discipline.

Bagley's legacy to the nation's Master Teachers stretches across numerous fields of educational study. In particular, his work in psychology, teacher education, educational thought, and school administration formed the foundation for today's schools of professional teacher preparation. The challenges that he faced with endless energy and impressive alacrity remain for 21st-century educators to address with equal effort. With additional educationists who work toward Bagley's (1920) practical goal of providing "A Competent Teacher for Every American Child," more children and youth should realize a classroom in which Bagley's Master Teacher is present. Toward this end, all institutions of higher education that seek to be truly educative should rededicate themselves to the education of teachers in the sense that Bagley understood this responsibility. Moreover, these properly prepared teachers, from Bagley's perspective, should possess the knowledge, the abilities, and the ethical commitment to the pursuit of wisdom and to the ideal of social service to their respective communities (Null in press). Only after more institutions of higher education in the United States have made such an ethical commitment to universal liberal education through the education of teachers will Bagley's ideal of a truly well-educated populace be realized.

References

Bagley Family Origins Genealogy. n.d. Personal collection, compliments of Norton R. Bagley, Plymouth, N.H.

Bagley, W. C. 1898. A study in the correlation of mental and motor ability in school children. Master's thesis, University of Wisconsin–Madison.

Bagley, W. C. 1900. The apperception of the spoken sentence: A study in the psychology of language. Ph.D. diss., Cornell University.

Bagley, W. C. 1902a. City and vicinity. *The Dillion (Mont.) Tribune* 24 August.
Bagley, W. C. 1902b. The city and county. *The Dillion (Mont.) Examiner* 27 August.
Bagley, W. C. 1902c. Qualifications of a principal. *The Dillon (Mont.) Tribune* 29 August.
Bagley, W. C. 1903a. Montana State Normal College. *Normal College Bulletin* 4 April, 1–2.
Bagley, W. C. 1903b. Montana State Normal College. *Normal College Bulletin* 4 August, 1–6.
Bagley, W. C. 1905. *The educative process*. New York: Macmillan.
Bagley, W. C. 1914. Fundamental distinctions between liberal and vocational education. *Journal of the Proceedings of the Fifty-Second Annual Meeting of the National Education Association of the United States* (July): 161–70.
Bagley, W. C. 1920. A competent teacher for every American child. Paper presented before the First Session of the National Citizens' Conference on the Crisis in Education, Washington, D.C. 19 May.
Bagley, W. C. 1924. The Army tests and the pro-Nordic propaganda. *Educational Review* 67(Jan.–May): 179–87.
Bagley, W. C. 1925. *Determinism in education: A series of papers on the relative influence of inherited and acquired traits in determining intelligence, achievement, and character*. Baltimore: Warwick and York.
Bagley, W. C. 1930. Howard Edwards, master teacher. *Journal of Education* 111(23 June): 713–14.
Bagley, W. C. 1933. Modern educational theories and practical considerations. *School and Society* 37(April): 409–14.
Bagley, W. C. 1935. Is subject-matter obsolete? *Educational Administration and Supervision* 21(September): 401–12.
Bagley, W. C. 1936. Some master teachers I have known. *Educational Administration and Supervision* 22(September): 427–36.
Bagley, W. C. 1937. Letter to F. Alden Shaw, 10 November, Hoover Institution Archives, William W. Brickman Collection, Stanford University, Box 52.
Bagley, W. C. 1938a. An essentialist's platform for the advancement of American education. *Educational Administration and Supervision* 24(April): 241–56.
Bagley, W. C. 1938b. Letter to F. Alden Shaw, 7 January, Hoover Institution Archives, William W. Brickman Collection, Stanford University, Box 52.
Bagley, W. C. 1938c. Letter to Flora J. Cooke of the *Chicago Schools Journal*, 14 April, Hoover Institution Archives, William W. Brickman Collection, Stanford University, Box 52.
Bagley, W. C. 1944. Letter to Arthur B. Moehlman of the University of Michigan, 12 December, Hoover Institution Archives, William W. Brickman Collection, Stanford University, Box 51.
Bagley, W. C. n.d. With Titchener at Cornell. Unpublished manuscript, Hoover Institution Archives, William W. Brickman Collection, Stanford University, Box 53.
Beineke, J. A. 1998. *And there were giants in the land: The life of William Heard Kilpatrick*. New York: Lang.
Boring, E. G. 1950. *A history of experimental psychology*, 2d ed. New York: Appleton-Century-Crofts.
Dewey, J. 1938. *Experience and education*. New York: Macmillan. *Dillon Examiner* Staff. 1903a. School board meets. *The Dillon (Mont.) Examiner* 7 January.
Dillon Examiner Staff. 1903b. The normal report. *The Dillon (Mont.) Examiner* 9 December.
Dillon Tribune Staff. 1903a. Another board meeting. *The Dillon (Mont.) Tribune* 23 January.
Dillon Tribune Staff. 1903b. Public school faculty. *The Dillon (Mont.) Tribune* 22 May.
Flugel, J. C. 1933. *A hundred years of psychology, 1833–1933*. New York: Macmillan.
Hall-Quest, A. L. 1938. *Kappa Delta Pi, 1911–1936*. New York: Macmillan.
Hoover Institution Archives. n.d. Miscellaneous letters, Hoover Institution Archives, William W. Brickman Collection, Stanford University, Boxes 52 and 53.
Intermountain Educator Staff. 1906. W. C. Bagley. *The Intermountain Educator* 1(July): 332.
Johanningmeier, E. V. 1967. A study of William Chandler Bagley's educational doctrines and his program for teacher preparation, 1895–1918. Ph.D. diss., University of Illinois.
Johnson, H. C., and E. V. Johanningmeier. 1972. *Teachers for the prairie: The University of Illinois and the schools, 1868–1945*. Urbana: University of Illinois Press.
Montana State Normal College. 1903. *Sixth annual catalogue of the Montana State Normal College*. Dillon, Mont.: *Dillon Examiner* Print.
Null, J. W. 2000. Progress in Dillon: William Chandler Bagley and Montana education, 1902–1906. *American Educational History Journal* 27(Fall): 64–70.
Null, J. W. 2001a. A disciplined progressive educator: The life and career of William Chandler Bagley, 1874–1946. Ph.D. diss., University of Texas at Austin.
Null, J. W. 2001b. Psychology, Cornell, and the Rockies: The graduate preparation and early career of William Chandler Bagley, 1896–1906. *Curriculum History* (Spring): 55–66.
Null, J. W. In press. *A disciplined progressive educator: The life and career of William Chandler Bagley*. New York: Lang.
Proctor, A. M. n.d. Arthur Marcus Proctor papers, Teachers College Special Collections, Milbank Memorial Library, Box 1, Folder: Education 415, class notes and syllabi.
Ravitch, D. 2001. *Left back: A century of battles over school reform*. New York: Simon and Schuster.
Rogers, D. 1961. *Oswego: Fountainhead of teacher education—A century in the Sheldon tradition*. New York: Appleton-Century-Crofts.
Shaw, F. A. 1937a. Letter to William C. Bagley, 8 November, Hoover Institution Archives, Stanford University, William W. Brickman Collection, Box 52.
Shaw, F. A. 1937b. Letter to William C. Bagley, 16 November, Hoover Institution Archives, Stanford University, William W. Brickman Collection, Box 52.
Snedden, D. 1914. Fundamental distinctions between liberal and vocational education. *Journal of the Proceedings of the Fifty-Second Annual Meeting of the National Education Association of the United States* (July): 150–61.
Spiegle, E. F. 1958. A historical study of the formation and early growth of Western Montana College of Education. Master's diss., Western Montana College of Education.
Teachers College. n.d. Teachers College School of Education announcements, 1918–1919, 1919–1920, 1920–1921. Teachers College Special Collections, Milbank Memorial Library.
University of Chicago. 1896. Matriculation card and transcript, William C. Bagley. Chicago: University of Chicago, Office of the University Registrar.
Wahlquist, J. T. 1942. *Philosophy of American education*. New York: Ronald Press.

Western Montana College. 1903. Faculty meeting minutes, Lucy Carson Library Archives and Registrar's Archives of Western Montana College, 23 February through 21 May, Dillon, Mont.

Western Montana College. n.d. History statistics studies of Western Montana College. Unpublished private collection.

Wolfe, D. C. P. 2000. Telephone interview, 4 January.

Chapter 2

Hollis Leland Caswell: Teacher, Principal, Professor, Dean, President, Mentor, and Friend

by Lynn Matthew Burlbaw

Hollis L. Caswell (1901–88) had a tremendous influence on the field of curriculum and instruction. He served education in nearly every capacity possible, and has left us a body of work that still resonates with our goals.

Life and Career

Hollis Leland Caswell was born to Hollis Leland and Lotta Hood Caswell on 22 October 1901 in Woodruff, Kansas. His early years were spent in western Kansas, where his father had a farm and later was the rural route mail carrier. Caswell's early education was typical of the day; small rural schooling in a multiage classroom. The education offered in the local high school was not up to the expectations of the senior Caswells, and in 1918 Hollis was sent to Hays, Kansas, for his final year of high school education and his first two years of college in the accelerated preparatory program at the Kansas State Normal School. After two years at Hays, Caswell entered the University of Nebraska at Lincoln, majoring in English, with the intention of becoming a lawyer; he also took the 15 hours required for certification as a teacher in case the law did not provide him a living.

Caswell's parents had committed to financial assistance while he studied for his baccalaureate degree. To supplement his parents' contribution, Caswell farmed wheat during the summers. In the early 1920s, with prices and crop yields for wheat low because of continuing drought, prospects for law school were bleak. Needing to make a living while saving money for law school, Caswell sought a teaching position.

Caswell began his public school career as a principal-teacher in Auburn, Nebraska, at the suggestion of his college advisor. The professor was a friend of the school's superintendent, who related to the professor that, during the past year, the older students had forced the principal to resign. The superintendent needed someone who could manage and control the older students. The professor recommended Caswell, and he was hired, as a 22-year-old, to "fix things." This began Caswell's career of "fixing things" in education, from classrooms and individual schools to state school systems and whole colleges. During his short tenure as a public school teacher and administrator, Caswell learned some valuable lessons that he would remember as he continued his education and worked as a consultant and professor. As Caswell (1977) related in his oral history, he learned more in his first year of teaching than he had learned in any one-year period up to that time. He learned that teaching could be rewarding, that classrooms could be exciting, and that bored students were likely to cause trouble. He also learned the value of providing a rich assortment of educational materials to engage students in their own learning.

After teaching for four years, Caswell, who had left his first position to become a school superintendent in a nearby town, chose to attend Teachers College, Columbia University. He intended to gain a master's degree in educational administration and then return to Kansas or Nebraska as a more-qualified, higher-paid superintendent in a larger school district. Caswell never mentioned when he gave up the idea of law school. Interested in administration, Caswell began studying with George Strayer, the acknowledged leader in educational administration in the United States in the 1920s. As part of his course work and an expectation for any student enrolled in the administration program, Caswell participated in several school studies that included schools in St. Louis and New Jersey. Through his work in these school surveys, Caswell learned the importance of multiple sources of information, both in data and perspectives, when proposing changes for schools and students. This knowledge was instrumental in the program for school reform he helped design when he became a professor at George Peabody College for Teachers in 1929.

Caswell never made it back to Nebraska or Kansas after receiving his master's degree in administration; Strayer had other plans for him. In Caswell's first semester at Teachers College, Strayer suggested that Caswell take the preliminary examination for the doctoral program. As Caswell (1977) recalled, "A suggestion from Dr. Strayer was pretty much what you did." Caswell passed the examination and stayed at Teachers College until 1929, when he was awarded his doctoral degree. Strayer was instrumental in making Caswell's stay at Teachers College possible by serving as a mentor, job counselor, and dissertation advisor.

While at Teachers College, Caswell took classes from many notable names in the field of education. In particular, Caswell (1977) mentioned four: Edward L. Thorndike, Paul Mort, Bruce Raup, and his adviser, George Strayer, as being especially influential in his developing educational philosophy and model of practice. From Thorndike, Caswell learned the importance of attention to detail and the need for precision in constructing evaluation questions so that the resulting answers would be meaningful. In Mort, Caswell saw a person who championed the need to attend to individual students as opposed to groups of students. After 50 years, Caswell (1977) declared that Mort's idea was still "one of the best techniques in all education. If we'd quit trying to devise ways of meeting these great-big-group needs, but, say, arrive at group needs by studying individuals—and then we get a lot of individuals who have the same kind of need, relatively. Deal with them as a group—we'd be a lot further along."

Raup, a leader in the progressive education movement, also helped Caswell see the importance of the learner in planning educational experiences. Raup's courses were forums for dialogues between students and the professor, a place where extended exchanges were allowed to clarify thinking. As Caswell (1977) said,

> *He did more to remake my educational point of view probably than any other single man in that year's time. I went there a confirmed liberal-arts-oriented person, feeling that the thing to do, in spite of the way I taught at Auburn, was to lay [content] on the line and make [the students] learn it. In spite of my experience there, I had not come to see the role that the learner really has to take in any meaningful and major significant learning experience.*
>
> *Dr. Raup had no way of knowing that he was making headway and influencing my thinking, but he did influence it tremendously.*

Raup also had no idea the impression his graduate assistance was having on Caswell; Caswell later married Raup's assistant. Raup was a member of the Social Frontier Movement, a group of progressive educators at Teachers College in the 1920s and '30s that included several of Caswell's professors. Caswell makes no mention of attending any of the organization's meetings or working on its publication, *Educational Frontier*, but the progressive thinking that appears in the group's work appears to have had an influence on Caswell's later work in curriculum revision. Perhaps the influence was indirect through Raup's course.

Strayer, finally, was the most recognized name in school administration reform in the United States during the 1920s. At one time in the 1930s, the superintendents of 16 of the largest school districts in the United States were former students of George Strayer, who served as Director of the Division of Organization and Administration of Education. Caswell learned research methodology from Strayer through practical fieldwork in school surveys. Working and studying with Strayer helped Caswell (1977) refine his vision of what education could be:

> *He affected my sense of the role and purpose of public education deeply and profoundly. It fit in with my earlier background, but I had never gotten the slightest feeling or vision, coming through my undergraduate program in arts and science at Nebraska, of the role that education could and should serve as a means of moving society ahead and helping it with its major problems, the responsibility of giving every boy and girl the optimum educational opportunity from which he [or she] could profit, the equal dignity of one part of a program with another.*

Caswell completed his dissertation in the spring of 1929 and accepted a position at George Peabody College for Teachers as an assistant professor and associate director in the Division of Surveys and Field Studies. While at Peabody, Caswell taught curriculum courses and directed the curriculum workshops held each summer for teams of teachers from throughout the South. It was through this work that he met various state superintendents and began working with curriculum-revision projects in Alabama, Florida, and Virginia. The curriculum-revision program, begun in Virginia in 1931, kept Caswell busy for the next six years. His work at the Division of Surveys and Field Studies also made him a recognized figure in the growing curriculum field. With the publication of *Curriculum Development* in 1935, a book he coauthored with Peabody colleague Doak Campbell, Caswell was able to summarize what he had been writing about during his work with the state school systems. In assessing the impact of his work, Seguel (1966) wrote that Caswell was one of the major figures in the second wave of curriculum leaders who helped define the field.

In the fall of 1937, Caswell returned to Teachers College at the invitation of Strayer and Jesse Newlon, Director of the Division of Foundations of Education. Caswell was appointed Director of the Division of Instruction, a new academic division created by President Russell in 1937, and the first head of the newly created Department of Curriculum and Teaching. Caswell's appointment was contested by L. Thomas Hopkins, who had been working with curriculum projects beginning in 1927 with the Denver Project. Hopkins felt he was more qualified for the position than Caswell, due to his longer involvement in curriculum work; however, Strayer's influence made the difference. Herbert Bruner, another professor at Teachers College, also contested Caswell's appointment; Bruner had run the curriculum laboratory at Teachers College since the mid-1920s and had collected more than 14,000 courses of study, which were used in the summer laboratory classes.

Prior to 1937, curriculum had been housed in Strayer's division. This action made a clear statement that curriculum, as a field of study independent from supervision and administration, was legitimate and important. Several years would pass before the new division would run smoothly; in time, Caswell and Hopkins developed a cordial but not collegial relationship. Caswell's experiences with curriculum programs in the South and the contacts he had made through the Division of Surveys and Field Studies at Peabody contributed to the success of the new division and department.

Often, when a person attempts to make changes to the status quo, his or her life is enmeshed in controversy. This was certainly true of Caswell. The curriculum-revision program in Virginia had brought Caswell into conflict with business and educational leaders, and his appointment at Teachers College had aroused the animosity of older, more established faculty members. His decisions regarding the Lincoln School and the Horace Mann-Lincoln Institutes again embroiled Caswell in controversy, over outside funding and the role philanthropic organizations had in the management of a university.

By the mid 1940s, the Lincoln School at Teachers College, a laboratory school dating back to the 1920s, had fallen on hard times. The endowment had not kept up with expenses, and some Teachers College Trustees were calling for the school's closing. Initially, Lincoln's endowment was combined with the endowment from the Horace Mann School, another experimental school. This failed to remedy the deficits, and the Horace Mann-Lincoln School continued to be a drain on college resources. After carefully examining the situation, following the model of collecting data from multiple sources learned from Strayer, Caswell determined that the school would be closed and the endowment transferred to the Horace Mann-Lincoln Institute of School Experimentation. Caswell's decisions about the Lincoln School generated several lawsuits by parents seeking to keep the school open. Supporting the parents' position were noted educational leaders such as L. Thomas Hopkins and William H. Kilpatrick from Teachers College and Ralph W. Tyler, from the University of Chicago. Despite the support of noted educators, the parents were unable to show that any of the innovations supposedly being developed at the school were being used in the public schools. The judge found that the school established for experimentation to provide model instruction to improve public schools was not fulfilling its purpose and sound financial management required that it be closed.

About the school and its closing, Caswell (1948, 2) wrote, in his final report on the school:

> *With the discontinuance of the School an achieved fact, it seems appropriate to reiterate the point made by representatives of the Administration of Teachers College upon many occasions during the review of this action by the Courts. Horace Mann School and Lincoln School unquestionably made contributions of great importance to educational advancement. Those who had a part in developing these schools should be proud of their handiwork. The fact that the College has turned to a new approach to experimentation believed to be more appropriate to the demands of the present day in no way detracts from the achievements of these schools. This action simply demonstrates the truth that times change and the old must give way to the new, even in approaches to experimentation, if the greatest accomplishment is to be achieved.*

In part, Caswell decided to close the Horace Mann-Lincoln School because of the limited impact of the work done at the school on public school instruction. To overcome the parochial view of the school and expand the influence of Teachers College on reforming public school practice, Caswell (1944, 2) had proposed the transfer of endowment funds to the Horace Mann-Lincoln Institute, a new organization established to conduct "a major research project in the field of Redesign and Improvement of Youth Welfare and Education; that the method be a plan of experimental work in elementary and secondary education with such investigations as are essential thereto; that preliminary conclusions be tried out in the Horace Mann-Lincoln School; that the results be measured objectively and tested out in other schools; that tested materials, capable of being used in other school be published." Caswell's (1944, 5) plan resulted in a collaborative group of institutions, both higher education and public school systems, who:

> *recognized that the problems involved are of such magnitude that much more significant progress could be made if a variety of resources could be brought to bear on them. Particularly it was noted that satisfactory ultimate solutions could be worked out only in practical school situations. It was further seen that it would be advantageous if schools with varying conditions and resources would attack these problems simultaneously and exchange experiences. Consequently, a carefully selected group of schools have been invited to participate in the study as cooperating schools. Ten school systems and three colleges have become associated with the project.*

Membership in the cooperating schools group changed over the next few years. Reports of the research projects at many of the schools were eventually published in *Curriculum Improvement in Public School Systems* (Caswell and Associates 1950). This book of case studies was widely used in administration courses at Teachers College and other institutions in the early 1950s. As Caswell (1977) stated, "There was more in that introductory section than many people have seen. That introductory section represented my analysis of the organized curriculum movement." The book would be Caswell's last detailed involvement with the field of curriculum.

In 1946, Caswell was appointed Associate Dean; he became Dean in 1948 and President of Teachers College in 1954. As Caswell (1977) recalled:

> *After 1945, I didn't have much opportunity to work with graduate students because I was so deeply involved in administration. That was the one thing I missed, frankly; in doing the administrative work, I was getting away from the students and the faculty, from the close association with the faculty on professional issues. I enjoyed that phase of my work very much, although I found administration challenging. Teachers College at that time was a fine place to work in administration.*

Caswell was President of Teachers College from 1954 until his retirement in 1961. Throughout his tenure at Teachers College, interest and concern for practice figured prominently in his work. As Dean and President, Caswell continued to write and lecture about what he saw as important issues for the nation's schools. Asked to deliver the

Burton Lecture given in 1954, for example, Caswell (1956) demonstrated his continuing concern about the education being provided for the children of the United States in his lecture, "How Firm a Foundation."

Impact on the Curriculum Field

George Strayer urged Caswell to look at classrooms and answer the question, "What did you see?" Caswell then spent his lifetime examining and thinking about the practice of education in schools. Often dissatisfied with that practice, he identified what he thought would be the focus of school activity—the development of activities to enrich the experiences of children. Caswell worked to develop school programs and ideas about such programs that would provide a better education for children.

Caswell's 20 years of active work in the curriculum field can be divided into three periods, each having a particular focus. The first period began in 1929, with his acceptance of a teaching and field-service position at George Peabody College for Teachers. These three years proved to be a period of professional exploration and intellectual discovery in what would become the curriculum field. Highlighted by his work with the state departments of education in Alabama and Florida, Caswell became discomfited during these years with the conventional practice of curriculum construction and began to formulate a new set of ideas about the curriculum and, specifically, about courses of study. The understandings that Caswell derived differed from those of most other curriculum workers and required new ways of conducting curriculum work in schools to involve all teachers and administrators.

The years from the launch of the Virginia Curriculum-Revision Program with State Superintendent Sydney Hall until Caswell resigned from Peabody, roughly 1931 to 1937, constituted the second period. During those six years, Caswell further clarified his ideas about curriculum development and worked to test them in practice. He conceptualized new roles in educational and, especially, curriculum improvement for several groups: teachers, administrators, students, and lay citizens (Burlbaw 1991; 1989).

During the third period, that time between his joining the Teachers College faculty and his assumption of the Assistant Deanship (1937–48), Caswell's efforts yielded the major legitimation of the curriculum field. As he helped organize and define the department, Caswell imprinted it with his own personal stamp. Amid his new teaching and administrative duties, Caswell continued to clarify meanings and improve practice in the curriculum work. He consistently focused attention on practical field studies for the preparation of school curriculum leaders. His seminal activities in the creation and developments of professional organizations, particularly the Association for Supervision and Curriculum Development, are recognized as significant contributions to the further recognition of curriculum as a field of academic study and professional practice.

Caswell's life was dominated by the study of curriculum in practice. Throughout his career, Caswell sought to answer Strayer's question, as well as others about school practice. What was happening in schools? How were schools effectively educating children? How could teachers be helped in their work? How could a better curriculum be developed that would focus on the needs of children? Answers to these questions could only be found in the schools in which the work of educating children took place, in individual classrooms under the guidance of individual teachers within specific social and physical contexts.

Caswell argued that schools and society had mutual responsibilities and, for them to be carried out, school must provide an education that would enable children to take their place in and contribute to a more democratic society. If schools were to provide improved educational experiences for children, certain practical matters required attention. A practical program of education would have primary concern for the student and his or her teacher and the needs of the society in which the program existed. Such a program would always include a concern for the individuals (students, teachers, and circumstances), their relationships with one another, and the resulting action.

Foremost in Caswell's attention was concern for the learner and the role of the student in the learning process. Caswell was slow in coming to this recognition. Despite what he had learned from his teaching successes, it was not until his doctoral work at Teachers College with Raup that the importance of the student in learning became prominent in his thinking. Once there, however, it never left him. Mort also helped Caswell understand the value of focusing on individuals rather than groups of students, in teaching and educational program development. Teachers in the Virginia Curriculum-Revision Program were carefully instructed about the need to focus on individual students in the process of developing classroom-curriculum activities. One section of the *Tentative Course of Study* (Virginia State Board of Education 1934) was directly intended to assist and encourage teachers to gather information about students that could be used to select appropriate learning activities.

In his work in Alabama and Florida, Caswell became dissatisfied with curriculum-construction procedures. He observed that the procedures virtually ignored students; student ability and interests were not considered in determining what was to be taught in schools. Similarly, the sharp focus on logically organized subject matter and textbooks was, to Caswell, a misdirected emphasis in schoolwork and was responsible, to a large degree, for the unpreparedness of children to take their place in society.

As important as were the interests of the individuals in the education process, Caswell recognized that individuals living in a democratic society had responsibilities to that society. The relationship of the individual to the larger society changed as the nation moved from a frontier/agrarian economy to an industrial society. Individuality had been replaced with interdependence, and school programs needed to change to reflect the new relationship.

Students, with their individual interests, went to school to learn those things they needed to participate effectively in their society. If the young people of the society were able to learn what they needed by themselves, schools would not be necessary. In the increasingly complex and interdependent society of the 20th century, children needed assistance to learn to be responsible members of society. Teachers, working in formal school settings, were needed to provide the experiences that would educate students.

As Caswell worked to define and frame the field of curriculum work, he contributed to the language used by educational workers. Early in his career, Caswell (1932, 301) defined curriculum as "all the experiences children have in school." This expansion of the meaning of curriculum to go beyond the course of study or the objectives students were to learn meant that people other than curriculum makers were involved in the education of students. This definition was adopted with such enthusiasm that, by the time the 1941 *Cyclopedia of Education* was published, Caswell's name was no longer associated with coining of the definition. He also began using phrases such as "curriculum development"—as opposed to curriculum making—to denote the evolving nature of the curriculum and the teacher's involvement in creating the experiences students had in school, "scope and sequence" to indicate the need for defining and relating what is taught by grade and to other learning experiences, and "action research"—the involvement of teachers in identifying and suggesting solutions to educational problems.

Though Caswell was not the first to use the phrase "curriculum development" (Smith 1925), he was the first major educational consultant to use it consistently and articulate the difference between the "making" and the "development" of curriculum materials. By using "development," Caswell expressed more clearly the idea that the curriculum was more than a listing of courses or activities or a rewrite of a table of contents; curriculum was, instead, the sum of all the experiences students had in school. Teachers, of course, had a highly influential role in seeing that students' experiences were educational and valuable. The curriculum was not static, not "made" and finished; instead, it was evolving based on day-to-day observation and choices made by teachers.

Caswell observed, as had others, that preparing courses of study had little impact on student learning. The teachers who helped write the courses of study had an investment in their success and used the course of study in the classroom; other teachers, not part of the development process, used the courses of study very little. This he attributed to the mentality of a made rather than a developing curriculum.

Caswell is probably best known for his work with the Virginia Curriculum-Revision Program, begun in 1931 and lasting into the 1950s, though his direct involvement with the program ended in the late '30s. This project, bearing the strong imprint of Caswell's beliefs about schooling and the purpose of education, was the blueprint for several revision programs done in the 1930s in the South and Midwest. Many of the teachers and state administrators who attended Peabody's summer workshops used the Virginia Program as a model when they returned to their states and revised their curricula. The story of the Virginia Curriculum-Revision Program (Buck 1952; Burlbaw 1989; 1991) is an example of Caswell's ideas on how to develop support for a program and assure that the widest number of individuals have a chance to provide input into the development process. The program is an example of the need to attend to teachers, students, and society as school curriculum is developed.

Since his early days at Peabody, Caswell has been recognized as a leader in the curriculum field, both for his practical work with schools and his contributions to the legitimation of the field as an arena of intellectual endeavor. Through his teaching and mentoring, he helped prepare the next generation of curriculum workers. His doctoral students included William M. Alexander, Roosevelt Basler, Arthur W. Foshay, Alice Miel, and Galen Saylor. Though few in number, Caswell's students became respected leaders in education, well known for their work in curriculum and several related fields. In his work as an administrator, Caswell helped define the field of curriculum as he led Teachers College through the last turbulent years of the Depression and the fearful years following World War II.

In March 1978, 16 years after his retirement from Teachers College and almost 30 years away from active curriculum work, Caswell was a special guest at the annual meeting of the Association for Supervision and Curriculum Development in San Francisco. Caswell (1978) delivered the address, "Persistent Curriculum Problems," in which he reminisced about the problems he and other curriculum workers had encountered over the previous 50 years. In his speech, Caswell (1978) wondered aloud "whether the chief source of continuity in our field may not be the persistent problems rather than developmental trends in thought and practice":

1. dealing with "the basics" in the curriculum in a way which recognizes both social needs and individual potential;
2. developing tested procedures to improve the curriculum; and
3. developing a viable general education curriculum.

Though Caswell, especially with his work in Virginia and with the Horace Mann-Lincoln Institute for School Experimentation, had directed major efforts to resolve these three problems, his candid assessment suggested, "We did not develop adequate solutions to them."

More than 25 years have passed since Caswell made his observations, yet educators seem to be no closer to solving the problems than they were 60 years before when Caswell began his curriculum career. The very ideas that Caswell identified as counter-productive have again become publicly popular and institutionalized in the nation's schools: programs of increased emphasis on basic skills to non-promotion for failure to achieve basic skills and neglect of programs designed for individual student abilities, a return to the analytic and mechanistic methods of determining school content used and abandoned in the 1920s, and increasing focus of schools on specialized knowledge. Caswell and his fellow curriculum workers in the 1930s and '40s recognized the inappropriateness of these types of solutions and tried to develop better approaches to educational program development. The fact that their solutions did not persist does not justify the return by educators and society to even earlier and failed practices. Rather, consistent with his and his contemporaries' practice, other ways of engaging the problems must be invented.

Today, Caswell would probably not change his assessment of curriculum work from what he pessimistically noted about the three problems he described in 1978: "From a sidelines view, I doubt that your generation of curriculum workers is solving them either." His observation may be heard as judgment, but it also demonstrates faith in the continuing necessity to engage curriculum practice on its own terms and on its own ground and in the intelligence of practitioners as they engage matters of students, teachers, and societal needs.

Caswell's Enduring Legacy

Caswell died 15 years ago. He retired from Teachers College more than 40 years ago and quit teaching courses more than 50 years ago. What then is his lasting influence on the field of teacher education and public schooling? Prior to Caswell's work, few people saw that teachers had a role in deciding what should be taught in schools. Through his early work in Alabama and Florida, he learned that, unless teachers were involved in the design and implementation of materials for students in the school, chances were slim that the materials produced by "experts" would be used. If teachers have a part in preparing the lessons they use with students, then they must know much more than how to implement a lesson plan. They must know how to observe and assess student readiness, identify appropriate materials and activities for students to use, and be intimately involved in the learning process. Teachers, especially in elementary school settings, have a responsibility to identify those characteristics, skills, and types of knowledge that will benefit the larger society and assist students in learning and acquiring those ideas.

Caswell's writings, especially his book with Doak Campbell, *Curriculum Development*, organized his thinking about the curriculum field and how curriculum work should be approached. A best-selling college textbook, *Curriculum Development* provided a sound basis for the emerging field of curriculum. His book *Curriculum Improvement in Public School Systems* provided examples of how all the members of the academic community, today called "stakeholders," worked together in large and small school systems to improve instruction.

Caswell, in his own quiet way, showed educators the way to improve schooling for children in a democratic society. From popularizing the term "curriculum development" to the involvement of teachers in curriculum work, Caswell tried to have practical results that would better the lives of children and society. His work continues today through the influence of his graduate students—and through the emerging work of their students. It is a rich legacy, all the more significant because Caswell never lost sight of his goal—to improve the teaching and learning environment in real classrooms.

References

Buck, J. L. B. 1952. *The development of public schools in Virginia, 1607–1952*. Richmond: Division of Purchase and Printing, Virginia State Board of Education.

Burlbaw, L. M. 1989. Hollis Leland Caswell's contributions to the development of the curriculum field. Ph.D. diss., University of Texas at Austin.

Burlbaw, L. M. 1991. More than 10,000 teachers: Hollis L. Caswell and the Virginia Curriculum Revision Program. *Journal of Curriculum and Supervision* 6(3): 233–54.

Caswell, H. L. 1932. Curriculum revision in rural schools. *Virginia Journal of Education* 25: 301–03.

Caswell, H. L. 1944. Report of the director for the academic year ending June 30, 1944. New York: Division of Teachers College Schools and School Experimentation.

Caswell, H. L. 1948. Report of the director for the academic year ending June 30, 1948. New York: Division of Teachers College Schools and School Experimentation.

Caswell, H. L. 1956. *How firm a foundation? An appraisal of threats to the quality of elementary education*. Cambridge, Mass.: Harvard University Press.

Caswell, H. L. 1977. Interview by O. L. Davis Jr., 17–18 October 1977. Audiotape recording. Austin: Oral History Collection, Center for the History of Education, University of Texas.

Caswell, H. L. 1978. Persistent curriculum problems. A paper presented at the Annual Meeting of the Society for the Professors of Curriculum, San Francisco, 3 March.

Caswell, H. L., and D. Campbell. 1935. *Curriculum development*. New York: American Book.

Caswell, H. L., and Associates (W. M. Alexander, E. A. Arnold, L. B. Cook, C. L. Cushman, P. Cutright, N. A. Fausch, R. S. Gilchrist, J. A. Hall, G. R. Koopman, A. J. Lewis, V. Martin, J. W. Menge, C. M. Olson, J. Sternig, and E. S. Ward). 1950. *Curriculum improvement in public school systems*. New York: Bureau of Publications, Teachers College, Columbia University.

Seguel, M. L. 1966. *The curriculum field: Its formative years*. New York, Teachers College Press.

Smith, E. E. 1925. *The heart of the curriculum*. New York: Doubleday, Page and Co.

Virginia State Board of Education. 1934. *Tentative course of study for Virginia elementary schools: Grades I–VII*. Richmond: Division of Purchase and Printing, VSBE.

Chapter 3

Ralph Tyler: A 20th-Century Innovator

by Daniel W. Stuckart
and Michael J. Berson

On the face of it, it would appear that public education in a democracy cannot avoid being a revolutionary force in the sense that I am using the term, that is, a force to improve our society so that it can achieve the ideals of democracy under the rapidly changing conditions that industrial life brings.
—Ralph W. Tyler (1947)

Ralph Tyler was a 20th-century innovator with a masterful ability to analyze a condition, devise a solution, and subsequently apply the solution using a meticulous design. Though the "Tyler rationale" was a phrase used to describe a specific formulation and application of learning objectives, the underpinnings of the logic were the common threads that guided all of Tyler's work and, at the same time, advanced behaviorist thought. Tyler believed that an examination of the environment provided the needs and context for modern education. Furthermore, learning was a change in behavior brought on by some external stimulus emanating from that environment. Tyler (1947; 1958a) honed his rationale early in life and used it to address important educational challenges that he attributed to the dynamics of industrialization. In the first half of the 20th century, he facilitated new methods for test construction, provided the blueprint and justification for behavioral-learning objectives, and created evaluation and appraisal standards for military personnel in World War II. In the second half of the century, Tyler assumed the role of the revered education statesman. His innovations sprang from his wide and varied experiences and manifested themselves in an assortment of directorships, speaking engagements, and contemporary commentaries. In assessing the role of technology in education, Tyler argued that technology was not an educational panacea, yet he noted that it offered great hope for educational enhancement and information management—two highly relevant themes today.

Despite Tyler's prolific contributions to the field of curriculum development, today he has become a relative unknown. The fact that his achievements were much more than educational products may help to explain his obscurity; Tyler offered intellectual innovations grounded in a subtle mixture of passion and logic set within the context of a newly industrialized society. These innovations were rooted in forces outside the education realm: economies of scale, the Great Depression, World War II, and the emergence of U.S. superpower status. Likewise, they were logical extensions of the great curriculum experiments of the late 19th century and were appropriate for the era. Yet, by the late 1960s, cognitivist models gained favor, and perhaps Tyler's innovations were superceded by an emphasis on mental structures over environmental influences.

There may be other reasons as well. His ideas appeared deceptively simple, and his intellectual innovations have become an integral part of both the teacher-training process and the general education classroom. Perhaps his ideas became so entrenched in educational thought that, along the way, his name became dissociated with the innovations. Or maybe his humble personality encouraged praise and acknowledgements to be showered on his intellectual predecessors and contemporary colleagues rather than himself. Or, conceivably, the man represented a bygone era in education; an era that was an image of the great industrial behemoth of the middle years of the 20th century. In any case, Tyler's contributions originated in the 1920s and proliferated into the 1990s, ending shortly before his death at the age of 91 in 1994.

Regardless, Ralph Tyler's extraordinary life, which spanned nearly the entire 20th century, was one of major innovations. His greatest accomplishments involved the curriculum experiments of the 1930s. Later, he engaged in social issues and addressed the role of technology in education.

Early Influences

Ralph Winfred Tyler was born into a pious family on 22 April 1902 in Chicago, Illinois. Four years earlier, his vexed parents reconciled a seeming contradiction between their secular and religious lives. Ralph Tyler's father was earning $5,000 a year as a Nebraska physician, a princely sum in 1898. Worried that they were worshipping "Mammon rather than God," Tyler's parents moved the family to Chicago while the father studied for the ministry. The family soon returned to Nebraska, where the young Ralph Tyler attended elementary school. As Tyler (1986–87, 37) later commented, "A guiding principle in the selection of curriculum content and learning experiences was that the material should be distasteful to students—not interesting but quite the opposite. The theory was that students really had to discipline themselves and work hard on topics they found unpleasant, while topics of interest would offer no challenge and require little effort." Nonetheless, he successfully pursued his education and attended Doane College. In 1921, he graduated with honors in science, philosophy, and mathematics at the age of 19. With the expectation of following in his father's footsteps, Tyler planned a career in medicine, but first he accepted a teaching assignment at a high school in Pierre, South Dakota. This brief stint (1921–22) profoundly affected Tyler's ambitions and set the course for one of the greatest educational careers (Stanford University News Service 1994).

Tyler's entry into the world of professional education occurred amid great economic and social upheaval. The industrial revolution was still in its infancy, and social institutions, such as schools, were evolving to fit into a new, modern paradigm. Tyler was influenced by his own experience as a secondary school teacher and the major curriculum experiments of the late 19th and early 20th centuries. He selected five major curriculum events that redefined the goals, purpose, and structure of education: Edward Thorndike's studies, John Dewey's monograph on *Interest and Effort in Education*, the 26th Yearbook of the National Society for the Study of Education (NSSE), the Society for Curriculum Study, and the curriculum experiments of the 1930s (Tyler 1986–87). Each event provided the foundation for subsequent innovations. By the 1930s, Tyler was at the forefront of curriculum experimentation as a logical extension of those innovators preceding him.

Tyler cited Edward Thorndike's early experiments as the most significant development in school curriculum (Tyler 1986–87). According to Tyler, Thorndike refuted two claims that defined education. First, Thorndike conducted empirical studies showing that specific subjects do not discipline the mind. Second, he refuted the notion that differentiated subjects enhance specific faculties of thinking. Geometry was believed to enhance the faculty of logic, while Latin and Greek developed the verbal faculty. Thorndike's studies compared the faculties of students who completed geometry and classical-language courses with those who did not. His studies suggested that a classical education neither disciplined the mind nor developed logical and verbal faculties. In seeking the purpose of an education, many education researchers and philosophers began to look at everyday life for answers.

Education dogma continued to shift from a classical paradigm to one grounded in the reality of the emerging modern world, and each event profoundly affected Tyler's thinking and ambitions. Dewey's (1913) *Interest and Effort in Education* advocated that students' interests should be considered when formulating curricular objectives. Tyler later reflected on his own elementary schooling. NSSE (in Tyler 1986–87) provided the justification and rationale for professional curriculum development. As a graduate student at the time, Tyler and his colleagues were enthusiastically debating the tenets of the yearbook: Current curriculum was not adequate for a modern democratic society and the promotion of universal education. As Tyler (1986–87) noted, the yearbook influenced him to make curricular development his life's work.

Tyler channeled his ambitions into revamping test construction in the 1920s, one of his earliest innovations. The essential principles guiding the process contained the seminal ideas that later would form the foundation of the "Tyler rationale" (Madaus and Stufflebeam 1989):

- formulating and defining course objectives in terms of student behavior;
- collecting and presenting specific situations to discern student exposure to the objective;
- evaluating student reaction in the context of the objective; and
- reexamining the objective in terms of evaluation and reliability.

Tyler's passion for curricular professionalism led to his involvement with a small group of graduate students meeting in 1930 to discuss their projects and ideas as a sort of precursor to the education think tank. Later, the group formalized as the Society for Curriculum Study. The group met two nights a week. Tyler (1986–87, 38) recalled that "discussions of particular projects were not only informative and instructive but that they raised significant issues for reflection, study, and discussion." Many years later, the group merged with the National Education Association's Directors and Supervisors of Instruction to form the Association for Supervision and Curriculum Development.

Many of these major ideological shifts occurred during Tyler's graduate years. Tyler enrolled at the University of Nebraska–Lincoln, where he achieved a Master of Arts degree in education and assumed the position of Instructor and Assistant Supervisor of Sciences (1922–26). Subsequently, he completed his doctoral work at the University of Chicago (1926–27) under Charles Hubbard Judd. At the same time, he worked as a research assistant to W. W. Charters. After completing his graduate studies, he joined the faculty at the University of North Carolina at Chapel Hill (1927–29). While there, Tyler assumed a leadership position in the state high schools' examination program. This position marked the formal beginning of Tyler's zealous dedication to improving testing and evaluation in U.S. schools. He carried this passion to his next position as a faculty member at The Ohio State University (1929–38).

Tyler entered the forefront of research at Ohio State by pioneering the field of educational evaluation. He used his position as research associate in the Bureau of

Educational Research to develop "a conception and rationale for achievement testing to measure a wider variety of instructional objectives than covered by tests and examinations then in existence and defining educational program objectives in behavioral terms" (Kolodziey 1986, vi). Because of his substantial accomplishments in educational evaluation, Tyler was selected as Director of the Evaluation Staff for the Eight-Year Study (1933–41), one of the great curriculum experiments of the 1930s.

The Eight-Year Study

Other than war, few events in human history affected so many people like the Great Depression. The 1929 stock market crash ushered in a decade of economic malaise and subsequent widespread unemployment. The collapse of the world economy impacted both individuals and institutions. Prior to the economic downturn, many teenagers entered the job market, foregoing a high school education; however, with the disappearance of gainful employment, school became a relevant place to channel both discontent and ambitions. The role of schools needed to change to meet the demands of society.

Preceding the Great Depression, only about 25 percent of young people attended high school; throughout the 1930s, school attendance doubled (Madaus and Stufflebeam 1989). Most high schools were designed for college preparation as well as a limited vocational agenda such as agriculture, homemaking, and automobile mechanics. The U.S. government, in conjunction with the Carnegie Foundation, commissioned the Eight-Year Study in 1933 to assess curriculum issues related to the changing functions of schools.

Tyler (1976, viii) recounted his years in the Eight-Year Study as a time of "the greatest satisfactions." He described an ambitious group of researchers in their 20s and 30s committed to substantive changes in education. Tyler and the rest of the committee members examined 30 schools with thousands of students. The culmination of the study was a report titled *Appraising and Recording Student Progress* (Smith 1942). The report was not meant to offer a critical evaluation of contemporary school conditions. Rather, committee members viewed themselves as facilitators in helping schools develop clear educational objectives and assessments of the processes necessary to achieve these objectives. Tyler's leadership at this critical juncture in world history shaped education policy in both the United States and other parts of the world. As he later related, Tyler's (1969, 34) basic concern was for students' learning: "Until students are involved in things they consider meaningful and significant, they will not put forth the effort or give it the attention required for this learning to become part of the student's own repertoire of behavior."

First, he incorporated the ideas of the Eight-Year Study into a course that he taught at the University of Chicago. Later, using the syllabus from his curriculum course, Tyler published the landmark treatise, *Basic Principles of Curriculum and Instruction* (1949). Educators designated the tenets of the book the "Tyler rationale."

Basic Principles of Curriculum and Instruction

Tyler (1949, v–vi) presented his rationale in a deceptively spare book of 128 pages, divided into four sections:
1. "What Educational Purposes Should the School Seek to Attain?"
2. "How Can Learning Experiences Be Selected Which Are Likely to Be Useful in Attaining These Objectives?"
3. "How Can Learning Experiences Be Organized for Effective Instruction?" and
4. "How Can the Effectiveness of Learning Experiences Be Evaluated?"

The first section of the book contained much more in its six paragraphs than a quest for education purposes; it provided the basis for the first part of the Tyler rationale and captured the systematic brilliance of the entire work. Part of this brilliance was a tacit approval and acceptance of the industrial world, manifested in changing notions of accomplishment and efficiency. Another was Tyler's use of a simple, concise vernacular suggesting practical experience and keen insight. As a primary source document, the first section of the book served as the opening salvo to modern curriculum development— a blueprint for education and modern industrial society that commented on the fragmented nature of education in the first half of the 20th century and offered a timeless solution. As Tyler (1949, 3) noted:

> *Many educational programs do not have clearly defined purposes. In some cases one may ask a teacher of science, of English, of social studies, or of some other subject what objectives are being aimed at and get no satisfactory reply. The teacher may say in effect that he aims to develop a well-educated person and that he is teaching English or social studies or some other subject because it is essential to a well-rounded education. No doubt some excellent educational work is being done by artistic teachers who do not have a clear conception of goals but do have an intuitive sense of what is good teaching, what materials are significant, what topics are worth dealing with and how to present material and develop topics effectively with students. Nevertheless, if an educational program is to be planned and if efforts for continued improvement are to be made, it is very necessary to have some conception of the goals that are being aimed at. These educational objectives become the criteria by which materials are selected, content is outlined, instructional procedures are developed, and tests and examinations are prepared. All aspects of the educational program are really means to accomplish basic educational purposes. Hence, if we are to study an educational program systematically and intelligently, we must first be sure as to the educational objectives aimed at.*

To Tyler, the most essential part of effective teaching was the identification of goals. Goals gave education a purpose—and only with a purpose can the study of education proceed "intelligently." Moreover, goals and purposes, key tenets of the factory system of the industrial revolution, belied a human capacity to improve on past performance. The first paragraph concluded with a suggestion—though many fine teachers teach with instinct, the modern world was predicated on order. Hence, the study of education required a systematic approach. The most basic foundation rested on identification of goals or objectives of education. In the second paragraph, Tyler (1949, 3–4) offered a rhetorical response to the forming of objectives: "How are objectives obtained? Since they are consciously willed goals, that is, ends that are desired by the school staff, are they not simply matters of personal preference of individuals or groups? Is there any place for a systematic attack upon the problem of what objectives to seek?"

By posing the questions from general to specific, Tyler focused his logic on a plan of "attack." He gingerly shifted from complimenting teachers who used natural instincts to select their objectives in the first paragraph to a "systematic attack" on a "problem" in the second. Along the way, Tyler (1958b) related that any decisions made were "consciously willed goals," reflecting the knowledge explosion of the industrial world and the inability of humans to acquire all knowledge. Tyler (1949, 4) answered his reasoned questions in the third paragraph, using measured responses:

It is certainly true that in the final analysis objectives are matters of choice, and they must therefore be the considered value judgments of those responsible for the school. A comprehensive philosophy of education is necessary to guide in making these judgments. And, in addition, certain kinds of information and knowledge provide a more intelligent basis for applying the philosophy in making decisions about objectives. If these facts are available to those making decisions, the probability is increased that judgments about objectives will be wise and that the school goals will have greater significance and greater validity. For this reason, a large part of the so-called scientific study of the curriculum during the past thirty years has concerned itself with investigations that might provide a more adequate basis for selecting objectives wisely. The technical literature of the curriculum field includes hundreds of studies that collected information useful to curriculum groups in selecting objectives.

In the third paragraph, Tyler responded to the questions with new ideas and innovations. Tyler (1949, 4) advocated a "comprehensive philosophy of education." Subsequently, he evoked scientific ideals with words such as "probability," "significance," and "validity." He also suggested that educators could begin their investigations with preexisting studies from the field of curriculum. In a sense, Tyler (1949, 4–5) suggested that education should operate more like an applied science of the industrial world for which knowledge is cumulative and scientific practices increase efficiency:

Accepting the principles that investigations can be made which will provide information and knowledge useful in deciding about objectives, the question is then raised what sources can be used for getting information that will be helpful in this way. A good deal of controversy goes on between essentialists and progressives, between subject specialists and child psychologists, between this group and that school group over the question of the basic source from which objectives can be derived. The progressive emphasizes the importance of studying the child to find out what kinds of interests he has, what problems he encounters, what purposes he has in mind. The progressive sees this information as providing the basic source for selecting objectives. The essentialist, on the other hand, is impressed by the large body of knowledge collected over many thousands of years, the so-called cultural heritage, and emphasizes this as the primary source for deriving objectives. The essentialist views objectives as essentially the basic learnings selected from the vast cultural heritage of the past.

In the preceding paragraph, Tyler acknowledged the range of opinions and competing ideologies. He did not take a position in favor of any particular perspective. Rather, in an excerpt from a subsequent paragraph, Tyler (1949, 5) argued that all perspectives were valid sources for constructing objectives:

The point of view taken in this course is that no single source of information is adequate to provide a basis for wise and comprehensive decisions about the objectives of the school. Each of these sources has certain values to commend it. Each source should be given some consideration in planning any comprehensive curriculum program. Hence, we shall turn to each of the sources in turn to consider briefly what kinds of information can be obtained from the source and how this information may suggest significant educational objectives.

As a primary source document, a stream of consciousness emerged from *Basic Principles of Curriculum and Instruction* that is lodged in the underpinnings of the industrial revolution and evident in the ideas and words of science. The main effects and perhaps the ultimate power of the document were how it fortified and lent legitimacy to the nascent field of curriculum development. Tyler masterfully bound curriculum history to the scientific thought of the modern world. The remainder of the book developed these notions with logic and clarity.

Tyler devoted nearly half of the book to the first question on identifying objectives. He argued that, with the advent of the Second Industrial Revolution, the body of knowledge increased substantially, making it unfeasible and undesirable for schools to transmit all knowledge. Therefore, school staff members should investigate and decide on a set of appropriate objectives based on the community's values and students' needs.

Tyler's argument transcended the polarized views between competing forces such as the essentialists (core-curriculum advocates) and progressives (reformists). Clearly, in Tyler's view, all sides were important in shaping the objectives. Moreover, Tyler emphasized that the school staff should formulate the objectives with consideration to contemporary life and the learners themselves. To obtain relevant data for the formulation of objectives, Tyler advocated the use of many sources, including public opinion polls, medical statistics, subject specialists, social philosophy, and learning psychology.

In addition to investigating and formulating objectives, Tyler emphasized the selecting and stating of specific objectives. The process of selecting occurred within the framework of social philosophy and learning psychology. For instance, if the purpose of a specific school was to track different students, then objectives should be selected to accommodate each track. Likewise, if learning research suggested that effective objectives were consistent with one another, then school staff members should select only concordant objectives. The final stage was to state concise objectives.

Tyler devised objectives with two parts. The first part indicated the type of behavioral change expected in the student. The second provided the context in which the expected behavioral change was to function. Tyler stressed that both parts were necessary to provide clarification and guide appropriate learning experiences.

Tyler (1949, 63) defined learning experience as "the interaction between the learner and the external conditions in the environment to which he can react." He argued that the teacher's responsibility was to choose appropriate learning experiences to evoke change in all students or to vary experiences to reach a heterogeneous group. Therefore, he articulated the problem with learning experiences as both one of choice and logistics.

Tyler offered general principles to facilitate learning experiences. His first general principle was the notion that students must be given an opportunity to act on the objective. As Tyler noted, a student must have an opportunity to solve problems to attain a problem-solving objective. Context was always the second part of any stated objective, regardless of content area.

Though the teacher controlled the first general principle, the learner largely influenced the remaining four principles. The second principle referred to the idea that the student must derive "satisfaction" from the learning experience. The third stated that the learning experience must be possible and appropriate for the student based on previous events and knowledge. The fourth acknowledged the availability of sometimes vast and varying experiences to achieve the same objective. And the fifth articulated the notion that a student may realize several outcomes from a single learning experience.

Tyler (1949, 83) argued that teachers should organize learning experiences for "a cumulative effect" and to promote instructional efficiency. He offered three criteria: continuity, sequence, and integration. Continuity referred to the reiteration of specific, essential skills. For example, if a social studies instructor offered a recurrent skill of interpreting maps while studying world history, then the instructor should provide consistent and continuous learning experiences in map interpretation for each unit. Sequence, according to Tyler, was an added dimension to continuity.

Tyler described sequence as a progressive movement toward deeper understanding of a skill. In other words, a fifth-grade student does not interpret a map at the same intellectual level as an 11th-grade student. Over time, learning experiences must build successively to provide increased levels of sophistication and mastery. Within the context of continuity and sequence, integration provided relevance.

Tyler explained integration as the development of learning experiences that transcend the individual disciplines. Tyler recounted the notion that students should be able to apply the skills to other areas of life, making them relevant. In the case of map reading, a student could use the concept of map scale in mathematics, measurement in the sciences, and so on. In the example, the teacher used the concept of maps as an organizing essential for learning experiences.

Because of the diversity of both content and student behavior, Tyler stressed a sort of trial-and-error process. He realized that organized learning experiences mirrored the interdependence of the nonacademic world as well. The student was dependent on his or her parents, the grocery store, the electric company, and all other entities necessary for survival in the modern world. Effectively organized learning experiences subtly suggested the interdependent nature of daily life.

Furthermore, Tyler offered guiding principles to organization. They occurred on many levels, from state curriculum legislation to specific choices made by the individual classroom teacher. Regardless of the organizational level, Tyler (1949, 86) emphasized that specific elements could be identified as "organizing threads." After the curriculum person identified the threads, he or she could use a variety of organizational techniques—including chronological, sequential, and theme-based organizations—while the classroom instructor organized with lessons, topics, and units. Tyler implied that the possibilities for organization were limitless.

After educators identified objectives, chose learning experiences, and subsequently organized those learning experiences, the evaluation process occurred. Tyler deduced that, because learning was a change in student behavior, evaluation measured the amount of change. Inherent in Tyler's conception of evaluation was the notion of appraisal, the teacher-measured student achievement before instruction began and again at least one time afterward.

Tyler articulated evaluation procedures as well. He ascertained that the evaluation process began with an examination of objectives. Because a clear objective consisted of a desired behavioral change within a specific context, the evaluation should reflect both. Consider, for example, this objective: "The student will be able to interpret the physical traits on a map of India." The proper evaluation would address the skill of interpreting maps in the context of India. Tyler argued that choosing a proper test instrument together with an appropriate record system provided the teacher a satisfactory mechanism for evaluating the learning experiences and, hence, either a rejection or a refinement of those experiences. Tyler (in Madaus and Stufflebeam 1989, 251) recounted how a colleague at Ohio State recommended him for a directorate because he based evaluation "on what the schools are trying to do" and did not "simply take a test off the shelf."

Tyler's Later Years: Testing, Evaluation, Social Issues, and the Emergence of Computer Technologies

With the success of *Basic Principles of Curriculum and Instruction*, the Eight-Year Study, and his course at the University of Chicago, Tyler continued to incorporate the rationale into the university curriculum and explore testing and evaluation. While serving as professor, dean of the Division of Social Sciences, and university examiner, Tyler also assumed the directorship for the examinations staff of the U.S. Armed Services Institute from 1943 through 1953. The final product was a standardized test offering college credit to military personnel. This test later evolved into the General Educational Development Test (GED), by which millions of high school dropouts have achieved a high school degree (Madaus and Stufflebeam 1989). In 1953, Tyler's mission at the U.S. Armed Services Institute concluded, and, in the same year, he departed from the University of Chicago to become the first director of the Center for Advanced Study in the Behavioral Sciences at Stanford University (1953–67).

Tyler's 14-year tenure at the postdoctoral research center marked a continuation of his curriculum development in the behavioral sciences. At the same time, he undertook the role of Chairman of the Exploratory Committee on Assessing the Progress of Education (1964–68). The Committee devised a plan for one of the first national and systematic ventures to collect and report data on child achievement. Tyler retired from the center in 1967 (Kolodziey 1986).

Tyler's retirement marked a new beginning for the robust 65-year-old. He wrote, lectured, consulted, and advised at every grade level in the United States and in various projects abroad. Being the true behaviorist, Tyler always looked to the systematic pulses of the tangible world for educational meaning. As Tyler (1980a, 1) commented, "The needs of education in a nation depend to a considerable extent upon the conditions in the country at that time." He viewed the social landscape of the late 1970s and '80s, recognizing that the gap between rich and poor had widened, that minority issues were surfacing, and that the changing composition of families was shifting vital responsibilities to the schools. Tyler (1974; 1975a; 1980a; 1989) began to report on the disadvantaged child's educational needs.

A common theme in Tyler's treatment of the contemporary problems of the last few decades was the simple logic conceived during the curriculum experiments of the 1930s, particularly the Tyler rationale. The logic sprang from observations of the world around him. With these observations, he articulated society's needs and schools' roles in satisfying those needs. Tyler (1951; 1969; 1980b) further asserted that U.S. history showcased a slow, deliberate process of shifting responsibilities from the home to schools. In the 1970s and '80s, he turned his attention to the plight of disadvantaged children. He reasoned that, because society placed faith in universal education, innovative programs must be developed to address the needs of the poor. As Tyler (in Lipsitz 1983, 10) argued, "Education has to derive its objective in terms of what our society needs, and what young people need, and *then* the problem is: How will these technologies help us do the job?"

Tyler (1974) further asserted that modifying middle-class programs was not adequate in addressing the issues of malnutrition, frequent illness, and a home life in which books and learning held no importance. Other issues included single parents with little or no education, examining the requirements of minority students, the increased need for educated and skilled workers, and the reluctance of taxpayers to finance education as services for an aging population demanded more resources (Tyler 1975b; 1980a; 1989). After presenting the issues, Tyler offered a rationale for dealing with problems, such as a systematic outreach program promoted by the federal government and supported by legions of volunteer organizations (Horowitz 1995; Tyler 1980a). Tyler believed that social issues were inextricably linked to larger economic trends such as the proliferation of computer technologies.

Tyler consistently based his ideas on the needs of society, whether he spoke of learning objectives, testing, evaluation, or social issues. The same held true for his observations on computer technologies (Tyler 1980c; Tyler and Cole 1985). Tyler (1965; 1983b) recognized early the potential of computer technologies for managing the burgeoning accumulation of knowledge. He argued that computers served useful purposes as mechanisms for record keeping and facilitators for drill-and-practice exercises, those tasks that are "distasteful or boring" (Tyler 1983b, 5). Likewise, Tyler (1978, 35) saw technologies "as aids to educators, not as substitutes for them."

Because Tyler died in early 1994, he was unable to see the Internet's force in molding a new, world economic and social order. Yet Tyler's immense writings and speeches offer hints to what he might say about technology today. Every one of his major innovations began with an examination of society's needs. These examinations served as the foundation for a logical, systematic treatment of that need. First and foremost, he recognized the teacher's unique and crucial role in shaping motivation and instilling the satisfaction of intrinsic rewards (Mickler 1985; Tyler 1977). Hence, the role of the teacher remained constant in a mediated environment. Second, he embarked on a systematic analysis of society's needs and education's function in meeting those needs. If he were alive today, he might conjecture that a technological society like the United States requires a citizenship versed in the gathering, managing, and manipulation of information. As Tyler (1983a, 282) remarked, "Technology is form, not content." As a form, he might suggest that schools follow a path of computer integration similar to society in general.

In the last decades of his life, Tyler addressed fundamental social issues and cultivated a relationship with Kappa Delta Pi, International Honor Society in Education (KDP). In 1976, Tyler was inducted into KDP's Laureate Chapter. Moreover, he aided in the endowment of the KDP scholarship that bears his name. In developing the scholarship, Tyler's humble personality shone. As Felix Robb (1986) noted in a letter, Tyler "expressed significant concern that the fund-raising effort not be done primarily to honor him but to put the emphasis where he thought it should be: on what could be accomplished by the students who would be the recipients of awards through the years." In the spring of 1986, Tyler reflected on the lessons of the past and the implications for the future in KDP's scholarly journal, *The Educational Forum* (Tyler 1986). Tyler never deviated, even in his last years, from his conviction that history and the environment provided guiding principles for the future of education.

The Tyler Legacy

Tyler left behind a cornucopia of books and articles reflective of his innovations and contributions to education. In fact, the sheer abundance, wide scope of content, and eclectic publishing outlets virtually guarantee that some writings remain uncataloged and perhaps lost (Kolodziey 1986). The impact of his publications is twofold. First, at the time of publication, his writings served as a conduit of expression, a way to enlighten education professionals and guide educational thought. Clearly, in the 1930s and '40s, his ideas were at the forefront of change. Later, they became more reflective and prescriptive. Second, the mass of published materials help to preserve a legacy. Future generations will know Ralph Tyler because of his writing contributions. *Basic Principles of Curriculum and Instruction* went through 36 printings during Tyler's life and became an international bestseller (Stanford University News 1994).

However obvious these contributions appear today, they are merely manifestations of a tour de force, a lifetime that profoundly shaped the structure and tenets of education. By most accounts, it is a forgotten legacy that should be remembered; some of the seminal minds in education today were former students of Ralph Tyler. Included in this auspicious group are John I. Goodlad and Robert H. Anderson. Both have reflected on their relationship with Tyler and the genius that belies his enormous, under-recognized legacy.

Tyler possessed abundant energy, intense self-control, and a driving passion to improve society's understanding of education. As Tyler (in Cohen 1986, 95) commented, "I find everything I do interesting and enjoyable, and I suppose as you get older and realize that your length of life depends on the activity you carry on, it becomes even more exciting." His energy did not wane until the very last years of his life. As an octogenarian, he continued to crisscross the globe at a frenetic pace, conducting meetings, leading seminars, and championing children's issues (Cohen 1986). He parlayed his photographic memory and keen sense of concentration into guiding generations of graduate students. As Goodlad (1995, 78) noted, "He disciplined himself to concentrate the whole of his incredible intelligence on the problem at hand. . . . One always became a little clearer on some matters in the company of Ralph Tyler."

Tyler demonstrated extraordinary focus in helping graduate students and people in general. As Anderson (2000) noted, "He was always ready to help." He was not an exciting speaker, but his message evoked admiration. There was a sense of greatness in his presence, as he already was a national educational figure by the end of World War II. Anderson (2002) remembered fondly the immediate postwar years, when the graduate ranks at the University of Chicago swelled to unprecedented levels:

> About a hundred of us, recently discharged from military service, descended upon the University of Chicago and entered a glorious period of about two years during which we pursued our doctorates. Ralph Tyler was then in charge of the Department of Education. He taught several courses in which many of us enthusiastically enrolled. Although his voice was less than sonorous and his teaching style was not dramatic, the range and depth of his ideas and his command of the field were unparalleled in the country. He exhibited a strong interest in all of us graduate students both as an entity and as individuals. It was in fact exciting to be exposed to his incredible mind. One couldn't ask a question or suggest an insight that was out of his range or that he couldn't embellish, explain, or expound upon in some marvelous way. In subsequent years, during which I had many opportunities to be and/or work with him, I learned that, although his demeanor was always modest, he had stored away for "instant retrieval" a literal treasury of information from which he could instantly draw in responding to a comment or a question. Often, he was able to quote with complete accuracy just about everything that he had ever read (or heard).
>
> Once, in response to a student's question about changes in curriculum thinking, he quoted from several relevant pages that had appeared in NSSE yearbooks about two decades apart. Later, when a bunch of us went out to dinner with Tyler, the student expressed amazement that he was able to recall the exact quotes. Her amazement was further heightened when Tyler explained that he actually had pages locked away in his memory. Furthermore, NSSE had adopted a different typesetting by the time the second curriculum yearbook

had come out, and he could remember how the words looked in the earlier, and then the later, printed versions.

Tyler made a memorable impression on students for his quiet (one could almost call it "modest") communications with students and faculty colleagues. Even in ordinary conversation his language was clear, precise, and, yes, publishable! He also had a remarkable sense of humor, including stories about almost every conceivable situation. That he may well have been one of the two or three most productive and respected educators in world history is clearly arguable; and the thousands of people who have regarded him as mentor and friend cheerfully acknowledge their enormous intellectual (as well as human) debt to him.

John Goodlad (2003) recently reflected on his introduction to Tyler:

My first class as a graduate student at the University of Chicago listed no instructor. Those of us assembled a little before the scheduled hour were not sure it would become a reality. A few minutes later, a slightly rotund, middle-aged man appearing to be in deep thought slipped through the doorway and into the seat at the desk in front of us. There was no eye contact. He studied some papers, his bald head lowered toward us. At precisely 4:00 P.M., he looked up, smiled, and softly greeted us. A murmur went through the room: "Ralph Tyler."

He stood up and introduced himself as "Mr. Tyler," following an unwritten custom within the university. Then he asked the two dozen or more of us to do likewise, he responding to each brief statement with a comment that personalized the process beyond the mere stating of name and home base. He was standing up, not writing down our names. It was a conversational class during which he called upon Mr. Bates, Ms. Carter, Ms. Howard, Mr. Jones, or Mr. Sand, never again asking us to repeat our names. Astonishing!

Clearly, Tyler made a strong first impression, particularly among his students. As Goodlad (2003) continued:

As I soon learned, his filling in for this scheduled class was characteristic. Yet Ralph was at the time dean of the division of the social sciences, university examiner (responsible for the development and maintenance of the institution's comprehensive examination system), and chairman of the department of education. And he regularly traveled two or three days a week to carry out his extraordinary involvement in the behind-the-scenes infrastructure of our educational system.

Because he was much sought out as a doctoral advisor, one would expect him to have little time for his advisees. He did not, but he was the most masterful manager of time I was ever to meet. He scheduled six individual appointments a week, of ten minutes each, all within a single hour reserved exclusively for his students. We didn't complain. Rather, we learned—as he probably intended us to—how to think through what we were puzzling over and get our heads clear. No matter what the problem or issue, it was bathed in light by the time he stood up, asked those with wives or husbands how they were doing, and smilingly escorted us to the door. I don't ever remember his providing me with an answer. Indeed, he usually asked me several questions he expected me to answer. The number of us who benefited from these brief sessions and, later, in other professional and social settings is incalculable.

When asked about Tyler's lasting legacy, Anderson (2000) responded:

> *I think we will always be in his debt for having provided leadership in the field of evaluation and especially curriculum theory. And I think his legacy is in people. I can't think of any other person in the world who, like John Dewey, had more influence on people in the realm of education. He was everywhere. He was respected. He was always in motion, even into his late eighties. He would start the day in California and fly out to Amherst, Massachusetts, and go from there to Cairo or Jerusalem or what not. His lasting legacy takes all kinds of forms. One of them is in literature. And there probably isn't anyone who has produced as much stuff as he has in education. And he gave more consulting help and was involved in the construction of new ideas, new materials, new procedures. His lasting legacy is as the all-purpose educational theorist.*

As an educator, Tyler touched the lives of thousands directly—and perhaps millions indirectly. His participation and leadership in the curriculum experiments of the 1930s, combined with the research and ideas of his predecessors like Edward Thorndike and John Dewey, led to the development of the Tyler rationale, the blueprint for modern curriculum study. However, the rationale evolved into something greater than a narrowly defined procedure; it offered a systematic approach for resolving educational and societal dilemmas: testing, evaluation, providing credit for military personnel, educational reform, the plight of disadvantaged children, emerging technologies, and many more. Tyler's contributions, tireless efforts, and longevity truly make him a unique 20th-century innovator.

References

Anderson, R. H. 2000. Personal communication, 27 June.

Anderson, R. H. 2002. Personal communication, 29 December.

Cohen, D. 1986. David Cohen talks with Ralph Tyler. *Curriculum Exchange* 4(3): 84–96.

Dewey, J. 1913. *Interest and effort in education.* Boston: Houghton Mifflin.

Goodlad, J. I. 1995. Ralph Tyler: The educators' educator. *Educational Policy* 9(1): 75–81.

Goodlad, J. I. 2003. Personal communication, 9 January.

Horowitz, R. 1995. A 75-year legacy on assessment: Reflections from an interview with Ralph W. Tyler. *Journal of Educational Research* 89(2): 68–75.

Kolodziey, H. M., ed. 1986. *Ralph W. Tyler: A bibliography 1929–1986.* Washington, D.C.: Ralph W. Tyler Project, National Foundation for the Improvement of Education.

Lipsitz, L. 1983. Some thoughts on the improvement of American public education: An interview with Ralph W. Tyler. *Educational Technology* 23(8): 7–12.

Madaus, G. F., and D. Stufflebeam, eds. 1989. *Educational evaluation: Classic works of Ralph W. Tyler.* Boston: Kluwer.

Mickler, M. L. 1985. Interviews with Ralph W. Tyler. *The Educational Forum* 50(1): 23–46.

Robb, F. C. 1986. Letter to Robert H. Anderson, 25 November. Indianapolis: Kappa Delta Pi Educational Foundation Archives.

Smith, E. R. 1942. *Appraising and recording student progress.* New York: Harper & Brothers.

Stanford University News Service. 1994. Ralph Tyler, one of century's foremost educators, dies at 91. *Stanford News*, 28 February. Available at: *http://www.stanford.edu/dept/news/pr/94/940228Arc4425.html.*

Tyler, R. W. 1947. Major issues in education today. *Ohio Schools* 25: 58–59, 86–87.

Tyler, R. W. 1949. *Basic principles of curriculum and instruction.* Chicago: University of Chicago Press.

Tyler, R. W. 1951. Trends in teaching—How research is affecting our understanding of the learning process. *The School Review* 59(5): 263–72.

Tyler, R. W. 1958a. Desirable policies for the certification of teachers: A symposium. *The Educational Record for July 1958,* 253–61.

Tyler, R. W. 1958b. Emphasize tasks appropriate for the school. *Phi Delta Kappan* 40(1): 72–74.

Tyler, R. W. 1965. The knowledge explosion: Implications for secondary education. *The Educational Forum* 29(2): 145–53.

Tyler, R. W. 1969. Curriculum for a troubled society. *NCEA Bulletin* 66(1): 32–36.

Tyler, R. W. 1974. Educating children of the poor: 1975–1985. ERIC ED 092 643.

Tyler, R. W. 1975a. Reconstructing the total educational environment. *Phi Delta Kappan* 57(1): 12–13.

Tyler, R. W. 1975b. Tomorrow's education. *American Education* 11(7): 16–19, 22–23.

Tyler, R. W. 1976. *Perspectives on American education: Reflections on the past . . . Challenges for the future.* Chicago: Science Research Associates.

Tyler, R. W. 1977. What technology cannot do. *Phi Delta Kappan* 58(6): 455.

Tyler, R. W. 1978. Technological horizons in education: An overview. *Journal of Technological Horizons in Education* 5(5): 32–38, 65.

Tyler, R. W. 1980a. The needs of elementary and secondary education for the 1980's. ERIC ED 194 480.

Tyler, R. W. 1980b. Parent involvement in curriculum decision-making: Critique and comment. A paper presented at the Annual Meeting of the American Educational Research Association, Boston, 7–11 April. ERIC ED 191 596.

Tyler, R. W. 1980c. Utilization of technological media, devices, and systems in the schools. *Educational Technology* 20(1): 11–15.

Tyler, R. W. 1983a. Tyler talks. *Contemporary Education* 54(4): 279–82.

Tyler, R. W. 1983b. Using technology to improve education. *CMLEA Journal* 7: 4–6.

Tyler, R. W. 1986. Continuing the quest for excellence. *The Educational Forum* 50(3): 345–49.

Tyler, R. W. 1986–87. The five most significant curriculum events in the twentieth century. *Educational Leadership* 44(4): 36–38.

Tyler, R. W. 1989. Educating children from minority families. *Educational Horizons* 67(4): 114–18.

Tyler, R. W., and B. Cole. 1985. Development and use of technology in education. In *Historical perspectives on American education: Program 5* [videocassette]. Bloomington, Ind.: Phi Delta Kappa.

By Their Leadership, They Taught

O. L. Davis, Jr.

Some teachers occupy prominent status in our memories. Typically, we remember the names of our favorite teachers and, as well, a few of those whom we recall as the worst that we have known. We remember our teachers for a great variety of reasons: some because of how they dressed, of their manner of responding to us; others as a result of some particular personal characteristic, of their special affinity for particular subject content or books or activities; and some because of the richly spun narratives that filled their presentations. To be sure, we also remember them as they were not. For example, my classmates and I routinely referred to our high school English teacher as "old lady Elzner" even though, as I learned years later, she was younger than 30 years of age when she was our teacher.

Other teachers are known for their professional and scholarly leadership. For some, this prestige continues long after they retire, even after their death. Especially is this attribute noteworthy for those significant teachers of ours with whom we never had a course, to whom we never submitted an assignment, in fact, whom we never have known except as the author of a book or an article that touched us. These teachers are ones who, by their leadership, taught.

The three men portrayed in this section of *They Led by Teaching* are such teachers. All were Laureates of Kappa Delta Pi, a signal recognition of their stature as giants in our common field of education. Early in their careers and by all estimates, each was a good teacher in public schools. William Chandler Bagley taught in an elementary school; Hollis Leland Caswell taught English and Ralph Tyler taught science in high schools. Subsequently, after they taught in colleges and worked with teachers in schools, each served as a university Dean. Their teaching and administrative experience, however, only partly contributed to their reputation as notable leaders. Likely much more central to their prominence as leaders were other factors: their extensive authorship of articles and books, their presentations at major conferences, and their participation in professional and scholarly associations. Their intellectual and scholarly leadership constituted a form of their teaching. Only a very few of us, if any, ever studied with one of them. Most of us probably never knew them personally, and many of us may never have read their names. Nevertheless, we continue to be their students because of their profoundly important leadership.

In the engagement with these three portrayals, I encourage each reader to reflect upon the lives of these three individuals, particularly about the influences they exerted during their lifetimes and their enduring legacies. As reminders of their humanity, each possessed flaws as well as strengths; each experienced frustration and failure on multiple occasions as well as knowing frequent and publicized successes; and each garnered, in unequal amounts, both timely praise and harsh criticism. They were human beings. They were teachers. They were leaders.

Most of the Time, They Pointed in the Right Direction

These individuals held important ends-in-view about American schooling. They recognized, especially, the considerable importance of the development of individuals and of the ways of democracy. They neither sought a type of "group think" for individual persons nor a homogeneity of student experience and achievement in schools. For them, because of their commitment to democracy, authoritarianism was anathema; they fostered collaborative decision-making. They were concerned about appropriate ends, and they also were concerned about consistent means by which those ends might be achieved. They understood that the ways of democracy included the possible modification of ends. Still, as they worked, they appeared uncommonly to point in right directions.

In his work with teachers in the 30 experimental schools of the Eight-Year Study, Ralph Tyler routinely opened discussions with a request: "Please talk about what you and your students are doing." Over time, teachers talked fully about the nature of their teaching; they described lessons recently taught, subject matter upon which they had focused, assignments tasked, tests given, and projects anticipated. As this conversation continued, Tyler might have asked teachers to infer possible objectives from descriptions of individual aspects of "what was going on." These inferences reasonably might relate, in specific cases, to particular individual student needs or interests about thinking skills or subject matter, for instance. With the possible objectives noted, the conversation continued. Tyler recognized no formulaic plan for the conversation. On the other hand, he was aware of the necessity to deal recursively with the several basic curriculum-planning elements that he and Hilda Taba had identified. Decisions were the teachers', but he clearly must have guided and influenced the course of the discussions.

Too many readers of Tyler's popularly studied *Basic Principles of Curriculum and Instruction* find it and reports of his practice startlingly inconsistent. Having carelessly read the book, they have failed to note the explicit caveat in his text that planning procedures need *not* be conducted in any specified sequence. For example, objectives *certainly need not* be stated as the initial steps in planning. On the other hand, he considered a teacher planning group's awareness of objectives within appropriate ends-in-view to be essential to their continued collaboration and discussion. These teachers reasonably might review and revise objectives as well as purposes, because Tyler understood that teachers' collaborative planning should much resemble democratic decision-making as it was understood at the time.

William Chandler Bagley early decried the popular racial psychology of the 1920s and opposed widespread use of IQ tests. He understood both advocacies to be discordant with his concern for the openness to the development of individuals' full potential in American society. Bagley, a founder of Kappa Delta Pi, also held that teachers should possess substantial personal scholarship of that which they taught as well as should practice their teaching to enhance individual student learning. For him, Kappa Delta Pi signified teachers' realization of their substantial beginning of a maturing scholarship.

On a March afternoon in 1938, Bagley reminded the educational community that substantive knowledge must not be neglected or deemphasized in school programs, that it was essential to all education. Stating his long-held belief about the nature of education, his address struck directly at the rhetorically popular progressivism of the times. Only hours later, John Dewey also criticized excesses of progressive education in his Kappa Delta Pi lecture "Education and Experience." Bagley's position, however, was the one pilloried as a return to an outmoded education. Bagley suffered this harsh criticism; but his position, in no small measure, reflected the reality of most American schools of the times.

To point in right directions is not to set arrival destinations. Nevertheless, awareness of ends-in-view is necessary to appropriate decisions about movement. These American educators' leadership continues to teach us about right directions.

By and Large, They Engaged the Practical

To be sure, these individuals understood the role of educational theory to raise the curtain on possibilities. They chose, however, not to reside in the arena of rhetorical visions; instead, they directed educators' attention to educational realities and problems of the moment.

About 20 years ago, an aging Ralph Tyler attended a regional Kappa Delta Pi conference. Only a few chapter members registered for the meeting, but Tyler happily addressed the small group. He spoke particularly of the hard times that were beginning to impact American schools. Then, he surprised his listeners. He opined that, in his lengthy educational experience, hard times gave birth to particularly important creative and significant innovations by educators. He understood that reality cannot be escaped and must be embraced. He described his vivid recollections of how teachers and administrators had little money during the hard times of the 1930s, but how they nevertheless improved practice with powerful, creative ideas. Tyler respected teachers' talents and encouraged their collaboration.

Hollis Leland Caswell gained his initial prominent national notice during his conduct of the Virginia Curriculum Study during the early 1930s. Rather than assuming that he could envision a program for all Virginia public schools, he and his associates mobilized the state's thousands of teachers to work on the project. They studied and discussed problems together, not for a short time, but for an extended period. Among other things, Caswell also asked teachers to describe the instructional units that they liked to teach to their students. From these numerous units, they worked to organize a scope and sequence that admitted the priority of teachers' lived curriculum realities and, in addition, moved many schools in the state toward improved practices.

To engage the practical is not at all to accept the constraints of the present as only enfeebling conditions. Rather, this engagement can deliver opportunities for educators to study the vexing problems they face and to make *decisions* for action. Of course, some understand *decisions* to be *solutions*, because the term *solutions* embodies the prestige of authority. Quite likely, Bagley, Caswell, and Tyler favored *solutions*. Some of us contemporary curriculum workers back away from that position. We know that *solutions* mainly are theoretical constructs that seldom work out in practice, whereas we expect *decisions* to be only approximate and likely to be modified. Though increased numbers of contemporary educators would do well to rediscover the attraction to the practical known by Bagley, Caswell, and Tyler, they certainly could improve practice with enriched understandings of deliberation toward decisions to act.

They Practiced the Art of the Possible

Significantly, these educators never waited for all the conditions to be *right* before they proceeded to *do* something. They certainly recognized that all conditions never would be *right* and, furthermore, that the decisions they and their colleagues made would *never make them right*. Indeed, rightness in social relationships can be only theoretic— only an imagined prospect, not a reality that emerges from the practical. They proceeded, consequently, to do what they could, in the language of card games, with the hands they were dealt. Such a stance enabled them not only to practice their leadership and teaching, but also to move successfully toward appropriate ends-in-view.

Bagley, for example, never was directly involved in efforts that would have converted American schooling into vocational training programs. However, he could and did speak out and write in forceful arguments against such programs and their supportive rhetoric and in favor of programs that included rigorous attention to cultural knowledge. Earlier, as a young psychologist with solid experimental credentials in E. B. Titchener's laboratory at Cornell, he became convinced that teachers should possess psychological knowledge; but he recognized that his talents and abiding interest lay in the improvement of teaching rather than in psychological experimentation. He never conducted another experiment even though he cofounded the *Journal of Educational Psychology*. He emphasized what he thought was the best of the choices that he perceived possible.

During World War II, the United States drafted millions of men into the armed forces who did not have high school diplomas, including even some dropouts from elementary schools. They were ineligible, consequently, for training in a number of highly needed military specialties. Recognizing that various life experiences reasonably enabled individuals to achieve a level of knowledge that was "equivalent" to high school graduation requirements, Tyler led efforts to develop the original GED test, passage of which qualified individuals to receive a high school education equivalency certificate. He never understood the GED test to replace the high school. Yet, he also knew that high school attendance for most of these school dropouts, but otherwise competent individuals, was out of the question. Thus, he sought and achieved a "better" possible practice. GED testing, a wartime innovation, continues today.

The arts of the possible ordinarily yield useful results. Still, like all political acts, they rely on subsequent workers and actions to extend their effects. They are seen as insufficient, almost always, when judged by the standards of a later day. Nevertheless, arts of the possible realize that steps taken are real and valuable, even if partial.

To Teach by Leading

This section's portrayals spotlight the lives of only a few good teachers. We know many others who led by teaching. Their lives and teaching practices also should not be forgotten. Our reflections about them, therefore, should be expansive and inclusive. In particular, I encourage our renewed attention to individuals whose leadership continues to teach.

Part Two
Teaching Young Children

Chapter 4
Patty Smith Hill and the U.S. Kindergarten
Rose A. Rudnitski

Chapter 5
'Democracy's Proving Ground': Alice Miel and
Democratic Citizenship Education in the Schools
Elizabeth Anne Yeager

Chapter 6
Maycie Southall: Elementary Educator and
Organizational Leader
Sherry L. Field

Laureate Commentary on Part Two
With Vision to Spare
Bettye M. Caldwell

Chapter 4

Patty Smith Hill and the U.S. Kindergarten

by Rose A. Rudnitski

"Happy Birthday to you. Happy Birthday to you"—when people are asked where this song came from, they usually respond that they assume it is a folk tune that has almost always existed. They are only slightly correct. In fact, the song, "Happy Birthday to You," though set to a folk tune, was published a little more than a century ago in a book of kindergarten songs written by two sisters with a strong interest in early childhood education (Hill and Hill 1896). "Happy Birthday to You" and kindergarten share that common feature—the assumption that it has always existed as it is; but actually the U.S. kindergarten is the result of years of experimentation, adaptation, and even controversy. Its development is an important thread in the tapestry that is the history of education in the United States, and few influenced its weave more than Patty Smith Hill.

Early Stages

The development of the U.S. kindergarten began in the mid-19th century, when German immigrants established schools that included kindergartens for their children. In the late 1850s, Margaretha Schurz, the wife of Carl Schurz, started a kindergarten in her home in Watertown, Wisconsin, for her children and those of her neighbors. She had studied with Friedrich Fröbel (1898), educational philosopher and developer of the concept in Germany, and she conducted the Watertown kindergarten in German (Jammer 1960). When visiting Boston in 1859, she happened to meet Elizabeth Peabody, who was enthralled by the kindergarten and theories of early childhood education they discussed in this first meeting. Peabody was so captivated that she started her own kindergarten in Boston the following year. The endeavor failed, she later recounted, primarily because she had not had formal training in Fröbel's methods and did not implement them properly (Peabody 1882). This setback did little to discourage Peabody, who became an ardent supporter of transplanting the kindergarten to the United States. She argued that those involved in early childhood education worked with God to shape the intellect, artistic nature, and moral character of children (Committee of Nineteen 1924). She even coauthored a book on the subject with her sister, Mary Peabody Mann, who was married to educational reformer Horace Mann (Peabody and Mann 1877).

After traveling to Germany in 1867 to observe kindergartens there, Elizabeth Peabody worked hard advocating for the establishment of kindergarten training schools under the supervision and tutelage of teachers from Germany. Her dream was realized in 1873, when Maria Kraus-Boelte opened the New York Seminary for Kindergartners in New York City. The school included a kindergarten and primary school that served as laboratory classes for the teachers in training. One of Kraus-Boelte's first students was Susan Blow (Peabody 1882).

Blow was from a wealthy, prominent family of St. Louis, Missouri, and was in the social circle of then Superintendent of Schools William Torrey Harris, who was well versed in German idealism. In 1873, Blow offered to supervise a kindergarten classroom without pay if the school district would provide a classroom, materials, and a teacher. A deeply religious woman who, like Peabody, believed that this was God's work, Blow would not accept compensation for her work with young children. She wanted to prove that the kindergarten would be a successful addition to the grade-level structure of the elementary school, so she financed this Fröbelian kindergarten fully (Cremin 1988). The project was a success, eventually earning Blow an appointment at Teachers College, Columbia University. That achievement, in conjunction with the publication of Blow's interpretation of Fröbel, *Symbolic Education*, in 1895, resulted in the swift spread of the "kindergarten movement" across the country. By 1900, there were more than 200,000 children in kindergarten in the United States (Cremin 1988).

Social Context

By the 1870s, the common school was well established in the United States. Horace Mann had waged his campaign for the common school with the hope that universal education would solve society's problems. He, like his wife and Elizabeth Peabody, saw the school as the center for instilling common values that would produce a moral populace ready to take responsibility for the democracy. As more immigrants, especially from eastern and southern Europe, arrived in the United States, their different ways and the grinding poverty under which they lived in the cities were perceived as sources of social discord and perhaps even unrest. Toward the end of the 19th century, commentary on the decline of the family, the fundamental social unit in the republic, began to appear. Because the family was also identified as the child's first teacher and "assumed to undergird all subsequent education" (Cremin 1988, 274), its decline was viewed as a national crisis. Indeed, the perceived decline of the family persisted through the 20th century, with the school seen throughout as the core of the solution to social problems. A story, frequently told to kindergarten children early in the 20th century, reflected the moralistic nature of the kindergarten curriculum and the tenor of the time. In the story, two children bring a flower home to their dingy tenement and present it to their mother. She places it in a glass of water near the window, but the window is too dirty to cast enough light on it to show its beauty. This inspires the mother to wash the window, which allows enough light in to show the dirt in the rest of the apartment. The mother is then inspired to clean the floors and the entire apartment. The father, who drinks too much and cannot keep a steady job, comes home to such a pleasant, clean apartment that he decides to spend less time in bars. Staying at home more, he quits drinking and is able to hold a steady job.

The large numbers of poor immigrants helped to encourage well-meaning progressive reformers in their quest to educate and assimilate them and their children into society and added impetus to the notion of the moral nature of public early childhood education. Diverse immigrant views on child rearing were dismissed as inadequate even by those who attempted to help the immigrants through settlement houses, religious clubs and clinics, and nurseries and kindergartens for their young children. As Cremin (1988, 276) noted:

> *Social settlement workers like Jane Addams and Lillian Wald were discovering as they reached out to their neighbors that children were locked in their homes for hours at a time or abandoned to the streets while their parents were at work and that assistance at child rearing was one of the most important services they could render. Moreover, they were finding that when immigrant slum families did devote themselves to child rearing, the folk wisdom they had brought with them from their native lands, particularly in matters of child health and nutrition, was insufficient to the task.*

With poverty and insufficient child rearing came child labor and juvenile delinquency. These persistent problems generated such works as Jacob Riis's *Children of the Poor* (1892), which inspired the development of pamphlets on prenatal, infant, and child care published by the U.S. Government Printing Office. In revised form, these pamphlets are still in print today. Immigrants, particularly Italians, were seen as exacerbating these problems as well. One book of the time described immigrants' views on education as "un-American." As Breckinridge and Abbott (1912, 66) argued, "The immigrant child frequently suffers from the fact that the parents do not understand that the community has a right to say that children under a certain age must be kept in school. It seems, for example, unimportant to the Italian peasant, who as a gloriously paid street laborer begins to cherish a vision of prosperity, whether his little girls go to school or not."

By 1918, all 48 states had some form of compulsory education law, and many were developing kindergarten programs to precede compulsory schooling (Cremin 1988). The problem of whether or not Fröbel's methods were suitable for children in the United States surfaced almost immediately.

Divergent Views on Kindergarten

The Fröbelian kindergarten was associated with perfection and was thought to be the perfect method by its disciples, because it was based on the idealistic premise that each person holds the "seeds" of all knowledge within. The purpose of education was to nurture the individual and the process of growth from within. Fröbel's methods were seen as the vehicle for this growth, which was held as potential in each human being. This gave the method a foundation in the ideal of unity; but, because the method accommodated some freedom of response to Fröbel's materials, it also allowed for individual differences and unique talents to develop.

Fröbel noticed that children played spontaneously and viewed that as the primary "impulse" of the child on which to base first educational experiences. He designed toys, small blocks, and other materials through which the child could, under careful guidance and in the prescribed order, come to understand the world. Each "play" or activity symbolized a universal truth, and, through repeated exposure, children would come to know the truths, at first subconsciously, but later, as they grew older, consciously. The materials were grouped into two categories, Gifts and Occupations. The Gifts were comprised of balls and small blocks that fit into larger geometric patterns. The teacher would dictate a design that the children were required to replicate. When the children were allowed to play freely with the Gifts, the teacher studied their work, analyzing it for signs of understanding. The Occupations were a series of activities such as sewing and painting, with dictated tasks comprising the majority of these activities as well. The beginning of the transfer of the derivation of motivation, the impulse, from instinct to duty was the aim of the curriculum that children received in Fröbelian kindergartens.

As Fröbel's methods became better known and kindergartens began to spring up around the country, there was a pressing need to educate kindergarten teachers in the methods. Kindergarten training schools also proliferated, but many were started by people who were not well versed in Fröbel's ideas. The need for teachers was so great that many of the training centers cut corners and shortened their programs, thus diluting Fröbel's methods and changing them. In addition, many of the kindergarten teachers who were sensitive to their students viewed a number of Fröbel's symbols, which were rural and based in nature, as irrelevant to the poor children living in urban slums. Conflicting views on the best way to educate young children in kindergarten emerged. Still, no matter what position they took, all involved in kindergarten education held Fröbel in high esteem. The focus of the dissension was whether or not his methods were suitable in the United States at the beginning of the 20th century. The leader of the reform point of view was unquestionably Patty Smith Hill. She, Blow, Peabody, Jane Addams, Lucy Wheelock, and others led what became known as the "kindergarten movement" to transform U.S. public education. They called themselves "kindergartners" to distinguish themselves from ordinary schoolteachers. These kindergartners, mostly middle-class women, shaped the course of the kindergarten curriculum in the United States, adapting the distinctly European concept to a nation with no national oversight of education to create a truly unique educational form ideally suited to U.S. society.

The U.S. Kindergarten at the Turn of the Century

Amidon (1927, 506) described a typical kindergarten, taught by Miss Emma and Miss Julia in the church basement of a "prairie town," in the United States of the late-19th and early-20th centuries in this way:

> In those days, one's chief responsibility in kindergarten, as in school, was to learn to do as one was told. There was a white circle painted on the floor. There was a locked cupboard to which Miss Julia kept the key. One sat on the white circle while Miss Emma told a story embodying some spiritual "lesson," and one did not squirm or ask questions. One sat in a little red chair, "hands folded at the edge of the table," when Miss Julia unlocked the cupboard, placing in front of each child The Gift, while Miss Emma explained precisely what was to be done with it. Richard might aspire to a pattern of his own design on his pegboard. Kathleen might feel more like clay modeling than paper weaving. Margery might prefer cutting paper doll dresses from her blue paper to folding it into a geometric form. But in the kindergarten one did as one was told, all except David who blew into tantrums of outraged dignity and thwarted ambition and was finally refused as a kindergarten pupil by Miss Emma.

Patty Smith Hill's reaction to a similarly critical student during circle time was quite different from Miss Emma's. As an educator, Hill was resolved to listen to her students and to learn from them. As Hill (in Amidon 1927, 508) stated:

> When I look back on my long experience in teaching, I am always grateful for what I have learned from the children. If one is not absorbed in administering "a system," one can learn so much in a school room!

There was little Howard, for instance, back in the first Louisville kindergarten. Howard could always manage to say what he meant. Every school room ought to have one child who is able to express to the teacher what others only feel. We were sitting in the traditional kindergarten circle, the children and I. In those days it was part of a good kindergartner's job to get over to the children "the topic of the day." I was earnestly holding forth looking to the right and left, to the front, and to the children on each side when Howard lifted his face to mine. "Say, Teacher," he demanded, "who are you talking to anyhow?" At once I realized what artificial nonsense the whole performance was. In the circle I was not talking to anyone. I was just spraying my ideas over a group of children, who had to listen whether they wanted to or not. The circle as a "symbol" was disbanded then and there. After this I did my talking with individual children and little groups who came to discuss matters of genuine interest. As soon as we ceased to make a rite of it, it was easy to get exchange of ideas and vigorous discussion among little children. This was an enormous gain in reality and directness, but given our small, spontaneous groups as working units, I found myself asking: How can we develop social consciousness in children of this age?

A Childhood Filled with Commitment

There is a lot to learn about fostering the development of social consciousness from the story of Patty Smith Hill's childhood. Born in the Reconstruction South in 1868, Patty was the fourth child of six (two boys and four girls), born into an educated, influential, but very nontraditional family of Louisville, Kentucky. The children were encouraged to be independent thinkers who worked hard for others as well as for themselves. As Chaffee (1925, 1–2) related, each of the Hill children, as they matured, "undertook some big piece of work and thirty years after the father's death Louisville people began to say that Louisville, like Rome, was built on seven Hills."

Patty Smith Hill's father, W. W. Hill, who, as a Presbyterian minister, was not eligible for service in the Civil War, "opened a college for the daughters of the South near Louisville, Kentucky, as his contribution to the reconstruction years" (Bailey 1931, 5). Dr. Hill, a graduate of Princeton University, believed that higher education should be available to women as well as to men so that they could be prepared to live an independent life. Reminiscing in 1925 about her childhood, Patty Hill (in Amidon 1927, 507) related that, though her family was financially comfortable, the Hill girls were encouraged to pursue a profession: "This was a radical thing everywhere fifty years ago, particularly in the South. My father had a horror of girls marrying 'just for a home' and he said that the only way to avoid this catastrophe was to prepare every young woman to 'stand on her own feet' economically. For this reason from our earliest years sisters and brothers alike discussed together and with our parents the type of work we wished to pursue when we were grown."

Patty Hill's mother was, it seems, a perfect match for a man who held such beliefs. She was a writer for the Louisville *Courier-Journal* who had grown up on an antebellum plantation. She valued literacy and human dignity, and as a young girl she taught all the captives who labored on her family's plantation to read and write. She had attempted admission to nearby Center College, but she was refused formal matriculation because of her sex. She was tutored privately by professors from the college, but she never was allowed to earn a degree.

Patty Hill's (in Chaffee 1925, 1–2) mother believed that children should be free to play and follow their own pursuits as well as learn the value of hard work:

> *My mother's philosophy of life was a happy one. She said children should have every pleasure that there was not some good reason they should not have—a radical point of view in those Puritanical times. . . . We children each had our own small garden. We were also allowed to play with hammer and nails. We used to work for days making playhouses, and our home was always open to other people's children. My mother used to say, she'd rather have other people's children at her house than to have her children at other people's houses. Then she'd always know what was going on. Our home was always hospitably open. The cook was told that what was good enough for us every day was good enough for company, so that if a guest came at the last moment, just an extra plate was all that was necessary. And we hardly knew what it was to sit down without guests.*

Patty Hill later attributed much of her philosophy and its success in classrooms to her upbringing in a home with an atmosphere of freedom where play was valued as much as work. She viewed her parents as role models whom she followed in the way that suited her most. Hill (in Chaffee 1925, 2–3) recalled that, by the time she was eight or nine, she knew what she wanted to do when she grew up, though she had never heard of kindergartens: "When I was about eleven, someone told me about a foundling's asylum, and I decided that a whole houseful of babies would be the finest thing in the world, and I went as far as to ask my mother to help me take charge of one when I grew up."

Mentors

There were, of course, other people to whom Patty Smith Hill attributed her success and ability to have such a deep impact on education. One was her first kindergarten pedagogy teacher, Anna E. Bryan, the director of a kindergarten training school in Louisville. Bryan had studied in Chicago and opened up the training school the year that Hill turned 18. Hill entered as one of Bryan's first students. As Hill (in Amidon 1927, 507) said, "I was the youngest in the class, but from the very beginning, Miss Bryan would say, 'Do not follow Fröebel blindly. I want to see what you, yourself will do.'" The free interpretation of Fröbel's philosophy was unheard of in kindergarten circles in the United States at that time, and one wonders whether Hill would have so persistently questioned the Fröbelian Gifts and Occupations if she had not had the encouragement of the courageous Bryan.

Bryan appointed Hill head teacher of the demonstration kindergarten in her training school the year that she graduated. Hill was a masterful teacher who inspired those around her, especially the children, to think creatively and independently. Hill (in Amidon 1927, 508) believed that she was actually following Fröbel's teaching, because she interpreted him as constantly searching, "sending out material to mothers and teachers urging them to criticize it after experimentation. Those who came after him did not have this fresh and adventurous spirit. In their hands his incomplete experimentation grew into a cult. The purpose of the kindergarten movement ceased to be a progressive scheme of education and became a 'system.'" Many educational leaders of the day were emerging as advocates of the Fröbelian system that Hill decried: Peabody, William T. Harris, and Blow. Blow was a national leader in kindergarten and a lecturer at Teachers College who would later become an intellectual adversary and close personal friend of Hill's.

Bryan and Hill experimented with different methods in their campus school kindergarten in Louisville, deciding that children would rather build houses and doll beds with Fröbel's Gift of rectangular blocks than the square dictated by the followers of his system. The two women traveled together to the National Education Association meeting of 1890, where Bryan presented a paper titled "The Letter Killeth," a critique of the dictation-like, systematized method of teaching children to draw so commonly practiced at that time. Hill illustrated the talk with drawings and students' original work, revolutionary techniques in the kindergarten of the 19th century. That summer they went to study with Francis Parker at the Cook County Normal School in Chicago. As Hill (in Chaffee 1925, 4) related, "Whenever there was anyone that either Miss Bryan or I could study with, we did so." They studied with G. Stanley Hall of Clark University in 1895, after receiving a questionnaire from him that was obviously critical of the traditional techniques. As Hill (in Amidon 1927, 508) later reported:

> *While a large number of kindergartners responded to Dr. Hall's invitation, at the close of his first class only two students remained for the exceedingly strenuous summer course he proposed—Miss Bryan and myself. This gave us a rare opportunity, as we had the whole summer for uninterrupted study under Dr. Hall and Professor Burnham. Here we were introduced to the new child study movement, to the necessity for changing materials, curricula, and methods in the light of new knowledge about both physical and mental health.*

Even as she was spending her summers studying with many of the leading Progressives of the day, among them John Dewey, William James, and Luther Gulick, Hill was adapting the Progressive philosophy to kindergarten methods. She had worked with the poor children of the ravaged Southern states of the Reconstruction era. She was deeply moved by the malnutrition, child labor, and high death rate among children of poverty. She had developed a lifelong commitment to democratic ideals and the importance of self-determination in activity, especially in childhood, as a means of empowering children to overcome social and economic disadvantages. As Hill (in an undated interview) put it, "Even tiny children have a right to 'life, liberty, and the pursuit of happiness.'"

In 1893, Bryan went to Chicago to study with John Dewey, leaving Hill as Principal and Supervisor of the Louisville Kindergarten Training School. That year, Hill mounted an exhibit on her new kindergarten methods in the Education Building at the Chicago World's Fair. By then, more than 3,000 visitors had signed the register as guests who had observed her kindergarten in Louisville, including Colonel Francis W. Parker; Jenny B. Merrill, supervisor of the kindergartens of the New York City Public Schools; Caroline T. Haven of the Ethical Culture School; and Milton Bradley, the first manufacturer of kindergarten materials (Fine n.d.).

The exhibit at the World's Fair drew a great deal of attention to Louisville and to Hill. She became a leader of the kindergarten movement, was a prominent lecturer at meetings of the International Kindergarten Union (IKU), and was appointed by that organization to head the Liberal Committee of the Committee of Nineteen in 1904. By

1905, when Dean James Earl Russell invited her to accept an appointment as lecturer at Teachers College, she had traveled all over the United States and twice to Europe, speaking on her progressive ideas and methods for teaching young children (Jammer 1960).

Hill had become a strong voice, not only for children but for their teachers as well. Her teacher education curriculum at the Louisville Training School included many academic subjects. She strongly encouraged the development of attitudes that would promote independence in teachers rather than dependence on the methods of others. It was only through the study of children, she felt, that teachers could know how to react to them in their classrooms, and it was only through independent thought that each teacher could develop a program suited for her particular children (Hill 1901). Late in her career, Hill (in Amidon 1927, 509) summed up her ideas on teachers this way:

> There are two great divisions of teachers, you know, cookbook teachers and check-erboard teachers. A cookbook teacher sits down every evening, measures out so much arithmetic, so much spelling, so much music, according to a pedagogical recipe and next day spoon-feeds it into his pupils. He calls the process education. But suppose he were getting ready for a game of chess or checkers. Would it do any good to take the board the evening before and figure out the campaign—first this move, then that move? When he sat down with his opponents, he would find that the vital factor had been entirely omitted from his calculations: the reaction of the other mind. I tell my students that that is our main concern as teachers—the reaction of the other mind. Of course cook book teaching is easier. But the other kind—well, from the child's point of view the other kind offers possibilities of real adventure. And for the teacher it is a lot more fun.

It is easy to see why Russell persevered in persuading Hill to leave Louisville to seek her fortune in New York City, though she was very reluctant to do so.

James Earl Russell

Of all her mentors, the last was one of the strongest and had the most profound effect on Patty Smith Hill's life and work. James Earl Russell was aware of the two opposing views in the kindergarten movement and already had a major proponent of the traditional methods as a lecturer at Teachers College. Susan Blow remained staunchly committed to Fröbel's methods throughout her career. Hill had attended Teachers College in the summer of 1905 and received an invitation from Dean Russell to lecture there that fall. She impressed everyone with her open-mindedness, sincerity, and dedication—so much that Russell (1937) asked her to extend the leave she had taken from the Louisville kindergarten to a full year, offering her an honorarium of $20 per lecture. When she demurred at the low pay and the prospect of an extended absence from her job, Russell (1905) replied, "You should take it as a compliment that we are so anxious to extend your period of residence, and at the same time attribute the scaling of salary to our unavoidable poverty. Nevertheless, I have telegraphed you that, womanlike, you may have your own way."

Thus began a friendship that lasted through the rest of Hill's career. Russell gave her the opportunity to experiment with her ideas in the kindergartens of the Speyer School and the Horace Mann Schools. He encouraged her to carry on her work and served as a sounding board for her complaints as well as an advisor in her dealings with her enemies. She had come to Teachers College as a "radical" who was too unorthodox for many kindergarten educators. Sometimes she did not feel up to the task.

Russell recounted the story of his offering Hill a full-time appointment in a 1927 letter:

> *When it became necessary to reorganize our Kindergarten Department, I found that there was sharp competition between two schools of thought. Miss Blow and her disciples adhered very religiously to the formal interpretation of Froebel's philosophy and practice. Miss Hill was one of the two or three prominent leaders of the more liberal wing. My plan at first was to have both sides presented in Teachers College, as it is part of my policy to see that no one mode of thought is here represented to the exclusion of the others. Consequently for some time, I tried to drive the team abreast by making provision for both parties to present their case.*

To achieve this goal, Russell first asked the two women to share a course of lectures that were open to the public in January 1906. Each lectured on her point of view every other week, alternating with the other (Jammer 1960). The prospect of facing the impressive and powerful Susan Blow, who had chaired the Conservative Committee of the Committee of Nineteen in 1903, almost caused Hill to decline Russell's invitation. She had already encountered Blow in her activities in the IKU. In fact, the Committee of Fifteen had become the Committee of Nineteen in 1904, when it became obvious that there were two opposing points of view in the kindergarten movement. The Committee later split into three groups, with Blow chairing the Conservative Committee; Hill, the Liberal; and Wheelock, the Liberal-Conservative, each of which then issued a final report (IKU 1913). The intensity of Hill's concern was evident, as Russell's (1906) reply illustrated:

> *Dear Miss Hill:*
> *I can hardly believe that your present mental condition is other than temporary stage fright. Otherwise, how can you explain the apparent despondency of an able-bodied young woman at the head of the graduate department in her subject in the leading Teachers College of the world when she thinks of the specter of one who is a master of the same field but who has at best a few months or a few years in which to work? . . . But it is still worse than even this. The younger woman occupies not only the headship of the department but has a permanent appointment; the specter to which I refer has merely a temporary lectureship contingent on gifts received.*

Hill (1906a) replied to that letter in the affirmative, with a vow to enter upon her new work with enthusiasm and determination to make it a success if the possibility was in her power. She and Blow lectured their views every other week, as planned. As Hill (in Amidon 1927, 508) related, she later found it amusing: "The same group of students were exposed to diametrically opposed points of view on different days. It's a wonder the class survived!"

Hill's Play Room

From the beginning, Patty Smith Hill, with the continuous blessing and encouragement of Dean Russell, began a process of change and experimentation that never ceased during her tenure at Teachers College. Her first students, mostly kindergarten teachers and supervisors from the New York area, had been staunch advocates of traditional ways and the students of Susan Blow. Hill's methods were sometimes too liberal for the New York audience. Russell, seeing this, allowed Hill to establish a "play" room at Teachers College in which Hill, along with Luella Palmer, could experiment with their new methods with children who had not attended traditional kindergartens. They recruited children from three to seven years of age with no previous school experience and set to work designing materials and a curriculum suited for the children they had rather than an ideal of what someone thought children should be (Hill 1906c; Palmer 1906).

Hill had studied with Luther Gulick in 1898, in what she called the first school of play in the United States. It was there that she had started to experiment with different size blocks to see whether the children, like she and her brothers and sisters, enjoyed building structures large enough for them to play inside. Her own childhood had an effect on her work long after she left Louisville. As Hill (in Amidon 1927, 509) recounted:

> *I looked back on my own childhood when my sisters and I tried to make houses big enough to get into but the available materials were not suited to our purposes. We tried placing boards on top of barrels but the construction was so shaky that we were compelled to lie down after creeping "upstairs." . . . We worked on this scheme twelve or thirteen years before we devised our present set of blocks which schools all over the world are using.*

Because the New York crowd was so conservative, Hill dared not call her first Speyer School Play Room a kindergarten in the beginning.

Gradually, however, her reputation grew, and her ideas gained acceptance. Hill led the move toward abandoning Fröbelian materials and developing materials based on activities relevant to the child's experience. Hill (in Amidon 1927, 509) maintained, however, that, true to her interpretation of Fröbel's experimental attitude toward his philosophy, she "kept the Fröbelian attitude and spirit." She never adopted Montessori's methods, feeling that they were too rigid and artificial for U.S. children.

The Child as Autonomous Learner

One of Hill's ideas that revolutionized teaching in the kindergarten was the notion that young children had minds and personalities of their own—that they were unique individuals with interests and needs important enough to be heeded. She could not see the connection between Fröbel's Gifts and Occupations and the way children took pride in their work. In her study of young children, she saw that children of two or three cared little for their products, but those who were four, five, or six cared a great deal. Why, then, she reasoned, should the product be dictated to the child, when the child has ideas of his or her own? As Hill (1906b, 11) related, "Show a boy of five the kite fold which, when completed, will form one of a series to be pasted in the flat in a scrap book; then show him the same form made of tough paper and sufficiently large to experiment with in the wind. Ask him which he prefers to make, and you will see whether products are of importance. Also, watch the difference between his passivity and eagerness in the two cases."

Hill was quite vocal in her position that young children had personalities and that they were capable, with the right teaching, of being taught to think for themselves. She argued that a teacher who knew his or her children could help each child to develop his or her own individuality. She encouraged teachers to keep detailed records of children's behavior, even during free play, so that they might know each child as a person. She encouraged parent interviews as a means of getting to know each child's personality and temperament and as a valuable lesson in recognizing that the child has a life outside of school. In this way, she argued, the teacher could develop the curriculum most suited to each child.

The Child as a Social Learner

Hill did not merely acknowledge the young child's individual needs. Based on years of observation, she knew the importance of the child's social needs as well. In addition to her study of children, she attributed the philosophical basis for her ideas to Fröbel. As she wrote in her part of the Report of the Committee of Nineteen, Fröbel believed that the organization of the subject matter, the curriculum of the kindergarten, grew out of the social life of the child (IKU 1913).

Hill related how she fostered cooperation through the use of large blocks too heavy to handle alone and how children worked together to solve problems in their play. A true sense of purpose, Hill (in Amidon 1927, 509) said, came from the child's own life rather than the purposes set out by the teacher in her lessons:

> *A group of six year olds taught me about this many years ago. They worked for a week over a model of a Fifth Avenue bus which they built with blocks. They criticized, discussed plans, and improved the model with undiminished enthusiasm, till they were satisfied. We had to learn through these children what real concentration is when a job challenges their interest. It is astonishing the difference between attention which is only a response to the teacher's demand and the concentration inspired by enthusiasm for a job.*

Hill firmly argued that young children could learn democratic principles only if they were involved in democratic group situations. Hill (1915) also declared that these principles could not be learned unless they were experienced in a meaningful context—the child's own interests. She fostered independence and leadership in much the same manner as it had been for her as a child growing up in Louisville and later as a woman apprehensive about coming to Teachers College to continue her work. She advocated allowing children the freedom to choose their own means and ends, yet also allowing for aid and encouragement if they needed it. As Hill (in Amidon 1927, 508–09) related:

> *Jack taught me about this. Jack was in Miss Garrison's group, here at Teachers College. A canary bird had been given to the children. When Miss Garrison carried the cage into the room, they all crowded about her, admiring and asking questions. The cage was finally placed in the window, and the children scattered to their various occupations. Presently Jack tugged at Miss Garrison's sleeve. "What's the bird's name?" he asked.*
>
> *"I don't believe he has a name."*
>
> *"Then I will name him," said Jack. "I will name him for myself: Jack."*
>
> *"But Jack, does the bird belong to you?" asked Miss Garrison.*
>
> *"No, he doesn't."*

"To whom does the bird belong?"

"I suppose he belongs to all of the children in this room."

"Well, then, who has the right to name him?"

"I suppose all the children ought to name him," Jack answered slowly. "Miss Garrison, please call the children together to name the bird!"

Miss Garrison waited a moment and then suggested, "But Jack, you are the one who wants the bird named. Can't you call the children together?"

It was a big undertaking for a five-year-old. Jack hesitated, uncertain how to organize a "town meeting," but convinced of the need of one. Finally he went from one group of children to another saying, "Our bird hasn't a name—come on, let's name him. You can nail that afterward—let's name our bird right away."

Jack persuaded Leland and Margot and Sally to help him arrange chairs. They placed them in a big circle, "so we can all see each other," with a seat for Miss Garrison. But when all the chairs were occupied, it was Jack, not the teacher, who began to hold forth. The group entered into animated discussion, Jack insisting that Jessie mustn't talk till Emily was through and that everyone must be quiet when Harold, who stuttered, began to talk. At last a name was chosen, the big circle broke up and the children returned to their sewing and carpentry and painting. But Jack had taught us something about kindergarten organization that we needed to know: the small, spontaneous group is the natural unit for work with little children. A common interest is the only basis for calling together a large group. Given such an interest, a large group can function simply and spontaneously, and through it the children gain experience as parts of a social whole.

Hill held forth with her beliefs, writing and speaking frequently in the two first decades of this century on the value of making the interests of the child the central motivating force in classroom activity. She knew that young children, in their play, imitated adult behaviors and work activities. Thus, she encouraged children to engage in all kinds of occupations in the kindergarten classroom: carpentry, cooking, gardening, and painting. Though the products may not have been perfect, she saw social value in exposing children to all kinds of labor (Jammer 1960). Respect for all occupations would, she asserted, help to reduce the divisions between social and economic classes. The kindergarten, as the first formal stage in education, was the first place to begin formal lessons in this process (Hill 1912).

The Importance of Play

Patty Smith Hill argued that, for the child, play was learning. She had observed many children and, though she made a distinction between free and directed play, realized through her observations that, for children, all play was valuable. Free play developed initiative, self-reliance, and freedom, while directed play helped the young child, who was rather "fragmentary," to grow less impulsive and more focused (Hill 1906b). She advocated a balance between the two, with free play as a time for the teacher to observe children and to promote the development of democratic ideals. More and more, she departed from the blind acceptance of European methods and materials, espousing the development of a truly "American" method of schooling young children, using domestic materials and activities as the basis for learning (Hill 1913).

Hill was appointed Head of the Kindergarten Department at Teachers College in 1910, and she moved her play room to the Horace Mann School Kindergarten. Students came from all over the country and the world to study kindergarten methods and supervision with Patty Smith Hill. She was able to report, at the time of her retirement in 1935, that there was a kindergartner trained in her methods in every state of the Union, and in many countries around the world (Chaffee 1925; Amidon 1927; Fine 1936). To continue the development of the U.S. kindergarten, she advocated that every city maintain at least one experimental kindergarten for research and development (Hill 1915).

There was, however, a danger in developing a kindergarten based solely on U.S. culture. The United States and its schools were founded on a Puritan ethic that valued work and devalued play as idleness. This ethic also implied an acceptance of the inherent drudgery in work and enjoyment in play. As Hill (1906b, 4) wrote:

> As long as we limit work to ends which authority considers sufficiently valuable to impose upon willing workers, secured through processes which are unendurable to them, and limit play to the pleasant processes which result from whim or caprice, there will necessarily be a battle in adjusting the motives of play and work in elementary education. Not only does such a conception of work apply more directly to drudgery, but such a conception of play is inadequate to explain the serious significance of play in the period of prolonged infancy. So long as we regard work as activity leading toward an end imposed by authority, and play as whimsical indulgence inactivities leading toward no end of worth to the child or society, the battle will wage between the kindergartner and primary teacher.

Though both Hill and advocates of the conservative movement in the kindergarten avowed a debt to Fröbel's teachings, her major points of departure in kindergarten curriculum and teaching were in the value of play. Hill (1907; 1925) also emphasized the acceptance of the child as an autonomous individual with needs and interests and the ability to be self-directed, along with the belief that democratic principles could be modeled in the early childhood classroom and that they could be learned through the experience of the child rather than through the dictates of adult authority. She was indeed a radical.

Other Innovations of Patty Smith Hill

Hill's years of labor at Teachers College were rewarded with honors and worldwide acclaim as a leader of the Progressive Education movement in the United States. In 1922, the trailblazing Hill was the third woman promoted to full professor at Teachers College. In 1929, she was awarded an honorary doctorate from Columbia University by Nicholas Murray Butler—again, one of the few women to be so honored. In his speech, Butler (in Fine 1936, 2) said, "Year in, year out, Dr. Hill is answering the age-old question of Epictetus, 'What constitutes a child?' In the spirit of Fröbel, she is finding new ways and means to make the child the father of the worthwhile man." She continued to write and lecture, and students continued to come to New York to study with her and her colleagues, including the aforementioned Miss Garrison, who had been a student in the famed Blow-Hill Lecture course of 1906 (Jammer 1960).

Hill's lectures were famous and had the hallmark of her style. She held court in Horace Mann auditorium, lecturing from the stage, standing next to a grand piano graced by a silver candelabra, which was brought onstage just before she arrived. She was a very popular teacher. On her retirement, Hill (n.d.) was pleased to announce, "We have people in charge of kindergarten work in almost every teacher-training school in the country and the world. In the 47 years that I've taught, I've seen the whole thing change. I don't believe there's a normal school in this country without one of our graduates substituting the new ideas for the old."

With the onset of the Great Depression, Patty Smith Hill became an even more strident voice in the call for universal preschool education and the coordination of the kindergarten curriculum with that of the primary grades. She also advocated parent education so that there could be greater coherence between the values of the home and those of the school. With great vision, which we can only now appreciate, Hill (n.d.) said, "Never has the kindergarten been more needed than in modern life, with its limited home space for play, its out-family mother employed in the mills, the factories, and mines, and in other commercial enterprises. These conditions were serious enough, but when the wave of unemployment swept the whole country, the dangers of neglect were multiplied a hundred-fold."

In her retirement, she opened the Hilltop Community Center in a building donated by the Jewish Theological Seminary on 123rd Street, one block from Teachers College, and equipped with furniture donated by the Salvation Army. There, doctors sent by the New Deal provided health care for neighborhood children and their parents. Teachers, again paid by the government, with the help of an experimental teacher-training program at Teachers College administered by Hill and Agnes Snyder, provided education. Hill had a vision of the Center being the focal point for all positive activities in the economically poor and ethnically and racially diverse neighborhood (Fine n.d.). Hill (in Fine n.d.) stated, "Whether the mother is economically employed or in search of a job, the New Deal has a grave responsibility in setting leaders to work to create a new code for the protection of young children, a code for which we will include in its plans proper and increasing care of pre-school children of all classes of society whether they are found in large cities, small villages, or rural communities." Hill worked at the Hilltop Community Center as a volunteer until her death in 1946 at the age of 78.

The U.S. Kindergarten Today

Children in kindergartens all over the world encounter Patty Smith Hill every day in their singing of "Happy Birthday to You" or when they do large motor movements, play in rhythm bands, paint freely at the easel, play with large blocks, choose their own activity centers, visit the school nurse for a school physical, drink from water fountains or from separate cups, or use paper napkins at snack time (Rudnitski and Erickson 1993). When the custodian comes into their classroom to wash the floor at night, it is due to Hill's work. Though the memory of Patty Smith Hill does not loom large in our minds, it certainly has been a large enough part of our early childhoods. As did William F. Russell (in Fine n.d.), son of James Earl Russell and Dean of Teachers College at the time of Hill's retirement, we can say, "Miss Hill brought me up!"

References

Amidon, B. 1927. Forty years in kindergarten: An interview with Patty Smith Hill. *Survey Graphic* 2(6): 506–09, 523.

Bailey, C. S. 1931. Who's who in the schools: Patty Smith Hill. *American Childhood* 17(1): 5–6, 55–56.

Breckinridge, S. P., and E. Abbott. 1912. *The delinquent child and the home.* New York: Charities Publication Committee.

Chaffee. 1925. Interview by Miss Chaffee, Summer 1925. *Patty Smith Hill: Miscellaneous biographical data 1925–1936: Patty Smith Hill papers.* New York: Teachers College, Columbia University.

Committee of Nineteen. 1924. *Pioneers of the kindergarten in America.* New York: Century.

Cremin, L. A. 1988. *American education: The metropolitan experience, 1876–1980.* New York: Harper & Row.

Fine, B. n.d. Patty Smith Hill and progressive education. *Patty Smith Hill papers.* New York: Teachers College, Columbia University.

Fine, B. 1936. Patty Smith Hill: A great educator. *American Childhood* 21(May–June).

Fröbel, F. (trans. J. Jarvis) 1898. *Friedrich Froebel's pedagogics of the kindergarten: Or, His ideas concerning the play and playthings of the child.* New York: Appleton.

Hill, M. J., and P. S. Hill. 1896. *Song stories for the kindergarten.* Chicago: Summy.

Hill, P. S. 1901. Simplification of gifts and occupations. *International Kindergarten Union Proceedings,* 94–96. Washington, D.C.: IKU.

Hill, P. S. 1906a. Letter to James Earl Russell, 25 January. *Correspondence of Patty Smith Hill and James Earl Russell, 1905–1925: James Earl Russell Papers.* New York: Teachers College, Columbia University.

Hill, P. S. 1906b. The relation of work and play in modern education: Address given at the I.K.U. Convention, Milwaukee, April. *Kindergarten Review* 17(1): 7–14.

Hill, P. S. 1906c. The Speyer school experimental play room. *Kindergarten Review* 17(November): 137–40.

Hill, P. S. 1907. Some conservative and progressive phases of kindergarten education. In *The kindergarten and its relation to elementary education: National Society for the Study of Education yearbook,* pt. II, ed. A. V. S. Harris, E. A. Kirkpatrick, M. Kraus-Boelte, P. S. Hill, H. M. Mills, and N. Vanderwalker, 61–85. Chicago: University of Chicago Press.

Hill, P. S. 1912. Democracy in the kindergarten. *Kindergarten Review* 22: 432–33.

Hill, P. S. 1913. Some hopes and fears for the kindergarten of the future. *Proceedings of the International Kindergarten Union,* 89–101. Washington, D.C.: IKU.

Hill, P. S. 1915. *Experimental studies in kindergarten theory and practice.* New York: Bureau of Publications, Teachers College, Columbia University.

Hill, P. S. 1925. Changes in curricula and method in kindergarten education. *Childhood Education* 2: 99–106.

Hill, P. S. no date. Interview. *Patty Smith Hill: Miscellaneous biographical data, 1925–1936—Patty Smith Hill papers.* New York: Teachers College, Columbia University.

International Kindergarten Union. 1913. *The kindergarten: Reports of the Committee of Nineteen on the theory and practice of the kindergarten.* New York: Houghton-Mifflin.

Jammer, M. C. 1960. Patty Smith Hill and reform of the American kindergarten. Ph.D. diss. Teachers College, Columbia University.

Palmer, L. 1906. Results of observations in the Speyer school experimental play room. *Kindergarten Review* 17(November): 140–47.

Peabody, E. P. 1882. The origin and growth of the kindergarten. *Education* 2(523): 507–27.

Peabody, E. P., and M. P. Mann. 1877. *Guide to the kindergarten and intermediate class and moral culture of infancy.* New York: Steiger.

Riis, J. A. 1892. *The children of the poor.* New York: Scribner's Sons.

Rudnitski, R. A., and M. Erickson. 1993. Student teachers' perceptions of play in early childhood classrooms. Paper presented at the annual meeting of the American Educational Research Association, April, Atlanta, Ga.

Russell, J. E. 1905. Letter to Patty Smith Hill, 2 February. *Correspondence of Patty Smith Hill and James Earl Russell, 1905–1925: James Earl Russell Papers.* New York: Teachers College, Columbia University.

Russell, J. E. 1906. Letter to Patty Smith Hill, 11 January. *Correspondence of Patty Smith Hill and James Earl Russell, 1905–1925: James Earl Russell Papers.* New York: Teachers College, Columbia University.

Russell, J. E. 1927. Letter to Ilse Forest, 23 February. *James Earl Russell Papers.* New York: Teachers College, Columbia University

Russell, J. E. 1937. *Founding Teachers College.* New York: Bureau of Publications, Teachers College, Columbia University.

Chapter 5

'Democracy's Proving Ground': Alice Miel and Democratic Citizenship Education in the Schools

by Elizabeth Anne Yeager

Alice Miel, a nationally prominent curriculum-development scholar and practitioner at Teachers College, Columbia University, frequently has been overlooked in research on the history of the social studies and citizenship education, even as attention to women in this field has risen. Miel made important contributions to the practice and theory of children's democratic social learning. Her work served as a strong historical antecedent to current research on diversity in the social studies and the elementary school classroom in general. Miel's career offers a valuable source for deeper understanding of an important era in U.S. schooling, as well as insight into women's contributions to social education.

Three themes emerge in Miel's work. First, she advocated democratic ideals and the development of democratic behavior as the ultimate goal of schooling. Second, she applied theories of social learning and democratic principles and processes to various aspects of the school curriculum. Third, she applied her ideas about a democratic social learning environment to specific areas of the curriculum, particularly to the social studies, and to the elementary school curriculum as a whole.

One important point must be made about historical interpretation of Miel's work. Above all, Miel's was a scholarship of the reflective, practical, and personal that she sought to make highly relevant and accessible to school practitioners and to her students. However, much of the historical and philosophical context of her scholarship cannot be documented in conventional ways. Miel often did not document in footnotes, memos, journals, and recorded conversations the nature of the context in which she lived, taught, and worked. She was an activist and intellectual who read widely, internalized many of the prominent ideas of her day, reflected these in her teaching and research, and generated practical ideas on how these might apply to elementary schools. The fact that she was not a textual scholar of, for example, John Dewey, George Counts, William Heard Kilpatrick, David Riesman, or Gunnar Myrdal—and did not always explicitly reference their work—is not evidence that she was unaware of their impact. Nor is it evidence that she did not understand their major points. Indeed, she extended some of these ideas into the classroom in highly accessible language. However, it must be acknowledged that she did not footnote extensively in many of her published articles. One must simply infer from reading her work and through knowledge of the context of her career at Teachers College, her professional relationships, and her activism in education that she knew a great deal both inside and outside the world of education. When possible, in this chapter, I will refer to contextual issues that likely influenced her thinking.

Biographical Sketch

The progressive movement in education emerges as the strong undercurrent in Miel's story. The formative years for what would become the centerpiece of her career in education can be traced to the University of Michigan, where she benefited from her association with Professor Stuart Courtis, a professor of educational philosophy who was the first "deliberately democratic teacher" she had ever encountered (Miel 1994). Other formative years were spent at Tappan Junior High School in Ann Arbor, Michigan, where she taught social studies and Latin in the early 1930s. Miel had a high regard for Otto Haisley, the Ann Arbor school superintendent who developed an educational environment in which local school faculty members and students could practice democratic skills of deliberation and decision making (Miel 1994). At Tappan, Miel collaborated with her principal, G. Robert Koopman, and other colleagues on several curriculum projects. Koopman, according to Miel (1994), led a "democratically run school" and nurtured her interest in the application of democratic principles to education; he also initiated the involvement of teachers, parents, and community members in curriculum development.

One of the collaborative curriculum projects in which Miel participated yielded a junior high social studies curriculum guide that reflected the awakening concern of Koopman, Miel, and their colleagues about the effects of the Great Depression on society and the schools. The guide also addressed their emerging conviction that "the breakdown in our social, economic, and political structure has brought into serious question the objectives and purposes which have dominated public education during the past quarter century" (Koopman, Avery, Miel, and Oakes 1933). Incorporating the ideas of John Dewey, as well as those of leading Progressive-Era educators Harold Rugg, Ann Shumaker, and William Heard Kilpatrick, Miel and her colleagues demonstrated that the school curriculum must be modified to emphasize the study of contemporary social problems. Rugg, Shumaker, and Kilpatrick advocated "child-centered" education, in which teachers and students worked together to determine what was worthwhile to learn and how to learn it. The curriculum guide (Koopman et al. 1933) drew upon several prominent strains of progressive educational thought. The first stressed Dewey's (1902) notion of education as experience and of the child and the curriculum as two limits that define a single process. Education was the continuous recreation of the individual through experience, curriculum was the organization of experience, and the school was society's agency for furnishing a selected environment in which directed growth could take place more effectively during certain periods of a child's life. A second aspect of the guide propounded Boyd Bode's (1927) concern for a new social order focused primarily on the development of the capacity of personality. Third, the guide also drew from ideas of Kilpatrick (1918) and Rugg and Shumaker (1928) about how the teacher's role could be reconceptualized to promote the concepts of freedom, individuality, and initiative in a child-centered classroom.

Another landmark experience for Miel was a 1936 session at The Ohio State University with Laura Zirbes, a prominent figure in the field of elementary education. Miel left that meeting with a commitment to understanding children, not just content, and to providing for their individual differences.

Indeed, "child-centered" progressive education during the late 1930s, according to Cremin (1961), had become the conventional wisdom in U.S. educational thought and practice. Miel moved into this company in the early years of her career in education. A 1938 *Time* cover story perhaps overstated its conclusion that no U.S. school had completely escaped the progressive influence; clearly, not all U.S. educators embraced these ideas (Cuban 1984; Davis 1976). By the 1940s, both internal divisions and external attacks led to a fracturing of the progressive movement (Bode 1938).

At this time of transition for the progressive education movement, the locus of Miel's story began to shift to Teachers College, Columbia University, where it would remain for the next three decades. Miel began as the doctoral student of Hollis L. Caswell, to whom she had been introduced by G. Robert Koopman in 1942. Caswell, then chair of the newly organized Department of Curriculum and Teaching at Teachers College, had already enhanced the visibility of the curriculum field. He developed the idea of method in curriculum making, focused attention on the process by which a variety of people interacted to make curriculum, tried to reduce the gap between theory and practice by defining curriculum as actual experiences undergone by learners under the direction of the school, and provided a curriculum design that helped teachers apply concepts from organized knowledge to the solution of social problems (Seguel 1966; Burlbaw 1989). Caswell encouraged Miel to attend Teachers College for her doctorate and offered her a part-time instructor position. He agreed to serve as her major professor and helped her to formulate the problem of curriculum change as a social process for her dissertation, which was later published as *Changing the Curriculum: A Social Process* (1946). Miel went on to serve as a professor at Teachers College from 1944 through 1971; she also chaired the Department of Curriculum and Teaching at Teachers College from 1960 through 1967.

Miel became more deeply involved in progressive ideas, even as the movement itself began to wane. Her career at Teachers College spanned the later years of the college's preeminence as the intellectual crossroads of the progressive education movement (Cremin 1961). Her tenure there also spanned the movement's alleged decline and disarray in the 1950s as the main target of conservatives who attacked progressive philosophy and demanded a return to the "basics" of schooling. In the 1960s, Miel's last decade at Teachers College, the national mood shifted again as Charles Silberman and other humanist educators decried conformity and rigidity in school curricula and urged that the focus of education return to the needs of individual learners.

In Miel's early years as a member of the Teachers College faculty, the postwar era brought turmoil to the world of education in general, and to Teachers College in particular. Conservative attacks on progressive education were led by such critics as Arthur Bestor (1953), Admiral Hyman Rickover (1959), and Mortimer Smith (1949), who advocated a return to "traditional" academic content in the schools. During the late 1940s and 1950s, Teachers College also experienced a number of internal struggles as the progressive movement splintered. Miel's work does not seem to have been directly attacked by conservatives, and, from all appearances, Miel maintained her strong convictions and continued on the same scholarly path. Later, Miel (1994) acknowledged problems within the progressive movement and criticized its lack of a unified base of support, as well as its lack of new ideas. Though she acknowledged that Dewey's ideas had been distorted by some—for example, in some educators' "overemphasis on the individual" and in "activities just for activity's sake"—Miel (1994) argued that most of progressive education was constructive.

Beginning in the 1950s, the Red Scare affected Teachers College, as it did all of U.S. society. Communist hunters looked askance at this institution in particular, regarding it as the de facto headquarters of left-wing subversive educators (Caute 1978). Miel had personal experiences with the Red Scare on several occasions and was subjected to vague accusations of Communist affiliation. In general, though, she remained largely insulated from the more extreme manifestations of anti-Communist activity throughout the nation. Her career did not suffer; in fact, Miel was promoted to full professor in 1952, a time when only slightly more than one-third of college faculty members were women. In an era when women often found promotion difficult in academia, Teachers College was a pioneer in this regard (Cremin, Shannon, and Townsend 1954). Miel (1994) recalled the large number of female professors and students who were "treated as equals," and she never felt that she was either "punished or promoted" because of her gender.

In terms of some of Miel's research accomplishments, two of her studies during her tenure at Teachers College merit particular attention. From 1958 to 1962, she directed the Study of Schools in Changing Communities. From this project, she developed her 1967 book with Edwin Kiester, *The Shortchanged Children of Suburbia*. A. Harry Passow (1995) characterized this research study as a "groundbreaker" in its emphasis on what suburban schools were failing to teach about human differences and cultural diversity. In 1967, Miel had worked with Passow on a separate study of the Washington, D.C., public elementary schools (Miel 1967).

Miel was one of the early presidents of the Association for Supervision and Curriculum Development (1953–54). In the 1970s, she became a guiding influence in the founding of the World Council on Curriculum and Instruction (WCCI). The establishment of the WCCI was a natural outgrowth of her interest in improved curricula for all children and her work with doctoral students from all over the world. She also played an active part in the Association for Childhood Education International (ACEI) for several years. One of the distinguishing features of her career was her advocacy of global understanding through cooperation in international educational activities. Through these activities, and through her supervision of more than 140 doctoral dissertations, Miel's influence was indeed widespread.

Miel, Democracy, and Democratic Social Learning: Contexts and Meanings

Meanings, manifestations, and enactments of democracy were at the center of Miel's career, though she never adhered dogmatically to a precise definition of democracy. She believed that, though certain fundamental ideas were embedded in the term, its meaning must be continually developed and nurtured by people who professed it. Like Dewey (1927), she conceived of democracy as more than a system of government; to her, democracy was a unique way of being, thinking, and living with others.

Miel's interpretation of democracy was developed in the context of the era of Franklin and Eleanor Roosevelt, whom she greatly admired. Dewey's (1916) ideas in *Democracy and Education* especially influenced Miel's beliefs. In particular, Dewey (1927) argued that, as long as the structure of schools remained undemocratic and repelled intellectual initiative and inventiveness, all efforts toward reform would be compromised and their fruition postponed indefinitely.

With regard to Miel's understanding of democracy in practice, especially her own opportunities for democratic participation in educational settings, she benefited from her experiences in the Ann Arbor public schools. There, Miel worked with and observed democratic leaders who created settings in which teachers and students could practice democracy. As a doctoral student at Teachers College, Miel developed her ideas in the context of the Teachers College democratic mission that the faculty had articulated during World War II (Cremin et al. 1954).

Importantly, as a professor and administrator at Teachers College, Miel took very seriously her responsibility to model democratic principles through her teaching and administrative tasks. She structured her courses in ways that promoted students' involvement while placing a responsibility upon them to think and plan cooperatively and creatively. Wendell Hunt (1994), a student and advisee of Miel's in 1950 who later became principal of Western Michigan University's laboratory school, recalled that Miel "put into practice (in the course) her principles regarding democratic teaching and cooperative planning." For example, class members were involved in the selection of curriculum issues and concepts that they wanted to address in the course. They also had a strong role in determining the nature and direction of class discussions. Hunt (1994) explained that Miel "structured the course around what the students wanted to learn and played a facilitator role." Other former students were impressed by the overarching consistency between Miel's beliefs and her actual classroom practices (Martinello 1994; Varis 1994; Passow 1995; Dwyer 1971; Corbin 1971; Berman 1992). As Berman (1992, 107) summarized, Miel's teaching was distinctive and influential: "Never were 'right' answers taught. Rather, preferred ways of solving problems, relating to others, and searching for knowledge were sought. Her teaching was quiet but penetrating; the questions she evoked in learners were lingering ones."

Moreover, Miel was noted for her democratic leadership of the Department of Curriculum and Teaching. As chair of the department from 1960 to 1967, Miel tried "to apply the democratic principles she had been crafting so carefully through the years," attempting to use group problem-solving approaches (Berman 1992, 108). Though she came to the position with a structured agenda, Miel was noted for her "willingness to entertain a wide range of alternative viewpoints" and for her willingness to facilitate the ability of professors to "pursue their individual research, writing, and other professional activities, while at the same time fostering consensus when consensus was essential to carrying out departmental affairs" (Bellack 1994, 1). Miel was able to survive in this sometimes rancorous environment because of her efforts to build consensus, develop democratic processes, and support her opinions with strong evidence (Passow 1995); she was "very skilled in human relations" (Alexander 1994).

Miel's study with Hollis L. Caswell had influenced her belief that schools should play an active role in helping to mold a democratic social order (Caswell and Campbell 1935). Miel (1986) believed that the school was democracy's proving ground, because it had a large share of the responsibility for socializing the nation's young people into participation in civic life. Though some critics may have demurred that democratic lessons could be gained from an institution that mandated participation, Miel viewed the school as society in microcosm, where people from many backgrounds learned about freedom and responsibility, individuality and cooperation—all with an eye toward democratic citizenship.

Furthermore, throughout her life Miel continued to develop a keen sense of the historical context of social problems that, for her, raised acute concerns for the future of a democratic society—postwar reconstruction, the Cold War and Red Scare, the social tensions between "haves" and "have nots," and the Watergate scandal. In particular, she was deeply affected by the state of race relations and civil rights in U.S. society. Miel (1994) often taught African-American students in her classes at Teachers College, and she had several formative experiences that brought racial issues into increasingly sharp focus for her as she learned about and sometimes witnessed her own students' experiences with prejudice and discrimination. Miel (1994) sought to move beyond the outmoded notion of racial tolerance—that, for her, connoted "putting up" with people who were different—to a more active, broader notion of intercultural understanding and appreciation.

Miel also sought to refute the claims of back-to-basics school reformers who were, in the 1970s, enjoying the spotlight. She argued that the "basics" also extended to the "moral-ethical-social realm" and that social and character issues should be given a prominent place in the school curriculum. Miel was convinced that students' understanding of freedom and responsibility should be high on the agenda of every school in the United States. She returned to these themes in 1986 in the context of the "educational excellence" movement, manifested in reports such as *A Nation at Risk* (National Commission on Excellence in Education 1983), which called for higher achievement in the schools in order to ensure U.S. competitiveness in the global economy. Miel (1986, 322) criticized remedies that "give little consideration to the individual. . . . Young people are being put under enormous pressure to perform for their society's sake. . . . It is distressing that those claiming our nation is at risk do not see how risky it is to overlook the power of a populace informed about, committed to, and competent in the ways of democracy." For Miel, the overarching responsibility in democracy was to know how the system of government worked and how to maintain it through changing conditions.

With all of these influences in mind, Miel focused her work on fundamental ideas about what she considered to be appropriate democratic social learnings for children. Furthermore, she connected these ideas to her interest in democracy by focusing on the development of social behaviors that would best serve a democratic society. Her writing featured a number of recurring themes, particularly in *More Than Social Studies* (Miel and Brogan 1957).

In these writings, Miel said that, first, a democratically socialized person saw democracy as an ideal arrangement for keeping individual and group considerations, freedom and responsibility, in balance. Such a person had respect for the individual, as well as for group intelligence, welfare, and cooperation. In a democracy, Miel argued, especially in critical times, students needed a better grasp of the tools of learning than under any other circumstances to safeguard against irrational thought and behavior. Miel conceived of these skills in terms of social learnings for which schools should share responsibility with the family and community. She specified that such learnings included bearing a friendly feeling; having concern for all mankind; valuing difference; being a contributing member of a group; seeing the necessity of a cooperative search for conditions guaranteeing maximum freedom for all; taking responsibility for a share of a common enterprise; problem solving and working for consensus; evaluating and cooperating with authority; refining constantly one's conception of the "good society"; and learning effective communication.

Throughout her work on children's social learning and how this learning contributed to democracy, Miel consistently emphasized the idea of the cooperative person. Given her typical awareness of contemporary intellectual currents, it is likely that she was influenced partly by Riesman, Glazer, and Denney's landmark 1950 book, *The Lonely Crowd: A Study of the Changing American Character.* Riesman and his colleagues discussed the changing nature of work in the United States and the gradual, necessary shift away from the highly individualistic work orientation toward that of what he called the "other directed" person, characterized by cooperation, teamwork, and concern for others.

Miel discussed this notion of cooperation and "other directedness" within the context of life in a democratic society, not just in the workplace. She reiterated the theme of cooperative learning to build good relationships—what she called the "fourth R"—in schools and specifically focused on getting along with people and the development of "friendly feelings" as essential components of democratic social learning. Miel recommended three approaches that teachers could use to help children improve human relationships: creating a friendly, respectful atmosphere in the classroom; teaching ways of managing group endeavors; and teaching about peoples' commonalities and differences. Miel also focused on social learning opportunities for world understanding, and she criticized "culture units" commonly taught in the elementary schools for encouraging unhealthy stereotypes of cultural and ethnic groups.

Miel argued that the elementary school was in a unique position, because it presented opportunities throughout the school day for practicing democracy through discussion, problem solving, consensus building, and learning "world citizenship." Miel's illustrations of these concepts in her writing were selected to show the practical possibilities of educative experiences centered on problems—many of which arose in school living or in the community—as children themselves met them. Most important, elementary school teachers could model democratic behavior and help children learn from those in society who exemplified the highest values.

Furthermore, Miel (1949) strongly argued that no single school subject, including the social studies, could be expected to carry the full load of children's social education. However, in terms of the unique contribution of the social studies to children's learning experiences and to their democratic socialization, Miel and Brogan's (1957) *More Than Social Studies* pointed to the field's capacity to place social learning at the center of the curriculum. Teachers could provide experiences designed to develop children's interpersonal and intergroup relationships through solving problems of daily living; satisfy children's curiosities about the world; solve problems of understanding and community action; and build positive attitudes toward others through organized individual and group studies. Most important, they could help children develop socially useful concepts, generalizations, and skills so that they could organize their experiences.

In fact, in bringing social learning to the forefront of the social studies curriculum, Miel and Brogan (1957) criticized traditional approaches to the organization of the social studies based upon compartmentalized subjects and separate textbooks. Also, Miel and Brogan asserted that children reaped no benefits of social learning when they were simply taken through the motions of choice and discovery. If, as the authors argued, the fundamental goal of social studies derived from its social-learning function, then any approach that relied too heavily on a preplanned scope and sequence could not help but fail. Myriad learning opportunities were embedded in the concept of "social" studies, but these would be wasted if social studies were "divorced from living [and] looked upon merely as a new way to cover subject matter" (Miel and Brogan 1957, 120). Instead, Miel and Brogan (1957, 120) added, the focus of the social studies class was to learn lessons "needed by people in a democracy."

This analysis notwithstanding, Miel's other publications rarely focused on the role of specific social studies subject matter in a social learning context. Miel (1962, 45) suggested how the social studies could "make much more difference in the lives of individual children and in the society educating them." However, her suggestions usually were quite general and did not delve into disciplinary perspectives. Miel (1962, 45) instead sought to discourage teachers from merely "conveying bits of information." Rather, teachers could help children "clarify, organize, and extend information . . . to see how facts are interrelated, and to draw useful generalizations" (Miel 1962, 45). Miel stated that social studies on the elementary level, though not always well developed, contained opportunities for thoughtful study of people, current events, societal movements, and global problems that required children to investigate, cooperate, and become better informed about their world.

Nonetheless, Miel recalled that her view of social studies was less than warmly received in some circles. Miel (1994) noted that social studies content in the traditional sense was important and was "well covered" by other scholars, but she argued that the field had "stopped with merely providing an information base. . . . There was no understanding of relationships, let alone caring and action." Her social studies focus, centered on problem areas and cutting across different disciplines, was different and not confined to the area of the curriculum labeled "social studies."

Perhaps the most concise, illuminating example of Miel's perspective on the social studies came in 1981, when she offered ideas for the development of sociopolitical "giftedness" toward useful social ends. Miel (1981, 257) adeptly characterized talent in this area as uniquely and totally "group linked. . . . It cannot be developed or demonstrated except in a social context." This feature, she claimed, placed a special burden on the social studies to help students understand themselves and others and to participate constructively in societal and global affairs. In a cogent statement of the mission of the social studies curriculum, Miel argued that social studies must be designed for understanding of the world, caring for others, and action on community problems with which students had a reasonable chance for success. Influenced by Dewey's books *The Child and the Curriculum* (1902) and *Experience and Education* (1938), Miel (1981, 268) averred that, with such a well-rounded, interdisciplinary, and interdimensional approach to the social studies, students would "see how the information they are gaining relates to existing bodies of knowledge." Moreover, teachers could help them "to organize their learnings and fill in gaps so that they are constantly building a more systematic view of the world" (Miel 1981, 268). If social studies content were selected to facilitate observation, generalization, evaluation, and application of learnings to new situations, students would become "lifelong social learners" (Miel 1981, 268). According to Miel, there could be no better equipment for leaders and all participants in democracy than knowing ways of gaining understanding, extending feelings of caring, and acting on convictions.

In some ways, Miel's ideas about caring anticipate the work of Nel Noddings in this area. However, Noddings (1984) elevated this concept to major public attention largely on the basis of feminist theory. Miel never characterized herself as a feminist scholar, but one may discern similarities to Noddings in her exploration of different types of caring that can be encouraged in children. A detailed exploration of Miel's thoughts on caring is beyond the scope of this chapter, but she elaborates on this topic in *More Than Social Studies* (Miel and Brogan 1957) and again in the 1981 book *Strategies for Educational Change: Recognizing the Gifts and Talents of All Children*. Also, Miel's 1960 speech to the Association for Childhood Education International, influenced by the 1959 United Nations Declaration of the Rights of the Child, illuminated her view of how education could contribute to children's rights to growth and the development of their abilities, judgment, values, and human relationships.

Miel identified three dimensions of the development of an educated person that schools must emphasize to guarantee those rights for children. First, *learning to care* meant caring about oneself, then caring about others, and then caring about moral and social responsibility. Included in caring about oneself and others was caring about ideas and their verbal and nonverbal expression. Second, *learning to make informed judgments*, one of the bases of becoming a useful member of society, supplied children with pertinent information and skills necessary for caring about ideas and responsibilities. Miel argued that the school can develop power in children to go on learning under their own direction for the rest of their lives, adding that such power is rooted, in part, in knowing sources of information and useful methods of learning from each on how to solve problems, test solutions, and evaluate consequences. Furthermore, the elementary school must reinforce children's trust in themselves as independent decision makers. Third, through *learning to take an active role in his or her world*, a child must use problem solving and relational skills to translate concerns and judgments into socially useful action. Miel said that the elementary school must help children go the complete circle—caring about unrealized human potential all over the world, deciding what will improve conditions, and taking useful steps (with others) in creating better conditions. The elementary school's role, therefore, was to provide an education that made sense to every individual. As Miel (1981) noted, such an education must provide useful attitudes, knowledge, and skills that make it possible and likely that an individual can continue to be a self-directed learner. Furthermore, education must help each individual lead a dignified and useful life.

An Assessment of Miel's Views on Social Learning and Social Studies

Several factors likely limited the acceptance of Miel's conception of social learning. First, Miel argued that social learning should be taught throughout the school day and not compartmentalized into one particular academic subject area—and especially that it should not be the exclusive domain of the social studies. This view posed problems for teachers and curriculum workers, who, even at the elementary level, increasingly tended to think in terms of discrete subjects, whether they were integrating these subjects or teaching them in traditional organizational forms. "Social learning throughout the day" was probably too nebulous a concept to fit into such a structure, especially one with a predetermined, written course of study. Moreover, teachers may have shied away from explicit attention to the complexities of moral development and social action as components of social learning, preferring instead to inculcate certain proper behaviors in their students, and social studies teachers may have felt no unique responsibility for these components in their curriculum.

Second, the circulation of Miel's ideas was restricted by the publication of *More Than Social Studies* during the conservative educational reform movements of the late 1950s. In this era, Cold War–inspired fear of, and competition with, the Soviet Union, especially after the launch of the Soviet satellite Sputnik, placed the U.S. educational system on the defensive and generated widespread criticism of schools for letting the Soviets gain the upper hand in science and technology. Experts from traditional academic disciplines were called upon to improve schools; educational reform emphasized the disciplines over students' individual and social needs. The publication of Miel and Brogan's book coincided with increasing criticism of U.S. schooling and demands that math and science, especially, receive priority in education. The Sputnik-inspired National Defense Education Act, linking federal support for schools with national policy objectives, ensured that social studies would be deemphasized and that traditional academic history likely would prevail in new federal guidelines for education. Miel's notions of social learning throughout the curriculum simply found no place in these antiprogressive times and perhaps were viewed with deep suspicion by some conservatives, who favored "traditional," "American" individualism, as advancing a socialist or communist agenda.

Third, Miel lacked affiliation with subject-matter experts in the social studies, and she did not consider herself to be a specialist in any of the social studies content areas. These factors likely limited her role in this area of the school curriculum. Somewhat ironically, considering her criticism of overly prescriptive written courses of study, Miel considered herself a weak teacher of history at the junior high school level, mainly because she had taken so few history courses at normal school and had to rely heavily on the textbook to supplement her background knowledge (Miel 1994). In all likelihood, her nontraditional views of the social studies, as well as her lack of academic history credentials, also precluded her involvement in the National Council for the Social Studies, of which she was never a member.

Significantly, too, the social studies became increasingly dominated by subject-matter experts—mostly male—in academia who viewed and shaped this field through the lens of their particular disciplines. Miel did not have the academic credentials or teaching background to be considered an "expert" in any of these academic circles. For example, during the 1960s, the research of Jerome Bruner (1960), Philip Phenix (1962; 1964), Joseph Schwab and P. E. Brandwein (1962), and others on the "structure of the disciplines" was in vogue in the curriculum-reform discourse (Mehaffy 1979). Bruner (1960), for example, suggested that each discipline had an inherent structure and that curriculum content should be presented in a form that helps students to comprehend this structure. Phenix (1964) argued that the curriculum should consist entirely of knowledge that comes from the disciplines, because the disciplines revealed knowledge in its teachable forms. Moreover, advocates of discipline-centered views claimed that curriculum developers should rely on the "expert interpretations of subject matter specialists who reveal the logical patterns that give shape to their discipline and imply the order in which its elements should be learned" (Schubert 1986).

Miel's work did not focus on inherent structures in particular realms of knowledge and the feasibility of "expert" agreement on the dimensions of that structure. Rather, much of her work revealed a strong commitment to other variables that influenced learning, especially those that related to social context. In fact, partly because of her concern that "problems of a modern society cannot be solved by specialists in any one discipline," Miel (1963, 80) produced at least one brilliant critique of the "structure of the disciplines" approach. She cautioned that no general agreement existed on what a discipline was or on what the structure of particular fields should be. Moreover, structure was not a thing, unchanging and unchanged, to be packaged and handed over "ready-made and full-blown" (Miel 1963, 82). Furthermore, Miel (1963, 86) criticized Bruner's (1960) neglect of the "interrelationships among disciplines" and of "the question of the structure of the curriculum as a whole within which the fields of knowledge are to find their place." Miel (1963, 84) was largely preoccupied with a "disciplined way of dealing with social policy questions, where values must be applied and strategies worked out."

Another highly fashionable social studies "movement" in which Miel did not become involved was the "new social studies" movement of the 1960s, particularly because this often resulted in written courses of study that she eschewed. For example, Miel (1994) traveled to Harvard University to hear about the new curriculum, "Man: A Course of Study," which she believed to be too narrow in its focus because it lacked emphasis on "modern man and his problems." Her interpretation of the role and function of the social studies in the school curriculum still diverged from the "conventional wisdom" that social studies meant the study of discrete subjects at particular grade levels.

A confluence of factors, then, circumscribed Miel's contributions to the social studies discourse and contributed to her remaining a lesser-known figure in this field. These included, certainly, the historical context of the school curriculum and her emphasis on social learning at the expense of deliberate attention to—and even criticism of—the common social studies disciplines. Though many of Miel's ideas and criticisms were well founded and well stated, her voice sounded one of only a few discordant notes in the increasingly loud chorus of approval for a more traditional, academic, subject-centered curriculum.

Diversity Issues in Miel's Research

One of the issues that most concerned Miel as she explored meanings of democracy and democratic citizenship was the diversity of U.S. society. In particular, she focused on problems of children who experienced intellectual, economic, or cultural deprivation because of their ethnicity and/or socioeconomic background. She viewed the solving of such problems as central to the mission of U.S. democracy, and she saw the schools as places where these children could have, among other things, positive social learning experiences. As a Michigan junior high school teacher, Miel (1994) worked in the Ann Arbor schools, which were, in many ways, a model setting. The Donovan School, at which Miel became a teaching principal, was in a low-income neighborhood. She retained strong impressions of the life experiences of the children with whom she had worked and of their particular social learning needs. These impressions later figured prominently in her career at Teachers College as she taught and wrote about the importance of children's cooperation, understanding, respect, and relationships.

Concern for diversity and equity issues surfaced early in Miel's work. For example, Gunnar Myrdal's *American Dilemma* (1944) took U.S. socioeconomic, cultural, and class issues in a profound new direction and seems to have influenced Miel, who cited Myrdal in her 1946 book, *Changing the Curriculum: A Social Process*. Myrdal focused on the disadvantages suffered by African Americans, criticizing in particular the inferiority of vocational training programs offered to African-American youth and, consequently, the discrimination and lack of opportunity they faced in the job market. More broadly, Myrdal excoriated the United States as a backward nation for its failure to provide appropriate educational opportunities and employment to its youth and for maintaining a socioeconomic underclass. Myrdal viewed education as the "great hope" for both individuals and society, as the foundation for equality of opportunity for the individual, and as an outlet for individual ability.

Nonetheless, Miel's concern about diversity and equity issues did not fully manifest itself until some of her later work. Most likely, these issues were brought into sharp focus for her by her experiences in the late 1950s and 1960s, as she heard about and witnessed her African-American students' struggles with racism and discrimination (Miel 1994). After years of a general emphasis in her work on social and democratic learning, Miel became deeply involved in several major research studies, especially case studies, that related to diversity and equity issues in schools. In the mid-1960s, Miel worked with A. Harry Passow on a comprehensive curriculum study of the Washington, D.C., public schools. Miel studied the elementary schools in the District. She in turn facilitated contacts and correspondence between her students at Teachers College and approximately 80 classroom teachers. Miel and her students set out to examine several aspects of the Washington, D.C., elementary program: the social-emotional climate; learning objectives; use of time, space, and human and material resources; organization and types of subject matter; and opportunities for learning the skills of information processing and democratic living. When their task got under way, they discovered a sterile physical and intellectual environment that emphasized efficiency at the expense of children's active participation in their own learning. The researchers concluded that most learning activities appeared to be designed to promote order, silence, passive conformity, rigid adherence to a time schedule, and uniform instruction of children. Challenging subject matter and intellectual stimulation were scarce, as were basic instructional materials. The report also stated that teachers seemed to expect little progress from the children and that there appeared to be no joy in the learning process. From the perspective of Miel and her students, the Washington, D.C., elementary schools were failing to meet either the intellectual or the social-emotional needs of the children. Data on the children's academic performance and teachers' impressions that the children were not learning confirmed their observations.

Foremost among recommendations from this study (Miel 1967, 28) was the suggestion that the District's elementary schools provide children with opportunities to develop a "social personality," characterized by individuality, autonomy, independence, respect, and a sense of well-being. Their creativity, decision-making skills, and participation in classroom activities must be encouraged and affirmed. Miel and her students also advised that instruction in these schools become more flexible and individualized, taking into account the special needs of various children. Finally, they emphasized that none of these recommendations could be fully implemented unless changes were made in teachers' self-concept and professional status. Miel and her students also recommended changes in the schools' subject matter. They criticized the curriculum for disregarding "actual events and problems in today's world" and suggested that the curriculum be more relevant to the students' lives (Miel 1967, 28).

Miel's concern for "relevance" was particularly significant because the Passow study directly addressed the large African-American population in the Washington schools. Years before the multicultural-curriculum debate moved to the forefront of educational discourse, Miel and her students drew attention to the educational needs of minority children. In a foreshadowing of the debate to come, Miel (1967, 28) advocated a culturally inclusive curriculum that went beyond "the introduction of a little Negro history into the social studies curriculum" and instead featured the contributions of African Americans from all walks of life to society and placed their stories and experiences in appropriate historical perspective. The "desirable direction" they recommended was for teachers to begin with the experiences of the children in their homes and communities. Teachers and students then work toward a general understanding of minority-group concerns, an examination of the contributions and interactions of different cultural and ethnic groups in society and around the world, and an analysis of "the way society makes decisions and solves problems" (Miel 1967, 48).

Concerns for intercultural relations and the problems of minority groups as key issues in U.S. democracy can be discerned throughout Miel's career. She advocated a "broadened" view that went beyond mere "tolerance" and "understanding" to actual improvement in relationships among all groups—not only those groups based on race, culture, and religion but also those based on gender, occupation, educational level, age, and regional identity (Miel 1967, 16). She criticized teaching approaches that emphasized only the strangeness or quaintness of other cultures. Miel argued that intercultural education, when properly conceived, had two primary, mutually reinforcing goals. First, it should help "children discover how much like other people we are"; second, it should help "children to understand why differences in cultures have arisen and to value differences as a way to enrich us all" (Miel 1967, 16).

Her concern for young people's cultural awareness and valuing of cultural difference eventually led Miel to a concern about the nature of suburbia in the United States. Certainly, the homogeneity and conformity that seemed so pervasive in suburban life was not a new topic; for example, Helen and Robert Lynd addressed it in 1929 in the book *Middletown*. This classic study emphasized the orderliness, routinization, and rote learning typical of schools in Muncie, Indiana. Later, James B. Conant's book *Slums and Suburbs* (1961) seems to have had a powerful impact on Miel's thinking. Conant provided a striking contrast between affluent, spacious, well-staffed suburban schools and run-down, understaffed, overcrowded inner-city schools. He argued strongly that the public must address these disparities or face the "social dynamite" of social disorganization, alarming dropout rates, and unemployment, all of which would largely harm minorities who lived in U.S. slums.

Miel first broached the incipient concept of suburbia and the "postwar rush to the country" in an article written with Betty Psaltis (1964). Though a city dweller and resident of the Morningside Heights neighborhood near Teachers College in New York City until her retirement, Miel nonetheless viewed with increasing dismay the suburban growth phenomenon on, for example, Long Island and other new developments near the city. Her central question was whether suburban children, raised and educated in homogeneous environments, were being deprived of important social learnings about similarities and differences among people. The article, based on the results of her five-year Study of Schools in Changing Communities, surveyed the attitudes of several hundred rural, urban, and suburban children toward themselves, their families, and their neighborhoods. Psaltis and Miel (1964, 440) determined that, significantly, the "dominant middle-class cultural values" of the time—for example, order and conformity of dress and behavior—were being transmitted on an unprecedented scale throughout school and society. Moreover, these values were being inculcated in all types of children, without regard for their cultural backgrounds, frames of reference, and experiences. Psaltis and Miel (1964, 440) viewed this as problematic because "a whole constellation of educative media" worked to standardize young children's opinions and attitudes, and the school itself "contributed its share in the achievement of such homogeneity." Furthermore, Psaltis and Miel (1964, 440) strongly argued that, "in a world with new problems, the full development of individual potential," creativity, and resourcefulness should take priority over fostering alikeness.

These concerns emerged fully in Miel's book with journalist Edwin Kiester, *The Short-changed Children of Suburbia* (1967), an outgrowth of her Study of Schools in Changing Communities from 1958 to 1962. This research project, conducted in suburban schools and funded primarily by the American Jewish Committee, was developed in the context of the social unrest and civil rights struggles of the 1960s. Indeed, the book's publication coincided with the onset of great civil disorder in inner cities across the United States. It focused on "how the public schools prepare children for a world peopled by men and women of many different nations, races, religions, and economic backgrounds" when misunderstandings about human differences "are precisely what the chief problems of our time are about" (Miel and Kiester 1967, 8, 10).

Miel believed that this book best represented her research efforts. In fact, she received the National Education Association's Human Rights Award in 1968 as a result of this publication. Like the Washington, D.C., study, *The Shortchanged Children of Suburbia* was prescriptive in a general sense. That is, Miel herself recommended an "action program" for teachers to broaden social learning opportunities for their suburban pupils. Passow (1995) described this project as a "groundbreaking" study of what suburban schools were failing to teach about human differences and cultural diversity. Fred Hechinger, education editor of the *New York Times*, wrote in the book's foreword that Miel's work analyzed problems in enclaves of affluent homogeneity, where status quo was a virtue and where children's horizons were artificially limited. Hechinger further criticized what he saw as the "self-satisfaction," "overwhelming preoccupation with material possessions," and "the distortion of values" of the children of suburbia (Miel and Kiester 1967, 6–7). Moreover, he argued, teachers in this environment often appeared more anxious to avoid than to answer troublesome questions, and to pretend that controversial issues and inequities did not exist in U.S. society and throughout the world.

In this major study, Miel and several doctoral students from Teachers College extensively researched the pseudonymous, ostensibly representative suburb of "New Village." They collected information on the community, administered questionnaires, and interviewed 60 teachers, 50 parents, more than 100 elementary children, and more than 100 community members (Miel and Kiester 1967, 9). Miel and Kiester (1967, 12) concentrated on the role of the elementary school as the "chief training ground for American children" and on the opportunities that children had in their schools and communities for social learning about life in a multicultural, pluralistic democracy.

Miel and her colleagues reached conclusions that troubled them. First, Miel and Kiester (1967, 13) found that "extraordinary effort was required to bring about any encounter between a child of the suburbs and persons different from himself." The suburban child's world remained highly circumscribed and insulated. Second, the children in their study reflected only a superficial "tolerance" of differences. Beneath the surface, prejudices toward people of different races and religions, especially toward African Americans, already were deeply ingrained in the children. Third, though New Village parents and teachers seemed eager to address religious differences, they were much more likely to ignore or avoid racial ones, especially those relating to poverty and economic inequalities. The children in this study did not—nor did they want to—know about people of different races or socioeconomic status. Furthermore, the children's strong preference for conformity and for a single norm of appropriate behavior underlay all of their attitudes. Finally, Miel and Kiester found that parents and teachers in New Village placed much higher value on skill acquisition and factual learning than on social learning. Teachers found it unrewarding to address social attitudes because this had little to do with "getting into the right colleges" (Miel and Kiester 1967, 55).

For these reasons, Miel and Kiester (1967, 14) determined that suburban children were being "shortchanged" in their social learning, and, despite the "many enviable features" of their environment, they were educationally "underprivileged." The "action program" that Miel and Kiester (1967, 57–59) suggested for suburban schools and communities emphasized greater attention to the development of "higher thought processes," to children's value systems, and to a "more realistic picture" of their own community in relation to others. They also made numerous specific recommendations for the study of race, religion, and socioeconomic status—all aimed at dismantling stereotypes, avoiding facile generalizations, studying different groups in their appropriate cultural and historical contexts, and understanding the concerns and struggles faced by particular groups in society.

Within the New Village scenario, then, Miel was able to reassert her conviction that human diversity was a proper subject for the school curriculum in a democratic society. Indeed, Miel and Kiester (1967, 68) argued that there was "no more urgent business in the schools of America," adding that "children must be educated to deal fairly and realistically with questions of social justice, civil rights, national unity, and international peace."

Miel's ever-present concern for international peace deepened after World War II, when she traveled to Japan in 1951 as a curriculum consultant. She spent much of her time in Hiroshima, where she witnessed the city's painful rebuilding process, visited schools and orphanages, and participated in the reconstruction of the educational system. Upon her return to the United States, Miel (1953) wrote and lectured about life in postwar Japan and tried to correct possible U.S. misconceptions about Japanese views of education and democracy. Miel's (1994) travels in Japan profoundly affected her and served as a formative experience in her increasing interest in global issues.

Though she was not involved in the global education movement per se, international peace moved to the forefront of Miel's interests in the 1960s and '70s, perhaps out of a growing disillusionment with the political and educational climate of the United States. Miel's leadership in these years in founding the World Council on Curriculum and Instruction (WCCI) was particularly noteworthy. The WCCI emphasized dialogue and action among educators from around the world to improve all aspects of education and contribute to a more peaceful world. By 1990, membership grew to about 700 throughout 50 countries. The WCCI continued to promote and participate in international conferences, exchange teaching, study abroad, cross-national research on common problems, and development of curricula that encouraged international understanding, cultural sensitivity, and the reduction of prejudice within and across national boundaries. The WCCI was Miel's primary outlet for her international interests; however, throughout the 1950s, '60s, and '70s, she often visited other countries, including Uganda, Tanzania, and Afghanistan, as a curriculum-development consultant, continuing to focus on democracy and democratic social learning for children.

Miel, Schools, and Democracy: Final Assessments

Because of the nature of the societal concerns she addressed in her work, Miel in many ways embraced and encouraged what Parker (1996) has referred to as "advanced" ideas about democracy and democratic citizenship education. That is, she raised issues related to human social and cultural diversity and saw these as central to the ongoing development and "deepening" of democracy in the United States. She also viewed democracy as a way of life that citizens undertake together through deliberation, reflection, and civic action (Dewey 1927; Parker 1996). For Miel, democratic citizenship education must necessarily begin early in school, where children would learn what Goodman, Kuzmic, and Wu (1992) termed a "connectionist orientation"—a sense of altruism, personal and civic responsibility, community, and connection to other living beings—as an essential characteristic of democratic citizenship.

Miel did not view the school merely as a reactive institution or only as the target of social-change efforts. Her conceptualization of the school's role in a democratic society was an active, albeit indirect, one. Miel (1994) claimed that the educational process—and the curriculum itself—should be "the beginning of helping children to understand social problems and to feel a responsibility for helping to solve them." Addressing social problems was a natural outgrowth of the development of relationships between school and community.

One of the foremost legacies of progressive education was its emphasis on the process of change, deliberation, and continuous renewal (Zilversmit 1993). Later historical evaluations of progressive education were somewhat more circumspect than those of Bestor (1953), Smith (1959), Rickover (1949), and other strident critics of the postwar years. Still, they agreed that the progressive education movement ultimately collapsed for similar reasons: professional infighting, ideological fragmentation, removal from the public discourse, overuse of slogans and clichés, inertia, and obsolescence in the face of the continuing transformation of U.S. society in the years following World War II (Cremin 1961). Zilversmit (1993) emphasized that progressive education, ostensibly a philosophy of change, had become a fixed set of methods and rhetoric for teachers to learn. Furthermore, the idea of a role for schools in the advocacy of social change aroused increasing public hostility, especially as the Cold War intensified. More important, teachers' involvement in social transformation was simply unrealistic, given the reality of power relationships, the authoritarianism under which most teachers worked, and the capacity of schools merely to reflect and reproduce community values and patterns of social organization (Zilversmit 1993). Perhaps an overarching reason for the demise of progressive education in the 1950s was the inability of progressive educators to respond forcefully and concertedly to calls for reassessment of the movement.

The apparent lack of sustained attention to Miel's work and ideas may have been a matter of the timing of her life and career within this context. Her work in academia, which began as progressive education, was not only on the decline but also under deliberate, if exaggerated, attack from conservatives. Her explicitly stated beliefs regarding democratic socialization and the value of diversity for schoolchildren were not among the favored educational ideas of the 1950s and early '60s. Moreover, the liberal sociopolitical perspective that Miel openly espoused became unfashionable throughout those years. To a number of people during that time, it was even unpatriotic. Unfortunately, because she was at Teachers College during a particular era, Miel also may have been unfairly associated with some of the more irresponsible manifestations of progressive education that came under fire in schools. Even though these manifestations had little to do with the work of Teachers College faculty members, they may have played a role in causing her work to be ignored later by academic traditionalists anxious to distance themselves from that movement. Later in the 1950s and '60s, the "structure of the disciplines" movement elevated the importance of subject-matter expertise, which Miel never claimed to possess.

Three other points must be made about how Miel's work should—and should not—be characterized. First, a logical question that arises from an examination of her work is whether she was simply a follower of trends and other people's ideas—a disciple of others rather than a leader in her own right. A fair assessment of her work, in my view, is that she practiced an effective model of professional development and practical scholarship. That is, she read numerous philosophical and theoretical works that others had written, internalized the ideas that held the greatest meaning for her, and then took a strong leadership role in determining how these ideas could be made real and meaningful in schools. Her views on children's social learning, diversity, cultural awareness, and democracy all were in some sense derivative, but her creative, thoughtful, and democratic leadership style helped these ideas make sense to her students and to practitioners. Second, much of Miel's work did not observe the traditional academic conventions of statistical, "objective" research. Much of it indeed appears to be based mainly upon a combination of Miel's firm convictions and her own sense of professional ethics, along with extensive observations and conversations in schools. Third, Miel was never an activist in the sense of high-profile political involvement in the issues about which she wrote. Her "activism" expressed itself through her teaching, research, and service to the profession through the Association for Supervision and Curriculum Development, the WCCI, and ACEI. After her retirement, she lived a quiet life in Florida, occasionally speaking or writing when invited, mainly to reemphasize ideas about democracy that she had advocated all of her professional life. Underlying all of these ideas was a deep concern for the intellectual growth and well-roundedness of all students, and her work revealed attention to a number of variables that influenced learning, especially those deriving from the social context of schooling.

Still, there remained a "timelessness about many of the problems the progressives raised and the solutions they proposed" (Cremin 1961, 352–53); their "authentic vision remained strangely pertinent to the problems of mid-century America." Poor slum schools still existed. So did wretched rural schools, as well as outmoded and harmful teaching practices that ignored the unique needs of students, glaring social inequities, and dehumanized approaches to knowledge. Clearly, Miel's work consistently illustrated her capacity to call attention to some of the nation's enduring educational and social problems.

This research was made possible by a Spencer Foundation/American Educational Research Foundation Doctoral Research Fellowship. The author is most grateful for this support.

References

Alexander, W. M. 1994. Interview with author, 14 October, Gainesville, Fla.

Bellack, A. 1994. Letter to author, 10 December.

Berman, L. 1992. Alice Miel. In *Profiles in childhood education, 1931–1960: A project of the ACEI Later Leaders Committee*, ed. L. P. Martin, 98–102. Wheaton, Md.: Association for Childhood Education International.

Bestor, A. E. 1953. *Educational wastelands: The retreat from learning in our public schools.* Chicago: University of Illinois Press.

Bode, B. H. 1927. *Modern educational theories.* New York: Macmillan.

Bode, B. H. 1938. *Progressive education at the crossroads.* New York: Newson.

Bruner, J. S. 1960. *The process of education.* Cambridge, Mass.: Harvard University Press.

Burlbaw, L. M. 1989. Hollis Leland Caswell's contributions to the development of the curriculum field. Ph.D. diss., University of Texas at Austin.

Caswell, H. L., and D. S. Campbell. 1935. *Curriculum development.* New York: American Book Co.

Caute, D. 1978. *The great fear: The anti-communist purge under Truman and Eisenhower.* New York: Simon and Schuster.

Conant, J. B. 1961. *Slums and suburbs: A commentary on schools in metropolitan areas.* New York: McGraw-Hill.

Corbin, H. 1971. On knowing Alice Miel as my advisor. Speech given at the Project Milestone Dinner, 7 May. *Alice Miel collection.* Columbia: Museum of Education, University of South Carolina.

Cremin, L. A. 1961. *The transformation of the school: Progressivism in American education, 1876–1957.* New York: Knopf.

Cremin, L. A., D. A. Shannon, and M. E. Townsend. 1954. *A history of Teachers College, Columbia University.* New York: Columbia University Press.

Cuban, L. 1984. *How teachers taught: Constancy and change in American classrooms, 1890–1980.* New York: Longman.

Davis, O. L., Jr. 1976. Epilogue: Invitation to curriculum history. In *Perspectives on curriculum development, 1776–1976*, ed. O. L. Davis Jr., 257–59. Washington, D.C.: Association for Supervision and Curriculum Development.

Dewey, J. 1902. *The child and the curriculum, 1859–1952.* Chicago: University of Chicago Press.

Dewey, J. 1916. *Democracy and education: An introduction to the philosophy of education.* New York: Macmillan.

Dewey, J. 1927. *The public and its problems.* New York: H. Holt & Co.

Dwyer, A. 1971. On knowing Alice Miel as my advisor. Speech given at the Project Milestone Dinner, 7 May. *Alice Miel collection.* Columbia: Museum of Education, University of South Carolina.

Goodman, J., J. Kuzmic, and X. Wu. 1992. *Elementary schooling for critical democracy.* Albany: State University of New York Press.

Hunt, W. 1994. Interview with author, 19 December, Austin, Tex.

Kilpatrick, W. H. 1918. The project method. *Teachers College Record* 19(4): 319–35.

Koopman, Avery, Miel, and Oakes. 1933. *Helping children experience the realities of the social order: Social studies in the public schools of Ann Arbor, Michigan (Junior high school).* Ann Arbor: Ann Arbor, Mich., Public Schools.

Lynd, H., and R. Lynd. 1929. *Middletown: A study in American culture.* New York: Harcourt, Brace.

Martinello, M. 1994. Letter to author, 27 December.

Mehaffy, G. L. 1979. Symbolic and occupational functions of curriculum discourse: An exploration of curriculum theory during the disciplines era. Ph.D. diss., University of Texas at Austin.

Miel, A. 1944. Living in a modern world. In *Toward a new curriculum: Yearbook of the Department of Supervision and Curriculum Development, National Education Association*, ed. G. Mackenzie, 11–21. Washington, D.C.: National Education Association.

Miel, A. 1946. *Changing the curriculum: A social process.* New York: D. Appleton-Century Co.

Miel, A. 1949. Toward democratic socialization. *Childhood Education* 26: 50–51.

Miel, A. 1953. Education's part in democratizing Japan. *Teachers College Record* 55: 10–19.

Miel, A. 1960. Speech. Wheaton, Md.: Association for Childhood Education, International.

Miel, A. 1962. Social studies with a difference. *Education Digest* 22: 45.

Miel, A. 1963. Knowledge and the curriculum. In *New insights and the curriculum*, ed. A. Frazier, 79–87. Washington, D.C.: Association for Supervision and Curriculum Development.

Miel, A. 1981. Social studies for understanding, caring, acting. In *Strategies for educational change: Recognizing the gifts and talents of all children*, ed. W. L. Marks and R. O. Nystrand, 257–68. New York: Macmillan.

Miel, A. 1986. Teaching for a democracy. *The Educational Forum* 50(3): 319–23.

Miel, A. 1994. Interview with author, 11–13 October, Gainesville, Fla.

Miel, A., and P. Brogan. 1957. *More than social studies: A view of social learning in the elementary school.* Englewood Cliffs, N.J.: Prentice-Hall.

Miel, A., and E. Kiester. 1967. *The shortchanged children of suburbia: What schools don't teach about human differences and what can be done about it.* New York: Institute of Human Relations Press, American Jewish Committee.

Miel, A. 1967. Study of the Washington, D.C. Schools elementary program: A report of the Task Force on the Elementary School Program, 1967 (final draft). *Alice Miel collection.* Columbia: Museum of Education, University of South Carolina.

Myrdal, G. 1944. *American dilemma: The Negro problem and modern democracy.* New York: Harpers.

National Commission on Excellence in Education. 1983. *A nation at risk: The imperative for educational reform.* Washington, D.C.: U.S. Department of Education. ERIC ED 226 006.

Noddings, N. 1984. *Caring: A feminine approach to ethics & moral education.* Berkeley: University of California Press.

Parker, W. C. 1996. 'Advanced' ideas about democracy: Toward a pluralist conception of citizenship education. *Teachers College Record* 98(1): 104–25.

Passow, A. H. 1995. Telephone interviews with author, 4 and 6 January.

Phenix, P. H. 1962. The use of the disciplines as curriculum content. *The Educational Forum* 26(3): 273–80.

Phenix, P. H. 1964. *Realms of meaning: A philosophy of the curriculum for general education*. New York: McGraw-Hill.

Psaltis, B., and A. Miel. 1964. Are children in the suburbs different? *Educational Leadership* 21: 436–40.

Rickover, H. G. 1959. *Education and freedom*. New York: Dutton.

Riesman, D., N. Glazer, and R. Denney. 1950. *The lonely crowd: A study of the changing American character*. New Haven, Conn.: Yale University Press.

Rugg, H., and A. Shumaker. 1928. *The child-centered school: An appraisal of the new education*. Chicago: World Book Co.

Schubert, W. H. 1986. *Curriculum: Perspective, paradigm, and possibility*. New York: Macmillan.

Schwab, J., and P. E. Brandwein. 1962. *The teaching of science as enquiry*. Cambridge, Mass.: Harvard University Press.

Seguel, M. L. 1966. *The curriculum field: Its formative years*. New York: Teachers College Press.

Smith, M. B. 1949. *And madly teach: A layman looks at public school education*. Chicago: H. Regnery Co.

Varis, F. 1994. Letter to author, 2 November.

Zilversmit, A. 1993. *Changing schools: Progressive education theory and practice, 1930–1960*. Chicago: University of Chicago Press.

Chapter 6

Maycie Southall: Elementary Educator and Organizational Leader

by Sherry L. Field

Maycie Katherine Southall's career as an educator spanned more than 50 years, from before World War I, when education in the United States was entering an era of scientific inquiry and methods of research, to the mid-1960s, when attention to school subjects, especially those of reading, science, and mathematics, was heightened dramatically following the launch of the Soviet satellite Sputnik in 1957. She lived through times of rapid change, as elementary education moved from an emphasis on rote memorization, elocution, and drill of facts to an emphasis on a child-centered, research-based approach to learning. During her career, she was a vital component of the movement toward a scholarly approach to teacher education, with increased course work providing theoretical and pedagogical emphases. This chapter highlights the influential life of Maycie Katherine Southall and provides vignettes from her childhood; public-school teaching, administration, and supervision; college teaching; organizational leadership; and retirement.

Being a Playful Child

Maycie Katherine Southall was born in 1895 in Maury County, Tennessee, to William and Mary Southall. Her father was a farmer and real estate trader. Southall was the ninth of 10 children. Though the family moved several times when Maycie was a child, several years, including those of Southall's early childhood, were spent in a large home called Vine Hill. The home was indicative of some financial success. It boasted two grand staircases, a second-floor ballroom, and a grand view of the rolling countryside and nearby counties (Southall 1979).

Southall recalled her childhood fondly, as one in which she could freely play outside and roam the Southall farm. There, she liked to climb into the hayloft, create and act out familiar stories, play dress up, and splash in the swimming hole (Brown 1981). As a young girl, Maycie Southall never lacked for playmates, either from her own large family or from families on nearby farms. She was both a loving sister and an independent child. Two stories from her childhood exemplify her youthful fearlessness and growing independence. According to a family story, Maycie Southall ran away from home when she was two years old. Her family searched frantically for her through the night, but young Southall was not discovered. It was not until morning that she reappeared, after having slept overnight in the nearby icehouse (Southall 1979). In later childhood, adept at many school subjects, Maycie Southall was only too happy to accept help with her mathematics lessons from an older sister. Once, after an argument between the two, the older sister refused to continue to help with the lessons. Not to be deterred, and certainly not to give up, Southall learned to work her own arithmetic problems independently. Being one of 10 children necessitated having a practical, informal mathematics education, especially when it came to dividing resources, treats, time, and money (Southall 1979).

School and schooling were topics of great interest to the young Southall, even before she was old enough to enter school herself. She regularly met her older sisters and brothers at the garden gate when they returned home from school in the afternoons. She awaited eagerly the time when she would be able to join them in their daily treks to school and back again. Her siblings' schoolbooks held a special fascination for her, and she taught herself to read before learning formal lessons about the subject. Another incident in early childhood profoundly influenced her interest in learning. Southall (in Brown 1981, 31) noted that "a director of a school permitted her, along with a few other students, to view his private library of books. At that time, the child had never seen so vast a collection and was utterly fascinated by the notion that anyone could own such a prize possession."

When Maycie Southall reached school age, her experiences in school were similar to those shared by countless other children who grew up in rural America. She began her formal education in a small, one-teacher school. Her intelligence and ability to learn were quickly recognized. She undoubtedly was able to help younger learners with their work. She enjoyed playing school, even when she was away from the schoolhouse. Following common practice of the day, she was able to complete seventh- and eighth-grade work during one school year. By the time Southall entered secondary school, she had responsibility for driving herself and her younger sister by buggy back and forth each day (Southall 1979). Southall completed secondary school in Columbia, Tennessee, in 1911. She received her diploma some two years ahead of most of her peers. She had attended one-room and multi-room, public and private schools and had learned to make adjustments necessitated by skipping grades (Brown 1981).

Upon graduation from high school, Southall traveled to Broxton, Georgia, to visit a married sister and to vacation before entering college in the fall. While there, a serendipitous chain of events was set into motion, which would prevent her from returning home to go to college. Southall did not enter her post-high-school life with the intention of becoming a teacher. She did, however, come from a family that valued education. Soon after arriving in Georgia, Southall was asked by a school trustee whether she would be willing to fill a newly vacant teaching position. She was interested, and she immediately completed and passed the required teacher examination to become certified to teach in the state of Georgia. One week later, she accepted the teaching position. She arranged to "board" with the family of one of her students-to-be, whose home was nearer Southall's new school than was the home of her sister and brother-in-law.

Becoming a Teacher

On 3 July 1911, Maycie Southall began her teaching career in Coffee County, Georgia. She was assigned to teach eight grades in a one-room schoolhouse near Broxton. Twelve students enrolled for the fall term. Southall was 15 years old.

Despite her youth and lack of preparation for a career in education, Southall was able to call upon the practical lessons she had learned from her mother and the teaching techniques she had observed from her own teachers. As the excitement of taking on the new, unexpected challenge of teaching school dimmed and the realities of teaching students who had many different learning levels became clear, she began to develop a daily routine. Each school day, she arrived at school before her students, readied the classroom, taught her students during the day, cleaned the classroom, went home, dined with the family with whom she was living, listened to their son (her only eighth-grade student) recite his lessons, and retired to her room to finish grading papers and prepare for the next teaching day. Likely, her weekends were spent visiting her sister, participating in church activities, and getting ready for the coming week of school.

Intent on meeting both the mental and physical needs of her students, Southall seemed to realize that each child required different structures for learning. She remembered that her own first-grade teacher had allowed her to go outside to run and play occasionally during the day so that she might be able to focus on her studies when she came back into the classroom. Consequently, she planned similar physical activities for her students. Of course, Southall realized the importance of reading, writing, and arithmetic in her daily lesson planning. Yet, she also began to think of the classroom in new ways, and extended its boundaries to the outdoors.

As Brown (1981, 38–39) noted, in taking advantage of her rural school setting and prior experiences of her students and their parents:

> *She developed a technique through which the principles of nutrition could be taught by her, practiced by the students, and the results, or harvest, used to supplement the limited diets of those in her charge. As a wider variety of vegetables was needed, suggestions were sought from the students; the aid of the larger boys was then elicited whereby unsightly ground beyond the fence was converted into a garden plot; and the surplus vegetables, cultivated by the students, were later canned, with the help of the rural families, for school use. Because the teacher wanted her students to develop an appreciation for the aesthetic as well as the practical, she encouraged them to work on beautifying the grounds by planting flowers along the fence inside the schoolyard and cultivating the vegetable garden in an adjoining plot along the fence.*

Southall's enthusiasm benefited the school and its students in other, measurable ways. She organized the community and held fund-raisers, such as ice-cream suppers and another, innovative measure. She sold eggs supplied by her students in order to purchase reading materials. Southall also bought playground equipment. She successfully engaged her students in lessons inside and outside the schoolhouse; and as people in the community learned of the interesting activities the young teacher carried out, they began to enroll their children in school. By the end of her first year of teaching, enrollment was 65 students (Brown 1981). This young first-year teacher had increased by 500 percent the number of elementary school students attending the country school in Broxton, Georgia.

Being a School Leader and Supervisor

As she completed her first year of teaching, Southall planned to return home and obtain a two-year diploma from Middle Tennessee Normal School. She sensed a need to become more fully prepared for the rigors of teaching and to learn more about the science of educating children. She taught fifth grade at Mt. Pleasant, Tennessee; and, later, in Columbia schools, she taught sixth grade as she completed her studies at Middle Tennessee Normal. Southall quickly realized that she desired to learn more about the energizing world of educational theory and pedagogy; and, in 1918, she enrolled at George Peabody College for Teachers in Nashville. Just as Southall was entering a new phase of her career in education, the United States entered World War I. Southall was recruited for a high-school principalship in Rover, Tennessee, and took on the responsibility of leading the school, comprised of four female teachers. She accepted this role as her part of the war effort (Southall 1979; Brown 1981).

In little time, Southall's skills as an educational leader were recognized in her new community. She quickly put into practice some of the same out-of-school activities that had served her well during her initial teaching assignment. As Brown (1981, 43) related:

> *Although community learning did not become a familiar term among educational circles until several decades later, Maycie Southall organized activities at Rover that involved the students, parents, and neighborhood in the cause of education. One such project consisted of an effort to beautify the school grounds, as well as to teach her pupils how to prevent soil erosion, through planting trees. Southall's efforts foreshadowed those of contemporary educators who view their work as facilitators of learning. First, the students shared their ideas about the project; next, the boys identified suitable saplings in nearby woods; on a designated Saturday, the adults provided teams of mules to haul the trees while the girls prepared a dinner for the workers; and, as a result of the plans initially developed by the students, the project found fruition. The patrons, through participation in setting out a large number of trees, demonstrated their support for the leadership of an educator who became a pioneer in school-community relationships many years prior to the launching of the 1930–1940's movement.*

Southall continued her course work at Peabody and subsequently received her Bachelor of Science degree in June 1920. Her acquisition of the degree was a prized accomplishment, but it also represented a period during which she had undergone serious disappointments. She had set out to become a mathematics teacher, but was advised that women should not seek roles as college mathematics teachers and, consequently, that she should continue to capitalize on her success in working with young children and their teachers. When she graduated, she moved to Greenville, North Carolina, to become a county school supervisor. Four years later, she took a position as a state supervisor of elementary education in Raleigh, North Carolina, where she continued for four years.

School state supervisors were required to travel about the state, visit schools in their assigned geographical area, and evaluate the educational programs in operation within specified districts. Southall's supervisory work, from 1924–28, was fraught with challenges. First, it required that she travel, alone, sometimes all over the state, and on roads that at times were nothing more than dirt trails. Second, it required that she stay overnight in motels and hotels, at a time when few women did so alone. Third, it required that she be ready to give both impromptu and planned demonstrations on a wide variety of topics to teachers and administrators at each school that she visited. She enjoyed sharing her expertise and making new research findings practical for teachers. Her presentations at schools were about topics such as child-centered approaches to teaching reading and mathematics; new assessment strategies, including teaching how to use standardized testing measures; and humanistic approaches to school administration and supervision. Southall approached her challenges with good humor and not insubstantial bravery. Once, when traveling in a new automobile, she bounced along on deeply rutted roads. The jarring movements dislodged the floorboards of the car, and her prepared lunch was lost through the gap. The bouncing also disengaged the headlights of the car. Southall did not turn back; instead, she finished her work for the day and hurried home in early evening, straining to reach her destination before total darkness, to see the roadway, and to keep her car on it (Southall 1979).

Rather than take a passive role as "inspector" of schools, which she found intimidating and divisive, Southall served as a motivator and change agent for the schools she served. She always alerted school personnel of her upcoming visit. She took on an additional substantial role during her years as a school supervisor. After assessing the physical plants and the curriculum materials available, she determined that high-quality curriculum materials were badly needed in the schools. Southall consequently became an informal lending library to her schools by "transporting books to the children. . . . She wanted the news of her visits, associated with anticipation of reading materials, to serve as a motivational device for the students in their reading programs" (Brown 1981, 49).

Southall was eager to continue her education to the next level, and to undertake graduate study. She was enlightened by her practical experiences and inspired by progressive theories about which she continued to learn. While serving as a school supervisor, Southall studied during the summer at Columbia University and the University of Chicago. She obtained the Master of Arts degree at George Peabody College for Teachers in 1926, and was awarded the Doctor of Philosophy degree in 1929. Only three women prior to Southall had achieved this degree at Peabody. Immediately following, she was recruited to become a Professor of Elementary Education at her alma mater. She would remain at Peabody for 35 years, becoming a major figure in elementary education, and a leader in various national and international organizations.

Embracing Life as a Peabody Professor

Maycie Southall immersed herself in the work of being a professor at Peabody, just as she had worked zealously at being an effective elementary school teacher, principal, and supervisor. She prepared conscientiously for her classes, which routinely included topics such as elementary school methods of teaching, elementary school curriculum, and supervision of elementary school education. She had high standards for her students, and many recalled rigorous assignments. Students were regularly sent to the library for research, and they reported their findings to their peers. Southall believed in planning a variety of learning activities for each class session. It was her practice to include some, if not all, of the following elements in a teaching segment: direct teaching, questions and answers, discussion groups, and group reporting. Former students recalled that she worked tirelessly for all her students, and she was especially adept at providing a great deal of written feedback on student research papers and assignments. In turn, her classes were large, especially during the summer. In the years following World War II, it was not unusual for her graduate classes to have enrollments of 125–50 people. A typical course load during the academic year included teaching four classes a quarter, with each class meeting four times a week for a total of four credit hours.

A critical aspect of the Peabody educational experience, and a required activity in Southall's classes, was to spend time observing in the Demonstration School at Peabody. As John E. Windrow (in Brown 1981, 65–66) recalled, in addition to sending her students to observe at the school, "she went with them; then they would come back [to the classroom], and all of them would discuss what they had observed. Many of the teachers at the Demonstration School were her own [former] students. . . . She recognized that the Demonstration School had limitations, so she would send her students out into the public schools to observe . . . situations there." Another former student recalled that such observations in the Demonstration School favored by Southall were accompanied by guided reflections, which required that the student record the time, place, setting, observed behavior, philosophy or theory undergirding the activity, and personal comments (Brown 1981).

A significant part of Southall's influence was wielded through her widespread involvement in campus activities. She led a number of conferences and workshops in summer sessions. Over the years, thousands of students attended these conferences at Peabody. Southall was appointed to a number of important faculty committees, and she was heavily involved in student activities.

Southall regularly organized summer conferences, and they made a significant impact on the students who attended them. She believed that preparing teachers to be leaders was an important task to be undertaken by college professors. Thus, a new summer series, called the Conference of Southern Leaders in Childhood Education, began in 1949. The following is an account from a campus publication indicating the success of the conferences (Lee 1959, 105):

> *One of the outstanding conferences on Peabody campus this summer was the second Conference of Southern Leaders in Childhood Education. Its purpose was to find ways of improving the education of children in the southern region by unifying and coordinating the efforts of the lay and educational leaders in this region with those of the state and national agencies. It brought together representatives from more than 17 cooperating organizations, all of which are vitally interested in the welfare of children. Under the capable leadership of Dr. Maycie Southall, who directed the conference, study groups attacked the following major problems affecting the welfare of children: Indecent Living Conditions in School; Indifferences to Children's Welfare; Teachers Poorly Prepared; Lack of Inspired Leadership; Unwholesome Pressures on Children; Three Isolates—Home, School, Community; Meager and Unbalanced School Living; Little or No Guidance Services for Children; School Living Which Miseducates; and Ill-Defined Goals. The conference closed with carefully laid plans for continued study and the distribution of its proceedings.*

Two significant college committees to which Southall was appointed were the Committee of Eleven in 1945–46 and the Ruml Plan Committee in 1959–60. The Committee of Eleven, consisting of professors appointed by President Henry H. Hill, met weekly to study the function and roles of Peabody. Twenty-two subcommittees were formed as the report was drafted. It was based partially on interviews conducted with educational experts nationwide, Peabody alumni, and members of various organizations. Peabody President Felix Robb (1961, 133) viewed the final report, which contained approximately 150 recommendations, as a success because of "the majority of [recommendations] which were eventually put into effect." The Ruml Plan Committee was convened in 1959–60 to evaluate the status of the college and to react to ideas proposed by Beardsley Ruml and Donald Morrison in *Memo to a College Trustee* (Ruml 1959). The committee's report was presented to the Peabody Board of Trustees in 1960.

No doubt, Southall was influenced over the years by many of her peers at Peabody, including Lucy Gage, Hollis Caswell, Willard Goslin, Harold R. Benjamin, Nicholas Hobbs, William Van Til, William M. Alexander, William Stanley, Susan B. Riley, Jack Allen, Fremont P. Wirth, Kenneth Cooper, James L. Hymes, Sam Wiggins, Clifton Hall, and Harold Drummond. Drummond described his years at Peabody as being intellectually stimulating, and he found Southall's substantial leadership evident on campus and in the larger world of education. Drummond (2001) recalled that Southall worked tirelessly and well on the various committees on which she found herself serving.

Influencing Lives of Students

During her three decades of teaching at Peabody, thousands of students clamored to study with Maycie Southall. A great many of her students went on to become college or university professors, school superintendents or principals, or school supervisors. The majority of her students began or continued careers as teachers. Southall had a special interest in foreign students studying at Peabody, and she made sure that they would have a rich experience while studying at the college. She advocated peaceful relations with all nations, even into her retirement. In her way, she deepened friendly relationships all over the world through her leadership at Peabody; in organizations such as the Association for Childhood Education International, Delta Kappa Gamma, and UNESCO; and on governing boards. In a speech in 1961, Southall noted that Peabody had attracted many students from China, Korea, Germany, India, Brazil, Japan, and the Philippines. Her students observed that she "made sure the international students got into her home" and that she "was especially considerate of the foreign students who studied with her. She often invited these students to her home for tea" (Brown 1981, 97). In 1973, Southall (in Brown 1981, 97) recalled that her students had "come from every state in the Union and fifty-two foreign countries."

Hilda Martin worked at the Ministry of Education in Lima, Peru, and studied with Maycie Southall in 1958 and 1959. Martin (in Brown 1981, 98) remembered the love, enthusiasm, and sense of humor Southall passed on to her students: "Dr. Southall's guidance helped me to become more sensitive and to develop a scientific attitude toward children. . . . [I] became more perceptive and more interested about children's needs, resources, and strategies on teaching."

Former student Sun Hi Lee Ro (in Brown 1981, 99–100), president of a junior college in South Korea, recalled particular kindnesses that were not unusual for Southall: "I can vividly remember one day when I needed help with my thesis. Dr. Southall, although very busy, agreed to look over my draft and return the paper the next day. When I received the corrected paper the following day, to my surprise, she had not only returned the paper but had also included a box of homemade cookies and some fresh strawberries."

Once they studied with Maycie Southall, students typically maintained a close relationship with her throughout their careers. In 1970, Southall (in Brown 1981, 101–02) visited Bangkok and was met at the airport by several former students: "I was greeted by the smiling faces of three who were preparing elementary teachers in three different colleges in Bangkok; one who was teaching English in the University; two who were principals of large secondary schools; one who was broadcasting a lecture series on child development from the King's Palace every Sunday morning; and one who is the private secretary to the King and writes all his speeches."

The late Dell C. Kjer (in Brown 1981, 75), former president of the Association for Childhood Education International and professor at Towson State University, related the following about Southall's relationships with her students:

> She loved beauty—art and music. She encouraged students to participate by attending concerts, etc. She gave things freely—tickets, books, material—to many students; she was generous . . .; for example, she had students to her apartment—an open house for every graduating class, but other students were included if she knew they were around. She was especially kind to foreign students, and there were many. Refreshments appeared as if by magic, always in the best of taste and in a comfortable but beautiful style. She had many conferences with students over meals that she had prepared. She was a popular guest for students to take to one of the many wonderful restaurants in Nashville. She had 'charisma.' . . . She accepted everyone and seemed to treat everyone alike.

Southall was also known to be very demanding of her students. She expected them to work hard and to follow a certain protocol in their responses in class, and outside of class in social settings. Every student was eventually invited to tea at Southall's apartment. They felt that their behavior at tea was as important as their classroom performance (Davis 2002a).

Sharing a Philosophy of Teaching

Basic principles for teaching young children were intuitively formulated by Maycie Southall when she was a beginning teacher at the age of 15. These were expanded as Southall immersed herself in the work of educational researchers and theorists such as William Heard Kilpatrick and Alice Temple. She believed that children should be treated with respect, as she would want to be treated herself. She believed that children should be reasoned with, not punished, when disputes arose. She believed that learning is best when it is done by doing. She believed that the walls of the classroom had no boundaries. She believed that parents should be involved in their childrens' educational experiences. At George Peabody College for Teachers, Southall's philosophy of education for children was adapted to suit the needs of her adult learners. Comments from several of her former students serve to illustrate her outlook on teaching.

A comment made by former student Nona Sparks (in Brown 1981, 67) reveals the nature of inquiry promoted by Southall, who taught her students:

> Children grow best in an atmosphere that is child-like. Their world is close to nature. Therefore, take them outside to explore, to see, feel, and touch. Bring some of that outside world into the classroom for further experimentation and enjoyment.

> *Encourage them to question, to make mistakes, and to use their imaginations. She helped us to understand that we as teachers will not be guides in this wonderful process of learning unless we understand their nature and needs and ways in which they grow and develop.*

Similarly, Rubie E. Smith, former chair of the Department of Elementary Education at Murry State University, was inspired by Southall's teaching. Smith (in Brown 1981, 67) noted, "One statement [made by Maycie Southall] has particularly guided my life, 'Don't scatter your fire; if you do, you won't have any.'"

Mary Louise Anderson, a teacher for almost 50 years, chose to attend Peabody because of Maycie Southall. Anderson (in Brown 1981, 68) remembered:

> *Dr. Southall's philosophy stemmed from Dr. Dewey's philosophy of Experimentalism as he meant it to be: liberty for children without license, freedom with responsibility, and exploration and discovery in learning. In the years since Dewey and Kilpatrick, we have moved toward smaller groups, child-centered classrooms, more study of individual children, and the value of teachers' listening to children in order to provide more meaningful learning experiences for them.*

Another former student noted that he enrolled at George Peabody College for Teachers to study with Maycie Southall. George T. Guess (in Brown 1981, 69–70), professor at Central State University in Oklahoma, extolled, "Elementary education was a 'sorry stepchild' until Dr. Southall . . . came on the scene. Her influence at national, regional, and local levels lifted the education of children from baby-sitting to profitable experiences for the child."

West Virginia educator Clemit O. Humphreys held similar memories. Humphreys (in Brown 1981, 70) reported, "Dr. Southall's thesis was the 'whole child.' She subscribed to Dewey's 'you learn to do by doing.' The thing that I remember is that she felt every room in the building should be equipped with . . . audio-visual equipment, mats, cooking stoves, refrigerators—anything that could be used in teaching . . . she put more emphasis on this than on textbooks."

Like Dewey, Southall urged teachers to engage children in meaningful activities and to utilize hands-on methods of inquiry. Dell C. Kjer (in Brown 1981, 67) related, "Her philosophy was a mixture of Pestalozzi, Dewey, Kilpatrick, Bode, and others with a lot of practical common sense; it was generally 'progressive.'" While a student at Peabody, she had studied with Thomas Alexander, Charles McMurry, Norman Frost, and A. L. Crabb. Indeed, Southall had studied with many luminaries in education during summers away from Peabody. These included John Dewey, Thomas Heard Kilpatrick, Edward L. Thorndike, Alice Temple, and Patty Smith Hill.

While her personal theories about education were crystallized long before educators endorsed constructivist approaches, Maycie Southall's approaches foreshadowed those of contemporary child-centered constructivists.

Leading Educational Organizations

Contributing to the larger world of education by way of leading educational organizations was also a role that Maycie Southall energetically embraced during her lifetime.

Several organizations were beneficiaries of Southall's leadership. She became a charter member of the Association for Childhood Education (now Association for Childhood Education International [ACEI]) in 1930, precipitated by the merger of the International Kindergarten Union and the National Council of Primary Education. By the time she became its president in 1945, the organization had grown to 38,000 members. The scope of the organization increased during Southall's term of office, for it was during this time that the name was changed to include the word *International;* likewise, the organization was reorganized to include all elementary school grades. Southall's stature as a leader expanded considerably during World War II. She was one of six educators called to Washington and assigned to guide the Extended School Program for Children of Working Mothers. In this supervisory capacity, she was required to travel in Texas, Louisiana, and New Mexico to help organize after-school programs in those areas affected by the war industries. Massive efforts were required to mobilize schools and communities to care for children whose mothers had taken war-related jobs (Field 1994; 1996).

Also during the war years, an ACEI meeting was held in Washington, D.C. Eleanor Roosevelt invited the group to the White House. At one of the meetings during the conference, Southall was seated in the East Room with Jean Betzner (president of ACEI), Jennie Wahlert, and Margaret Mead. Clearly, Southall was considered an influential educator whose opinions were sought on many levels. Frances Mayfarth, who served as ACEI publications editor from 1936 to 1950, was impressed with Southall's leadership skills and the poise she demonstrated during her presentation of "The Nation and Its Children" report to President Harry Truman. Southall asked Truman to consider the report from "citizens concerned for our nation's children, and not as politicians seeking favors." President Truman replied, "My dear Dr. Southall, you are a politician whether you want to be or not." Southall responded, "We are willing to be called politicians if you so desire and if you will see fit, as an avowed politician, to carry out our recommendations in this report." The President agreed to "give them serious consideration and see what action can be taken" (Brown 1981, 202–03).

Southall's leadership extended into other organizations as well. In 1943, she was elected to the Educational Policies Commission of the National Education Association. She served two terms and worked on several publications with others on the Commission. Most notable of these are *Education for All American Youth* (1944), *Educational Services for Young Children* (1945), and *Education for All American Children* (1948). Among the 21 members of the Commission during Southall's tenure were the presidents of Harvard, Cornell, University of Louisville, American Association of School Administrators, National Education Association, Department of Classroom Teachers of the NEA, and American Council on Education. Other members included a state commissioner of education, and several school superintendents and assistant superintendents.

Southall was summoned to the White House for three important conferences on Children and Youth—in 1940, 1950, and 1960. She considered her role in another White House Conference, on Women in Policy Making in 1944, to be equally important. This conference brought together presidents of 73 nationally recognized women's organizations to discuss opportunities for women to take a greater role in policy-making decisions at the local, state, and national levels.

Other educational organizations were the beneficiaries of Southall's leadership skills and energies. Delta Kappa Gamma, an honor society for women in education, was founded in Texas in 1929 by her friend Annie Webb Blanton. Persuaded by Blanton to join the organization and to become its state founder, Southall became the Tennessee Delta Kappa Gamma state president in 1935. Just three years later, in 1938, she was elected as the Society's fourth national president, an office she held until 1940. Her presidency was highlighted by the recognition and encouragement of research in the field of education, establishment of the first Delta Kappa Gamma scholarship, planning for the construction of a headquarters building, and negotiating a staff to run the organization. Southall was recognized by the organization in 1941 with the society's Achievement Award, bestowed upon one member per year; and in 1962, with the establishment of the fifth international scholarship in her name. While Southall (in Brown 1989, 175) expressed disappointment in her later years that "the Delta Kappa Gamma Society had . . . not [generated] more action to improve education and the role of women in education," she did note that many of her major goals as president were addressed and achieved as she had planned. These included study of several issues facing women: the status of the teaching profession, discrimination against married teachers, the selection of candidates in teacher training institutions, unjust discriminations, tenure and retirement, leadership in international crisis, and enrichment of women teachers' personal lives.

The Association for Supervision and Curriculum Development was another organization upon which Southall made an impressive impact. She joined the organization when it was established and from the beginning "was active in the new organization and served as an elected officer longer than any other person" (Davis 1978, 613). She contributed to the Board of Directors as a member for many years, helping to guide the organization through its formative years.

In her last academic year of teaching at Peabody, Southall was initiated into the Laureate Chapter of Kappa Delta Pi. Membership in the Laureate Chapter is the highest honor that may be bestowed upon educators. Limited to only 60 members, the Laureate Chapter has included, through the years, such educational leaders as Jane Addams, William C. Bagley, George Washington Carver, Hollis L. Caswell, James B. Conant, John Dewey, Albert Einstein, Patty Smith Hill, William Heard Kilpatrick, Margaret Mead, Jean Piaget, Eleanor Roosevelt, Lewis Terman, and Edward L. Thorndike. Four other Laureate members were initiated with Southall in 1964: Paul R. Hanna, Lee L. Jacks Professor of Child Education, Stanford University; Francis Keppel, U.S. Commissioner of Education and former Dean of the Graduate School of Education, Harvard University; Ralph Emerson McGill, Editor and Publisher of *The Atlanta Constitution*; and Howard Taylor, Vice Chairman of the National Committee for the Support of Public Schools and former President of Sarah Lawrence College.

Living after Retirement

Felix Robb (in Brown 1981, 151–52), President of George Peabody College for Teachers, related the following about Maycie Southall at the time of her retirement from Peabody, in 1964:

> *I stood in awe of [Dr. Southall's] tremendous accomplishments, her world-wide fame, her driving energy, and her reputation. The mantel of the fabled elementary education professor, Miss Lucy Gage, had fallen upon her capable shoulders; and for decades she was one of that bright group of stellar professors who made Peabody*

*College both famous and great. . . . If there were a Hall of Fame for elementary educa-
tion, Maycie Southall would be in it. My hat is off and doffed to this great lady, this
master teacher, and this personal and professional guide to thousands of students
who found their way to her classroom.*

Maycie Southall remained very active during retirement in her local community of
Nashville and in the national and international organizations she led vigorously during
her career. In 1981, she helped found the International/Intercultural Education Center
in Nashville. It was established during the International Year of the Child to promote an
international perspective related to children's literature, art, and music. The Center's
ultimate mission, to promote global understanding and peace among nations, had as its
focus the good of children everywhere—in Nashville, Tennessee, and in the larger world.
Southall's rationale for the Center's being (quoted in Gilstrap 1990, 247), and likely the
reason she energetically supported it, is best reflected by her thought that "since wars
are made in the minds of men, it's in the minds of men that the defenses of peace must
be." Southall sought to reach those minds at a young age, through learning about other
cultures and reading quality children's literature. Today, the center 's holdings—comprised of English-language children's books and copies of popular children's titles from
non-English speaking countries—are divided between the Southeast and Richland Park
Branch Libraries. Commenting on the value of the collection to the community, Southeast Branch Children's Librarian Toni Ross (2000) said, "One patron found a copy of the
very first book her mother had ever read to her when she was a child in Iran, *The Little
Black Fish* by Samuel Bahrang (1971). She was thrilled to be able to check out a copy of
the same book to read to her little girl in their native language."

In 1985, Southall was asked to relate her ideas about educational changes that had
transpired during her career (Gilstrap 1990). She noted several, including more educational opportunities for children, better preparation of teachers, more concern for individualized education, and greater attention to disadvantaged children (Gilstrap 1990).

George Peabody College for Teachers honored its former professor by establishing
the Maycie K. Southall Distinguished Lecture Series in 1985 to emphasize public education for, and the well-being of, children. Sarah Lawrence Lightfoot, Professor of Education at the Harvard Graduate School of Education, gave the first address. In recent years,
lectures have been presented by Virginia Richardson, Gloria Ladson-Billings, John T.
Bruer, and Barbara T. Bowman. Before her death in 1992, Maycie Southall must have
looked back on a rewarding life, friendships made and maintained, and her life's mission of promoting practical educational practices for the good of all children. She saw
the status of education and the methods by which it is achieved change dramatically
during her lifetime, and she was widely recognized as an influential educational leader.
Yet, she most likely would have wanted to be remembered not as an educational leader,
but as a teacher who had children's learning at the heart of her work.

Major Contributions

Why is it beneficial to learn about the life of Maycie Southall? She authored few
publications during her lifetime. Her scholarship was often part of larger, committee-
driven pieces of work and perhaps raises more questions than answers, given that most
of her writings were done in the early part of her career. We might wonder how her lived

experience—and her experiences as a woman who grew up and worked in the segregated south—influenced her philosophy of teaching in the midst of the Civil Rights Movement. We might also wonder whether she supported women's issues, especially those of women's suffrage and equal rights. Both major social movements occurred during her lifetime, but she spoke directly to neither. Instead, speculation based on the theory and pedagogy she shared with others, and from the causes she supported publicly, informs us. Even as Southall's legacy of scholarship is lean, there is sufficient evidence to support the notion that her legacy as a teacher, especially for pre-and in-service teachers whose lives she touched, is especially rich. Perhaps the primary reason for looking into the life of Maycie Southall is to provide greater insight into women teachers and teacher-leaders. While a growing body of educational biographies about influential figures in education exists (Crocco and Davis 1999), more research is needed.

Several themes emerge that appear to be framing forces in Southall's life. These themes speak to contemporary teachers. Southall supported equity in education, interdisciplinary education, out-of-classroom educational opportunities, women in school leadership positions, salient supervision practices, advanced methods in teacher education, intercultural and multicultural education, and peace education.

Primary among Southall's philosophical underpinnings were strongly held beliefs about how to meet the needs of learners, and how to plan, organize, implement, and assess instruction for young children. Equity in education was perhaps an overarching belief throughout Southall's career. She held that children's individual needs and strengths should be supported in schools. Additionally, her preferred strategy for curriculum planning and instruction was that of interdisciplinary instruction. Helping children make connections between one content area and another made sense to Southall. She utilized interdisciplinary instruction as an elementary teacher, modeled it as a school supervisor, and taught about it as a teacher educator. Another key instructional strategy was to provide numerous out-of-classroom learning opportunities for children. This idea resonated as well with other influential female educators during Southall's time (Field 2001; Bohan 1999), and support for this strategy appears to be growing in contemporary times (Alleman and Brophy 2002).

Southall enthusiastically supported her female colleagues in seeking leadership positions—in schools and in the organizations to which she belonged. She clearly saw merit in taking advantage of women's unique knowledge, skills, and experiences (Belenky, Clinchy, and Tarule 1986). Salient school supervision practices were also a major interest for Southall. Her major contribution to school supervision was in the practical manner in which she believed the process should take place. That is, the supervisory process should be efficient, helpful, and embedded in best practice. Southall viewed the supervisory process as one in which teachers' ideas and experiences should be taken into consideration, never losing sight of education's larger purpose—meeting the needs of every child. This guiding principle was reflected in her beliefs about teacher education. Southall spent the greater portion of her life as a teacher educator—directly as a Peabody professor and indirectly as a school administrator and supervisor. She strongly embraced collaborative efforts, and the identification and acknowledgment of trends that were successful.

Southall also should be remembered for her efforts in intercultural and multicultural education and in peace education. She joined other luminaries, such as during the intercultural education movement (Davis 2002b) and forged her own strategies for sharing its ideas with her students. She lived through the devastating years of World War II and determined that the best way to build a peaceful world was to promote common understandings and respect among diverse people. As her students attest, she modeled this behavior throughout her life.

References

Alleman, J., and J. Brophy, with B. Knighton, contributor. 2002. *Social studies excursions, K–3*. Portsmouth, N.H.: Heinemann.

Bahrang, S. 1971. *The little black fish*. Minneapolis, Minn.: Carolrhoda Books.

Belenky, M. F., B. M. Clinchy, and J. M. Tarule. 1986. *Women's ways of knowing: The development of self, voice, and mind*. New York: Basic Books.

Bohan, C. H. 1999. Lucy Maynard Salman: Progressive historian, teacher, and democrat. In *Bending the future to their will: Civic women, social education, and democracy*, ed. M. S. Crocco and O. L. Davis, Jr., 47–72. Lanham, Md.: Rowman and Littlefield.

Brown, D. L. 1981. *Maycie Katherine Southall: Her life and contributions to education*. Nashville, Tenn.: McQuiddy Publishing Co.

Brown, L. 1989. A rose among her roses. *Delta Kappa Gamma Bulletin* 55(3): 20–31.

Crocco, M. S., and O. L. Davis, Jr., eds. 1999. *Bending the future to their will: Civic women, social education, and democracy*. Lanham, Md.: Rowman and Littlefield.

Davis, O. L., Jr. 1978. Symbol of a shift from status to function: Formation of the Association for Supervision and Curriculum Development. *Educational Leadership* 35(8): 609–14.

Davis, O. L., Jr. 2002a. Interview by author. Austin, Tex., 22 September.

Davis, O. L., Jr. 2002b. Rachel Davis Du Bois. In *Building a legacy: Women in social education, 1784–1984*, ed. M. S. Crocco and O. L. Davis Jr., 169–84. Washington D.C.: National Council for the Social Studies.

Drummond, Harold. 2001. Conversation with author. Orlando, Fla., 8 November.

Educational Policies Commission. 1944. *Education for all American youth*. Washington, D.C.: EPC.

Educational Policies Commission. 1945. *Educational services for young children*. Washington, D.C.: EPC.

Educational Policies Commission. 1948. *Education for all American children*. Washington, D.C.: EPC.

Field, S. L. 2001. Lucy Sprague Mitchell: Teacher, geographer, and teacher educator. In *Bending the future to their will: Civic women, social education, and democracy*, ed. M. S. Crocco and O. L. Davis, Jr., 125–48. Lanham, Md.: Rowman and Littlefield.

Field, S. L. 1994. Scrap drives, stamp sales, and school spirit: Examples of elementary social studies during World War II. *Theory and Research in Social Education* 22(4): 441–60.

Field, S. L. 1996. Roosevelt's World War II army of community service workers: Children and their teachers. *Social Education* 60(5): 280–83.

Gilstrap, R. L. 1990. Later leaders in education: Maycie K. Southall—A special leader for special times. *Childhood Education* 66(4): 244–47.

Lee, R. 1959. Summer conferences and workshops. *The Peabody Reflector* 23(April): 105.

Robb, F. C. 1961. President looks at Peabody's problems, needs, aims, hopes. *The Peabody Reflector* 34 (September–October): 133.

Robb, Felix C. 1981. Letter to Dorothy Louise Brown. In *Maycie Katherine Southall: Her life and contributions to education*, ed. D. L. Brown, 151–52. Nashville, Tenn.: McQuiddy Publishing Co.

Ross, T. Nashville Public Library's International Collection to Grow. 2000. *TLA Newsletter* 8(1–2). Available at: www.lib.utk.edu/~tla/news0004.html.

Ruml, B. 1959. *Memo to a college trustee: A report on financial and structural problems of the liberal college*. New York: McGraw-Hill.

Southall, M. 1979. Interview by O. L. Davis, Jr. Nashville, Tenn., 20 April.

With Vision to Spare

by Bettye M. Caldwell

This part of the book deals with three remarkable women—women of vision, commitment, and iron wills; and women ready and eager to make a contribution to education in spite of their gender and the low status of their field of endeavor (Patty Smith Hill and Maycie Southall) or the intermittent unpopularity of the major tenets of her educational philosophy (Alice Miel). Their ideas and their energy stimulated at least two generations of students who were fortunate enough to encounter them. Their key ideas are very much alive—and influential—today. Even so, their names are not exactly household terms in education circles. In view of the tendency among all the scholarly fields to assume that what is new is *ipso facto* better than and significantly different from what came before, this is perhaps not too surprising. It is, however, unfortunate. Other fields have sacred names that no contemporary or modern scholar is allowed to obliterate—names like Newton and Darwin and Einstein. Though others may disagree with me (and it is probably too early to assert the position too definitively), I don't think education has produced a name since John Dewey that always is recognized and is non-obliterative.

Privileged to Repeat

One of the most common adages we often verbalize is the statement by George Santyana, engraved over the National Archives Building in Washington, D.C.: "Those who cannot remember history are condemned to repeat it." Sometimes the repetition is perhaps more a privilege than a condemnation. There is no question that great ideas recycle, and I think that young investigators should not hesitate to recognize the important historical antecedents of the problem areas with which they are dealing—and perhaps even the solutions they offer. Doing this identifies them as vital marchers in the parade of intellectual history, an achievement which, at any juncture in history, is entirely noble and acceptable. A common statement by professors of philosophy is that all philosophy is but a footnote to Plato. (Others are bold enough to suggest that Plato is but a footnote to Parmenides of Elea.) Then, of course, after that acknowledgment, they immediately proceed to discuss more modern philosophical ideas, and, unless the course is designed for philosophy majors who must plow through the *Dialogues*, the subject is closed. Perhaps it is the same in education; we pay a bit of lip service to historical personages, and then rush ahead to current gurus and contemporary ideas. There is no need to apologize for being, at least in part, a footnote to the women of vision highlighted here.

Of the people profiled in this section—Patty Smith Hill (who is always known by all three of those names)—has been especially important for early childhood, my own field. For some reason, however, the field of early childhood is very ahistorical. Maybe it is because we deal with young children, who have much more future than past. In my courses, I always included a fairly lengthy section dealing with the history of the field and briefly profiling many of the individuals who moved and developed it. To my dismay, I found that students migrating into early childhood from some other branch of education had never heard of most of the intellectual and advocacy leaders of early childhood—or, if they had heard of them, the names didn't register. Mention Pestalozzi or Fröbel, and you would get a furrowing of brows that seemed to indicate, "I've heard that name, but I can't quite remember where." Mention Margaret MacMillan or Susan Blow, and you would get a blank stare. Maybe, just maybe, the name of Patty Smith Hill would elicit a timidly raised hand and an apologetic answer offered in the form of a hesitant question, "Didn't she write "Happy Birthday?" The only name that generated unanimous recognition was Maria Montessori, and that was because of the spread of Montessori schools across the country in recent years. Even so, if you had asked about Montessori prior to around 1965, you most likely would have drawn a similar blank. If you had followed your inquiry with another asking for a statement of a few of the main ideas of Montessori's pedagogy, the student you called on most likely would have held a grudge against you for the remainder of the semester.

This ahistorical bent is especially puzzling in that many, if not most, of our historical *heroes* are *heroines*. There are few, if any, other critically important areas of professional education in which this is true. We need to be aware of the fact that much of the intellectual leadership and much of the effort involved in gaining societal acceptance of the importance of the early years have come from women. To me, it would be a good thing to have the new wave of practitioners and idea-generators who are appearing on the horizon, most of whom are women, rejoice in the fact that most of their important predecessors were women—women who worked against apathy and outright resistance to get across the idea of the critical importance of learning in the early years. And with that acknowledgement, it would be appropriate to hold on a little more steadfast to some of the names of the people who have made a difference.

Names Change, Dilemmas Remain

Anyone who is currently active in either early childhood or elementary education and who reads the chapters on our three indomitable ladies will be prompted to sigh and say, "So what's new?" Patty Smith Hill sparred and debated for years with Susan Blow over the extent to which the kindergarten curriculum should be prescribed according to an invariant pedagogical formula (in this case, Fröbel) or adapted to the interests of the children with whom a teacher must currently work. Believe me, that debate was still very much alive when I entered the field almost 40 years ago; and it is still continuing today, as most early childhood specialists try to counteract pressures to fit all kindergarten children into a heavily academic preliteracy program. All of those who champion play as an essential technique for learning in young children—and have observed the children joyfully and purposefully moving around the large wooden blocks— have inherited the legacy of Patty Smith Hill.

Maycie Southall is a little more difficult to categorize than the other two women. She was a true generalist who helped legitimize elementary education and who fought for the acceptance of the individuality of each child in a classroom. I especially like Field's suggestion that her thinking foreshadowed the currently popular constructivist theories of child learning.

Alice Miel, it seems to me, was perhaps less an innovator—in terms of campaigning for the admission of new areas of endeavor into the fold of professional education—than a voice basically asking the field to look at itself and determine whether the procedures it practiced were compatible with those it espoused. Thus, she was like Socrates, who proclaimed that the unexamined life was not worth living. The same is true, she might have said, for the unexamined field. Let's examine our teaching procedures, she urged, and make certain that they exemplify those we are telling teachers to adopt. Personally I am convinced that her ideas are going to recycle many times during this century, as those who guide education try to steer American education through the Scylla of over-regimentation and packaged curricula and the Charybdis of classroom chaos and scorn for accumulated knowledge. Miel had, perhaps, the misfortune of advocating democracy as the hub of all social learning (her vastly improved term for "social studies") during the time when public opinion would be captivated by the impressive achievements of clearly nondemocratic educational approaches. Hopefully, history will catch up with her before too long.

Similarities among the Visionaries

As I read these biographies, I was struck by a number of similarities among these indomitable women:

1. **There are noticeable personal similarities.**All grew up in middle-class environments that encouraged their early intellectual interests and cultivated their individuality. Additionally, two out of the three are from the South. Most scholarly disciplines seem to have a bias in favor of the Northeast or the Midwest, and the South doesn't always get its due as a place where great ideas are generated and developed. (Of course, I have to add that two of the three migrated to the Northeast and spent most of their careers there. Only Southall stayed in the South; maybe it was the power of her name.) To the best of my knowledge, none married or had children; the children whose lives were enhanced by their professional work were their descendents. Lastly, all lived to a ripe old age.

2. **All had been classroom teachers before becoming professors, and all remained close to classroom life.** The modern divorce of university professors from life in "real" classrooms continues to be a major problem in teacher training. All three continued to enrich their training of older students by their own involvement in live classroom experiences.

3. **All were advocates as well as teachers.** Public school educators have recognized the importance of advocacy for a number of years; but people in early childhood have developed that awareness only recently. Perhaps because of the stigma associated with "being for welfare families" and the fact that the field has assimilated and used less than fully trained professionals, early childhood leaders have learned the hard way that they have to work to gain acceptance for the field and better salaries for its participants. All three of these visionaries worked as advocates—Hill for universal preschool education, integration with elementary education, and recognition of a role for parents; Southall for the development of after-school programs for children whose

parents worked; and Miel for greater recognition of diversity among children and the need for adopting educational programs to that diversity. None of the three rested within the shade of their universities; all played important roles in the community.

4. All could deal with controversy. This must have been an important skill in an era when women professors lacked status and clout. Hill fought to what most would consider a victory in her ongoing challenges to Susan Blow. Southall would not have been able to help elementary education at Peabody College out of its "sorry state" had she not been willing to deal effectively with controversy. All of us who have served on university faculties know how resistant to innovation those faculties can be; yet, change seldom comes without controversy. And Miel addressed eloquently her opponents who charged that a democratic approach to education was merely an endorsement of *laissez-faire* practices that were allowing American children to fall behind.

5. All had an international perspective. Hill took her original inspiration from the great German educator, Friedrich Fröbel. Southall cherished her students from abroad, and it was during her tenure as President of the Association for Childhood Education that the word International was added to the name. Miel was the founder of the World Council on Curriculum and Instruction and lectured widely in many foreign countries. There was nothing provincial about any of our visionaries.

6. All were concerned with character development. What a delight to find this concern in all three women—especially at a time in history when some are challenging the role of the school in moral and character development. Hill realized the need for early education to nurture some of the personality characteristics in impoverished children that they would perhaps not develop in home environments weighted down by poverty. Southall was concerned that children have freedom, but with the addition of responsibility. And what Miel called "social learning" is but another term for character; it involves acceptance of responsibility for one's actions and respect for the actions of others. All basically advocated the position that the only way for children to assimilate democratic values was by being participants in a democratic environment. Further, they did what they could to get this idea across in the universities in which they were employed and in the organizations they established and supported. Perhaps most importantly, they all labored to help create a large cadre of teachers who could put that principle into action in the lives of children.

Summary

It is a joy to read these brief histories of three women important to the history of education. Southall wrote little, so summaries by people like Field are important "for the record." Hill wrote a good bit; but, in today's limited library space, older materials often get "de-acquisitioned" (that's the word libraries use). Miel wrote a great deal; but, to some extent, her writing was defensive—reactive rather than proactive. This was necessary for her, as her position went in and out of favor several times during her lifetime. The objective portraits in this section provide a valuable resource for current and future students.

What I hunger for upon reading these chapters is for an opportunity to have met these women in person, to have sat in one of their classes. Rudnitski's picture of Hill's having a silver candelabra brought on stage just before her lecture filled me with a longing for a world that has disappeared. Such panache! I wish I had had the courage to do something like that just once!

Yet, one doesn't have to look back on the world of these visionaries with nostalgia and longing. Perhaps the most common characteristic of the three is that they looked forward—forward to a time when adoption of their ideas would make for happier and more competent children and a better functioning democracy. So we should all rejoice that these women were out there smoothing the way for those of us who follow. Consider their contributions in the context of their time and place. Criticize as well as praise them. But don't forget them. And let's just hope that we do as well as they did.

Part Three
Forging New Cultural and Social Ground

Chapter 7

W. E. B. Du Bois: 'Race Man,' Teacher, and Educational Theorist

Derrick P. Alridge

William Edward Burghardt Du Bois (1868–1963) was an educator, historian, philosopher, and social scientist who contributed immensely to the development of African-American education and the study of the black experience during his 70-plus years of research, writing, and activism. As one of the most prolific scholars of the 20th century, he produced more than 22 books, 100 articles and essays, and 15 edited volumes encompassing such issues as black health, education, economics, politics, and the family, to name just a few.

A true interdisciplinary scholar, Du Bois crossed many boundaries in research and activism and made major contributions to several disciplines. For example, his book *The Souls of Black Folk*, published in 1903, is a classic in U.S. literature. In 1899, Du Bois published the first major sociological study on African Americans in an urban community. *The Philadelphia Negro* was a groundbreaking study that marked Du Bois as one of the founders of urban sociology. Finally, in 1935, Du Bois (1935a) published *Black Reconstruction*, further establishing himself as a major historian, despite the reluctance of many historians during his time to consider it a major historical work (Lewis 1995).

Despite Du Bois's many contributions to various disciplines and to U.S. society, until recently he has been overlooked as a major figure in U.S. history. During more than 70 years of scholarship and activism, Du Bois contemplated and wrote about a number of issues that directly influenced his ideas about education, particularly about the education of African Americans. Many of his educational views anticipated the educational perspectives and issues prevalent in education today. Du Bois, for instance, discussed Afrocentric, multicultural, and global education decades before they were major issues in U.S. education.

Unfortunately, educators and educational historians continue to neglect Du Bois as a significant educator and theorist. This chapter illuminates Du Bois's life and work as an educator and teacher, in the truest sense, by examining how his scholarship, activism, and thinking on a variety of social and educational issues helped teach the world about issues surrounding race, equality, and democracy. Du Bois was more than a teacher to the world; his thinking on the education of African Americans makes him one of the most influential figures in 20th-century U.S. education.

This chapter will progress chronologically and thematically. First, I shall examine the influences on Du Bois's thinking from his entrance into Fisk University in 1885 to his graduation from Harvard in 1895. Second, I shall place Du Bois's thinking within the intellectual context of other African American educators such as Booker T. Washington, Anna Julia Cooper, and Carter G. Woodson. Third, the chapter will examine the development of Du Bois's educational thought from 1896 to 1963. The chapter concludes with an overview of several themes that emerge from Du Bois's thinking on education over his lifetime.

Education and the Making of a 'Race Man,' 1885–1895

Du Bois was born on 23 February 1868 in Great Barrington, Massachusetts, into a working-class family. His father, Alfred Du Bois, a mulatto of Haitian and French descent, abandoned Du Bois when he was still a toddler. Du Bois's mother, Mary Silvina Burghardt Du Bois, and the Burghardt clan provided young Will, as Du Bois was called, with a nuclear family structure during his formative and adolescent years. With the support of his family and his school principal, Frank Hosmer, Du Bois excelled in college-preparatory classes, and community members helped provide him with books. With the exception of an incident in which a European-American female classmate refused to accept his greeting cards, Du Bois (1968) reported that he encountered a relatively minimal amount of racism in the schools and town of Great Barrington.

While Du Bois was still quite young, many people in his community recognized his potential as a leader of his race. Du Bois graduated from high school in 1884 and in 1885 headed south for Fisk University in Nashville, Tennessee.

Nashville was unlike anything Du Bois had experienced in Great Barrington. Fisk and the surrounding community exposed him to the harsh realities of Jim Crow society, with all of its mores and beliefs about the position of Negroes* in the U.S. social order. As Du Bois (1968, 108) stated, "I came to a region where the world was split into white and black halves, and where the darker half was held back by race prejudice and legal bonds, as well as by deep ignorance and poverty."

Despite these harsh realities, Du Bois was attracted to the rich black culture of Fisk, Nashville, and the surrounding areas. As Du Bois (1968, 107) noted, he was "thrilled to be for the first time among so many people of my own color or rather of various extraordinary colors." This rich culture, juxtaposed against the rigid racial caste system of the South, shaped the young scholar's thinking about education as a means to free "his people" from the shackles of Jim Crow. At Fisk, Du Bois gained a greater appreciation and understanding of what it meant to be a Negro in U.S. society. He identified the Negro spirituals he heard at Fisk with the ones he heard his relatives sing in Great Barrington. His appreciation of music encouraged him to join the Fisk choir and to acquire a taste for classical music.

At Fisk, Du Bois looked at himself and his young classmates as the future leaders of the race. Messianic in tone, he reflected on their mission of uplifting the race. It was during his Fisk years, perhaps, that he began to claim his role as a "race man" (Carby 1998) committed to addressing the problems that confronted the Negro race in the United States. As Du Bois (1968, 112) declared, "I replaced my hitherto egocentric world by a

---

* I use the term "Negro" in reference to African Americans periodically throughout this essay to provide a historical sense of the periods in which it was used. I use the term "African American" and "black" instead of "Negro" in discussing more recent history. For a discussion of these terms in their historical context, see Barry and Blassingame (1982), especially 389–96.

world centering and whirling about my race in America. For this group I built my plan of study and accomplishment. Through the leadership of men like myself and my fellows, we were going to have these enslaved Israelites out of the still enduring bondage in short order."

Du Bois later noted that his education at Fisk prepared him for race leadership. He studied Greek, chemistry, and physics, vociferously devouring works in philosophy and ethics with Fisk president Erastus Cravath. He also praised Fisk's liberal arts curriculum for preparing him to study the so-called "Negro problem" and praised Cravath for being "truly committed" to helping uplift the Negro race (Du Bois 1968; Myrdal 1944).

With a strong academic foundation from Fisk, Du Bois set out to free the "Israelites"—his people—by taking a teaching job in the backwoods of Tennessee. There he observed the debilitating impact of Jim Crow—the perpetual cycle of poverty further entrenched by substandard education—on Negroes' social and economic conditions. Nevertheless, he was excited about teaching young black children and thought nobly about his role as a teacher. Early in his career, Du Bois began to appreciate his obligation as a teacher and educator. For two summers, he taught school in rural Tennessee, paving the way for a lifelong career as a teacher and educator. Du Bois (1899, 99–104) recognized the awesome responsibility that awaited him: "I trembled when I heard the patter of little feet down the dusty road, and saw the growing row of dark solemn faces and bright eager eyes facing me. . . . There they sat, nearly thirty of them, on rough benches, their faces shading from a pale cream to a deep brown, little feet bare and swinging, their eyes full of expectation."

After his education at Fisk and teaching experiences in Tennessee, Du Bois set his sights on fulfilling one of his earlier quests—to attend Harvard University. With the help of Principal Hosmer in Great Barrington, President Cravath at Fisk, and other Fisk professors, Du Bois enrolled at Harvard in 1888. By this time, he saw Harvard as a means of enlarging his view of the world. However, he stated that he did not consider it to be the beginning or end of his education. Du Bois (1968, 133) also noted that Harvard's teachers were no better than his teachers at Fisk; they were just better known.

From 1888 to 1890, Du Bois studied for a bachelor's degree in philosophy, taking courses from a variety of scholars across disciplines, including William James in philosophy and psychology, Albert Bushnell Hart in history, and George Santayana in philosophy. After completing his bachelor's degree in philosophy in 1890, Du Bois received a master's degree in history from Harvard in 1892. Under the guidance of Hart, he started research on the African slave trade in the United States and began work on a doctorate in history. Outside the contact he had with his professors and a few classmates, Du Bois had very little social interaction at Harvard, immersing himself primarily in the black community of Boston. As Du Bois (1968, 136) expressed it, "I was in Harvard, but not of it."

To develop his thinking and scholarly skills, Du Bois took a leave of absence from Harvard in 1892 to study abroad at the prestigious University of Berlin. Like Fisk, Germany had a profound effect on his intellectual development, particularly on his views about the importance of education and social reform. In Berlin, Du Bois encountered three scholars who influenced his thinking about education, social reform, economics, and politics: Heinrich Von Treitschke, Adolf Wagner, and Gustav Schmoller. Interestingly, none of these scholars came from the discipline of philosophy, the field in which

Du Bois had focused much of his study at Harvard. Instead, Du Bois's Berlin professors trained him primarily in the area of political economy—a predecessor of sociology. In addition, Du Bois's Berlin professors were acutely interested in social problems, particularly those affecting Germany and other parts of Europe. Such exposure helped broaden Du Bois's thinking and challenged him to place the "Negro problem" within a global context (Barkin 2000).

Under Von Treitschke, Du Bois studied politics and was exposed to Von Treitschke's German nationalist views and criticisms of the United States' "uncivilized" practice of lynching in its Southern states. Wagner equally exposed Du Bois to his German imperialistic views and harsh critique of laissez-faire economics and its divisive practice of polarizing Germans between the rich and poor. Less nationalistic than Von Treitschke and Wagner, Schmoller also rejected laissez-faire liberalism; not to be confused with contemporary U.S. liberal views on economics, for a political economy grounded in scholarly research with clearly defined questions. Along with his colleagues, Schmoller believed that the state should help dictate the role of the economy.

The extent to which Du Bois's Berlin education influenced his emerging ideas on education and reform as ameliorative tools for addressing the Negro problem is debatable. However, Du Bois's Berlin diary and his coursework there show the influence of his German education, particularly his use of history and the social sciences, to address the modern-day problems of the Negro in the United States. Upon celebrating his 25th birthday in Berlin, Du Bois reflected on his educational experiences at Fisk, Harvard, and Berlin and committed himself to uplifting his people (Broderick 1959). In a solitary candlelight ceremony, Du Bois (1893) dedicated himself to becoming the Moses of his people, whose duty it was to uplift the race: "These are my plans: to make a name in science, to make a name in literature, and thus to raise my race." After a year in Germany, Du Bois abandoned plans to complete a Ph.D. in economics from the University of Berlin. Inadequate credits at the university and the lack of future financial support forced him to return to the United States to continue his work toward a doctorate from Harvard.

Upon returning to the United States, Du Bois was faced with being a full-time student, but instead he accepted a position at Wilberforce University in Ohio, where he taught Latin, Greek, and English. Wilberforce, Du Bois later noted, was a good place to begin his career, but he felt restricted by the administration, the school's fervent religious culture, and the school's reluctance to allow him to teach sociology. In 1895, Du Bois completed his doctoral degree and defended his dissertation, "The Suppression of the African Slave-Trade to the United States of America, 1638–1870." In 1896, he published his dissertation as a book.

Du Bois in Context: Jim Crow and Black Educational Thought, 1896–Early 1900s

Life for many African Americans during the 1890s and at the beginning of the 20th century was not much better than it was during the era of slavery. One of the first signs that the South would return to a racial caste system was the Compromise of 1877, which resulted in the removal of federal troops from the South. A second sign was the historic *Plessy v. Ferguson* Supreme Court decision in 1896, which legally permitted the "separate but equal" policy that upheld the segregation of the races (Logan 1997). These two events helped return the

South and other parts of the country to a system of institutionalized and legal servitude for blacks.

The social, economic, and political conditions of African Americans during the late 1800s through the early 1900s were so harsh that Logan (1997) has called this period the "nadir" of the black experience in the United States. Rigid Jim Crow laws restricted blacks from integrating into mainstream society and its institutions. African Americans, particularly in the South, were not permitted to vote or go to the same schools, hotels, restaurants, or theaters as European Americans. Nor, in most cases, could they attend church with whites. In addition, violence against blacks escalated in the early 1900s.

Following Reconstruction and well into the 20th century, the incidence of lynching blacks increased significantly. During the 1880s, lynchings averaged 100 per year, peaking at 161 in 1892. The new century did not fare better, with an average of 214 lynchings in its first two years. Between 1892 and 1901, 2,000 blacks were lynched, 68 of them women (National Association for the Advancement of Colored People [NAACP] 1919; Trotter 2001; Franklin and Moss 2000). Throughout the country, Negro life was of very little value to some European Americans, and even some white scholars of the period argued that Negroes were intellectually inferior and should never become integrated into U.S. society (Myrdal 1944).

Harsh conditions were also reflected on economic, political, and educational fronts. Large numbers of African Americans were impoverished, and many were restricted from voting, thereby locking them out of the political process at the beginning of the 1900s through half of the 20th century. The education of blacks also reflected the harsh times. In *The Negro Common School*, Du Bois (1901) reported that, in 1870, 79.9 percent of blacks in the South were illiterate, while at the same time many Southern whites resisted the establishment of black schools (Anderson 1998). Such social and educational problems, Du Bois and others believed, would pose a serious challenge for Negroes in the 20th century.

Du Bois and other black educators believed that education could play a major role in advancing black civil rights and in pulling blacks up from the doldrums of entrenched racism and poverty. In 1895, Booker T. Washington (1980, 194) delivered his famous Atlanta Compromise speech at the Atlanta Cotton Exposition, in which he called for blacks to forego demands for immediate civil rights: "Cast down your bucket where you are—cast it down in making friends in every manly way of the people of all races by whom we are surrounded." Washington was born into slavery, graduated from Hampton Institute, and became the president of Tuskegee Institute in Alabama. Based on his personal history, he strongly believed in and preached a doctrine of self-help. He advocated for Negroes to obtain vocational skills and training that would lead to employment and support for their families. Industrial education, Washington believed, was the most pragmatic approach to helping build Negro work and artisan skills during the late 1800s and early 1900s.

During the early 1900s, Du Bois supported a liberal/classical education focus for black education, while Washington advocated an industrial/vocational emphasis. It is important to note here that neither was entirely opposed to either form of education as a component of their educational perspectives. In reality, Du Bois and Washington both promoted uplifting the Negro race, though they favored differing educational approaches (Alridge 1999a).

Prior to Du Bois and Washington presenting their views on education, Anna Julia

Cooper, a teacher and scholar at the prestigious M Street High School (later Dunbar High School) in Washington, D.C., argued for education that incorporated aspects of both industrial and liberal education for her students. Cooper (1892) articulated many of her views on black women and education in *A Voice from the South*. In particular, Cooper focused on providing black women with education that would help them address the dual hegemony of racism and gender discrimination. While Cooper's and Du Bois's relationship was minimal, she encouraged Du Bois to educate the world, teach the truth about Negro history, and answer revisionist historians' argument that Negro leadership was detrimental to the South during Reconstruction. Cooper would go on to earn a Ph.D. from the University de Paris Sorbonne in 1925 and become president of Frelinghuysin University in Washington, D.C., in 1930 (Alexander 1995).

Carter G. Woodson was another contemporary of Du Bois's who believed that education would help uplift the Negro. Like Du Bois, Woodson held a Ph.D. in history from Harvard and believed that Negroes should learn about their rich cultural history. As a result, he spent much of his life educating the black masses, writing several textbooks on blacks. In 1915, he helped found the Association for the Study of Negro Life and History to correct the miseducation that Negroes received in both segregated and integrated schools across the country.

Washington, Cooper, and Woodson were only three of Du Bois's contemporaries who proposed cogent educational philosophies and strategies for U.S. Negroes. In addition, educators Mary McCleod Bethune, Alain Locke, Ambrose Caliver, and Ida B. Wells Barnett, among many others, were in the forefront of forging educational strategies for U.S. Negroes. These black educators and intellectuals developed their thinking in the context of Jim Crow society. Throughout the 20th century, their educational views helped provide the intellectual milieu within which Du Bois's educational thought evolved.

Development of Du Bois's Educational Views as a Teacher and Educator, 1896–1963

The year 1896 was eventful for Du Bois. In the fall, the University of Pennsylvania appointed him "assistant instructor" in sociology. Du Bois (1968) suspected that the faculty might have demurred at giving a black man any title, but he did not allow the low title to deter him from the opportunity to be the principal investigator and researcher on a project examining the social conditions of Negroes in Philadelphia. Finally, he would have the opportunity to apply the knowledge and methods learned at Fisk, Harvard, and Berlin to the study of "his people." Philadelphia provided a laboratory for the young social scientist to delve into the new field of sociology, using his education as a means of solving a real-world problem rather than discussing abstract problems.

In *The Philadelphia Negro*, Du Bois (1899) concluded that Negroes played a role in helping sustain the poverty and decadence in their communities, though the residuals of slavery, discrimination, racism, and social oppression had perpetuated a racial caste system that kept Negroes in a state of semi-slavery. In 1897, after 18 months of research, Du Bois accepted an offer from Atlanta University to establish a sociology department and oversee a series of research projects on the Negro problem, entitled the Atlanta University Studies. These projects gave Du Bois an opportunity to realize his dream of conducting comprehensive studies on the Negro condition, backed by a black university. Du Bois worked on the studies from 1897 to 1914, even though he left Atlanta University in 1910.

Du Bois also relished the opportunity to teach at Atlanta University. Again, he saw himself in the messianic vision of training a cadre of scholars to lead the race. Education and teaching were at the center of this vision (Du Bois 1903, 75): "Education must not simply teach work—it must teach Life. The Talented Tenth of the Negro race must be leaders of thought and missionaries of culture among their people. No others can do this work, and Negro colleges must train men for it. The Negro race, like all other races, is going to be saved by its exceptional men."

While a teacher at Atlanta University, Du Bois inspired his students and encouraged them to take up the mantle of leadership necessary for addressing the Negro problem. Though some students noted his aloofness, most appreciated his intellectual abilities and many appreciated his academically rigorous courses (Yancy 1978). Du Bois was known, for instance, to call students by their last name or not to greet them at all. His stylish dress and punctuality to class and to his office also contributed to students' perception that Du Bois was a very formal man. Some students also noted that as a teacher he was a "hard taskmaster" and at times antisocial. Most students, nonetheless, admired and had tremendous respect for him and the role he was playing in uplifting the race (Yancy 1978). In reflecting on his role as teacher at Atlantic University, Du Bois (1968, 283), noted, "I stimulated inquiry and accuracy. I met every question honestly and never dodged an earnest doubt. I read my examination papers carefully and marked them with sedulous care. But I did not know my students as human beings; they were to me apt to be intellects and not souls."

In 1899, Sam Hose, a black sharecropper, was lynched in Atlanta by a white mob. This event had a profound effect on Du Bois, and he began to question the effectiveness of scientific research in addressing the race problem. As Du Bois (1968, 222) declared, "One could not be a calm, cool, and detached social scientist while Negroes were lynched, murdered and starved; and secondly, there was no such definite demand for scientific work of the sort that I was doing."

As a result, Du Bois began engaging in scholarly activism by helping found civil rights organizations and by writing essays and books on the Negro problem directed at the general reader. In 1905 he was a founding member of the Niagara Movement; editor of *The Moon* in 1906 and *Horizon* from 1907 to 1910, a founder of the NAACP in 1909; and editor of the NAACP's *The Crisis* magazine in 1910. The greatest impact of Du Bois's scholarly activism during this period, however, came from his book *The Souls of Black Folk* (1903), which established Du Bois as an important leader among many U.S. Negroes and brought him national and international acclaim in literary circles. A collection of both previously published and new essays, *Souls* used allegory, history, and literature to chronicle events in Du Bois's life and to examine the condition of the U.S. Negro.

A well-publicized chapter in *Souls*, "Of Mr. Booker T. Washington and Others," laid out Du Bois's ideas about education for Negroes and critiqued Washington's plan of vocational education. Acknowledging the importance of vocational education as a component of a broad vision of education, Du Bois argued that liberal/classical education should be the focus of education for the most capable African Americans, whose purpose it was to uplift the race. He criticized Washington for focusing on vocational and industrial training at the expense of immediate civil rights.

From the early 1900s through the 1930s, Du Bois continued to educate the African-American masses, along with European Americans and the international community, about the Negro problem. Throughout this early period, he shifted from social science research, literary history, and fiction to editorials and activism, trying to reach the broadest possible audience. In novels such as *Quest for the Silver Fleece* (1911) and *Dark Princess* (1928), Du Bois illuminated the lives of Negroes navigating a society that challenged their very humanity. Du Bois also published several historical works on black history, such as *John Brown* (1909) and *The Gift of Black Folk* (1924), and a children's magazine entitled the *The Brownies' Book* (1920–22).

By the late 1920s, Du Bois began integrating Marxist economic theory into his ideas about the Negro problem. As a result, he began openly calling for a strong economic African-American community, advocating voluntary separatism for the time being to build a "nation within a nation." Du Bois's advocacy of voluntary separatism, however, put him at odds with the integrationist stance of the NAACP, which eventually led to his resignation from the organization and from his position as editor of *The Crisis* in 1934.

In 1934, Du Bois returned to Atlanta University as Professor of Sociology. Moving back into the academic world prompted him to focus again on scholarly work addressing the Negro problem. Responding to the racist scholarship of historians William Dunning, Ulrich Phillips, and others, Du Bois offered his own interpretation of life during the antebellum and postbellum eras. *Black Reconstruction* (1935a) argued that slavery was the main cause of the Civil War, primarily because it was the economic staple of the South. Du Bois also refuted the stereotypes of total incompetence that were ascribed to blacks during Reconstruction by arguing that blacks played a significant role in establishing free public education in the South.

From 1934 to 1944, Du Bois produced a number of other important works on African-American history and the African-American experience. *Black Folk, Then and Now* (1939) and *The World and Africa* (1947) expanded on his previous works in Negro history. In his usual role as a teacher, Du Bois sought to illuminate the achievements and contributions of African Americans. Another significant work during this period was *Dusk of Dawn* (1940), which was an autobiographical analysis of race. In 1940, Du Bois also published and became editor of a scholarly journal that examined black life called *Phylon*.

In 1944, Du Bois left Atlanta University for a second stint at the NAACP. However, after much squabbling with its director, Walter White, he was again forced to leave the organization in 1948. The last two decades of Du Bois's life were spent focusing on issues of world peace, nuclear disarmament, and African affairs. In 1948, he became co-chairman with Paul Robeson of the Council on African Americans. He helped organize the Scientific Conference for World Peace, held in New York in 1949, and he became chairman of the Peace Information Center in 1950. The U.S. State Department and the Federal Bureau of Investigation closely watched Du Bois's activities in these organizations, indicting him in 1951 for failing to register as a foreign agent.

Du Bois was eventually acquitted, but he saw his indictment as an example of the increasing level of U.S. suppression of revolutionary ideas. During the later years of his life, Du Bois continued to write about the African-American condition. Between 1959 and 1961, he wrote a trilogy called the *"Black Flame": The Ordeal of Mansart* (1959), *Mansart Builds a School* (1959), and *Worlds of Color* (1961). The series focused on the life of a black educator named Manual Mansart, who struggles with many of the problems of racial identity, oppression, and discrimination. Written during the birth of the modern civil rights movement of the 1950s and '60s, the trilogy reflected the struggles of the movement and its possible aftermath.

During his later years, one of his intended contributions to education was to be the publication of his *Encyclopedia Africana*. This project was to be financed by Ghanaian President Kwame Nkhrumah, a longtime friend. In 1961, Du Bois moved to Ghana and became a member of the Communist Party. Unfortunately, the encyclopedia never came to fruition. Du Bois died on 27 August 1963, the day before the March on Washington. The day of the historic march, NAACP president Roy Wilkins announced that it was Du Bois's spirit and voice that had called them to Washington that day to illuminate the plight of the Negro in the United States.

Overview of Du Bois's Educational Thought

Du Bois never articulated a cohesive and comprehensive philosophy of teaching or education. However, he wrote and spoke directly to the role of education in uplifting African Americans and in teaching the world about the Negro problem. Such themes emerge throughout his thought and work. Because of the complexity of Du Bois's thought and the long period in which his thinking evolved, his educational views often over-lap—and he adjusted his thinking over time. Thus, the futility of trying to categorize or pigeonhole Du Bois within one philosophical camp has made him a difficult figure to study (Alridge 1999a; 1999b).

Significantly, Du Bois did not see education as a panacea for the ills in U.S. society; nor did he see it as the sole means for eliminating the yoke of Jim Crow. Instead, his educational thought was always buttressed by a belief that alleviating African-Americans' oppression must be accomplished through social, economic, and political means. Though he acknowledged this reality, particularly during his later years, he pro-moted the value of education as a powerful tool for improving society for all races.

During the early years of his career, Du Bois was particularly disturbed by the social status and condition of his people. Slavery and miseducation by whites, he believed, had done great harm to blacks' racial identities, contributing to negative views of them-selves and ignorance about their African cultural and historical roots. To help address this problem, Du Bois advocated that African Americans learn about Africa and its contribu-tions to history and society. Thus, a focus of much of his early work on education for blacks was on *racial identity* and *ethnic and cultural awareness*. If blacks were to navigate U.S. society effectively, he believed, their education should be grounded in a knowledge and apprecia-tion of their African ancestry and homeland and the Negro experience in the New World.

Du Bois vocally supported this African-centered educational perspective to varying degrees throughout his life. From books and projects such as *The Souls of Black Folk* (1903), *Dusk of Dawn* (1940), *Black Folk, Then and Now* (1939), *The World and Africa* (1947), and his plans for an *Encyclopedia Africana* (1961), Du Bois advocated what today might be con-sidered Afrocentric education. In fact, Du Bois (1961; 1962) used the term "Afrocentric" to describe the worldview that his encyclopedia was to take and to demonstrate the importance of Africa and African peoples at the center of this educational endeavor.

Even earlier, Du Bois discussed the importance of an "Afrocentric" educational per-spective and emphasized the role that historically black colleges and universities should play in such education. As Du Bois (1973a, 95) suggested, the black university "seeks a beginning of the history of the Negro in America and in Africa to interpret all history;

from a beginning of social development among Negro slaves and freed men in America and Negro tribes and kingdoms in Africa."

Such education, Du Bois argued, should also be given to children. Between 1920 and 1922, Du Bois published a children's magazine that stressed an "Afrocentric" perspective. Called *The Brownies' Book*, its purpose was to "make colored children realize that being colored is a normal and beautiful thing, to make them familiar with the history and achievements of the Negro race, to make them know that other colored children have grown into beautiful useful, famous persons, to teach them delicately, a code of honor and action in their relations with white children." *The Brownies' Book* was consistent with Du Bois's idea that, within a culturally centered framework, blacks also should have an understanding of the larger white society and learn to navigate within it.

Such education and elevation of African and African-American culture, he believed, should be given to the masses via a cadre of black intellectuals that he called the *talented tenth*. Trained in classical/liberal education, the talented tenth, he believed, should be responsible for uplifting the social conditions and status of the black masses: "Just as far as the race can afford it we must give to our youth a training designed above all to make them men of power, of thought, of trained and cultivated taste; men who know whether civilization is tending what it means" (Du Bois 1973c, 14).

Du Bois also advocated education that focused on both *higher learning* and *living skills* that addressed the realities of living in a white-dominated society. For African Americans to navigate society collectively, Du Bois realized, they needed an understanding of the institutions, government, and political and economic principals that undergirded that society. At the same time, he recognized the need for technical and vocational skills within the black community, because they provided jobs and could create an economic base for the community. As Du Bois (1973c, 15) stated, "After we have sent our most promising to college, then not only the rest, but the college men too, need training in technical schools for the actual technique."

Du Bois also saw promise in engaging the community as a means of educating African-American youth. He argued that education should be integrated into the daily lives of African Americans. He therefore advocated education that promoted *community uplift*. Using an analogy with Yoruba, Sudanese, and Bantu tribes of Africa, Du Bois stated that education should occur first in the home and community with the mother and father, where children should learn the basics of living, such as sowing, reaping, and hunting. Tribal elders, he believed, should transfer knowledge about community history and culture to the children.

Ideally, Du Bois suggested, there should be no disconnection between the community, education, or its people. Within such a society, he believed national culture and art would develop. Du Bois noted that, despite the negative aspects of segregation, black children in the United States benefited from the close and insulated contacts that were fostered within closed communities. For example, Du Bois noted in *Does the Negro Need Separate Schools* (1935b) that future generations might lose much in terms of learning about their culture and history if their African-type communal environments were eliminated as a result of integration.

Though Du Bois was always concerned about the economic status of African Americans, he began to incorporate a Marxist economic perspective into his thinking about black education during the 1920s–'40s. Greed and capitalism, he argued, subsumed his talented tenth and made them compromise their mission of uplifting the race. Expressing his disappointment, Du Bois (1995, 348) stated, "I assumed that with knowledge, sacrifice would automatically follow. In my youth and idealism, I did not realize that selfishness is even more natural than sacrifice."

By the 1940s, Du Bois was calling for the education of the Negro masses for leadership within and outside the African-American community. Advocating a broader educational strategy than he did in the early 1900s, he called for education that provided all African Americans with opportunities for leadership at every level of society. He also called for the college educated to receive education in industry and the vocations and for the vocationally educated to receive education in the arts and sciences. Du Bois (1995) called this strategy of educating the masses for leadership the *guiding hundredth*. Thus, another focus of his ideas of optimal education for Negroes was on the development of *mass* leadership.

Within Du Bois's educational strategies of the talented tenth and the guiding hundredth, he saw the education of black women as a critical aspect of the struggle. By no means would Du Bois be considered a feminist by today's standards, given his sexist language and some of the ideas he expressed about women. However, Du Bois was an advocate for women's equality and believed that women educators should play a pivotal role in uplifting the race. Corresponding with Anna Julia Cooper, Mary McCleod Bethune, Ida B. Wells Barnett, and other black women, Du Bois benefited from their advice and considered the education of black women an important element in advancing the freedom struggle.

During the last three decades of his life, Du Bois called for education that would promote the establishment of strong *pan-Africanist* and *political* alliances to address black oppression in the United States and around the globe. His belief that African Americans should connect culturally and politically with the global community was also reflected in his educational thought. Reiterating his educational ideas of identity awareness, Du Bois argued that African Americans' education should focus on learning about their connections with Africa and the rest of the world.

Such education, he believed, would help anchor African Americans' identity and worldview while also placing their collective experience and psyches in a global context. As Du Bois (1973b, 144) stated, "We must understand the differences in social problems between Africa, the West Indies, South and Central America, not only among the Negroes but those affecting Indians and other minority groups."

Du Bois also saw African-American colleges and universities as important communal and cultural focal points for the dissemination and transfer of knowledge within a global community. These institutions, he believed, should help provide the foundation for ameliorating the oppressive conditions of African people and other oppressed people around the world.

One of Du Bois's major concerns in educating African Americans about the world was his fear that the Cold War environment of the 1950s would curtail education that liberated people's minds. Du Bois (1970, 230) warned that the government might attempt to sabotage such education, stressing that African Americans and oppressed groups should press on: "Especially we should insist upon the right to learn, upon the right to have our children learn, and upon keeping our schools, uncoerced by the dominant forces of the present world, free to exercise the right to join with the great Goethe in a worldwide cry for 'light, more light.'"

Conclusion

Du Bois's contributions to African-American and U.S. education are many. First and foremost, Du Bois's many studies on the conditions of African Americans from 1895 until 1963 educated all races about the history, culture, and dilemmas of African-descended people. Second, Du Bois's insistence on the need for schools to teach accurate history about African-descended people helped pave the way for black and multicultural studies during the four decades since his death. Many black studies scholars, for instance, trace the roots of their discipline to Du Bois and his work during the first half of the 20th century (Stewart 1984). Third, Du Bois's critical analyses of black education have been prophetic. He predicted problems resulting from the dismissal of black teachers after desegregation and the limited amount of black history that black and other children would learn as a result. He also advocated the importance of black studies programs.

Throughout his life, Du Bois hailed education as a powerful force that could help emancipate African Americans and the white world from the problem caused by racism and capitalism. He reminded us that education alone could not solve the problem of African Americans and other historically oppressed groups. Instead, he suggested, education must be linked to social, economic, and political improvements to alleviate substantively the conditions of the world's oppressed.

Du Bois is among the most important U.S. teachers and educational thinkers in the 20th century. It is my hope that teachers, scholars, and students will discuss and learn from his writing, work, and life. Du Bois's dedication to teaching the world about the principles of democracy and equality should resonate with teachers and educators of all races and backgrounds who are committed to the liberation of the mind.

References

Alexander, E. 1995. 'We must be about our Father's business': Anna Julia Cooper and the incorporation of the nineteenth-century African-American woman intellectual. *Journal of Women in Culture and Society* 20(12): 336–39.

Alridge, D. P. 1999a. Conceptualizing a Du Boisian philosophy of education: Toward a model for African American education. *Educational Theory* 49(3): 359–79.

Alridge, D. P. 1999b. Guiding philosophical principles for a Du Boisian–based African American educational model. *Journal of Negro Education* 68(2): 182–99.

Anderson, J. D. 1998. *The education of blacks in the South, 1860–1935*. Chapel Hill: University of North Carolina Press.

Barkin, K. D. 2000. 'Berlin days,' 1892–1894: W. E. B. Du Bois and German political economy. *Boundary 2: An International Journal of Literature and Culture* 27(3): 79–102.

Barry, M. F., and J. Blassingame. 1982. *Long memory: The black experience in America*. New York: Oxford University Press.

Broderick, F. L. 1959. *W. E. B. Du Bois: Negro leader in a time of crisis*. Stanford, Calif.: Stanford University Press.

Carby, H. V. 1998. *Race men*. Cambridge, Mass.: Harvard University Press.

Cooper, A. J. 1892. *A voice from the South*. Xenia, Ohio: Aldine.

Du Bois, W. E. B. 1893. Diary, 23 February. In *The papers of W. E. B. Du Bois, 1803 (1877–1963) 1999*. Amherst: University of Massachusetts.

Du Bois, W. E. B. 1899. *The Philadelphia Negro: A social study*. Philadelphia: Published for the University.

Du Bois, W. E. B., ed. 1901. *The Negro common school: Report of a social study made under the direction of Atlanta University*. Atlanta: University Press.

Du Bois, W. E. B. 1903. The talented tenth. In *The Negro problem: A series of articles by representative American Negroes of today*, ed. B. T. Washington, W. E. B. Du Bois, C. W. Chesnutt, W. H. Smith, H. T. Kealing, P. L. Dunbar, and T. T. Fortune, 75. New York: J. Potts and Co.

Du Bois, W. E. B. 1935a. *Black reconstruction: An essay toward a history of the part which black folk played in the attempt to reconstruct democracy in America, 1860–1880*. New York: Harcourt, Brace.

Du Bois, W. E. B. 1935b. 'Does the Negro need separate schools?' *Journal of Negro Education* 4(July): 335.

Du Bois, W. E. B. 1961. Provisional draft: Not for general distribution: Proposed plans for an Encyclopedia Africana, dated 21 September. Rare Books Room, Pennsylvania State University.

Du Bois, W. E. B. 1962. For cooperation toward an Encyclopedia Africana. Info. report #2, Accra, Ghana.

Du Bois, W. E. B. 1968. *The autobiography of W. E. B. Du Bois: A soliloquy on viewing my life from the last decade to its first century.* New York: International Publishers.

Du Bois, W. E. B. 1970. The freedom to learn. In *W. E. B. Du Bois speaks: Speeches and addresses, 1920–1963*, ed. P. S. Foner, 230. New York: Pathfinder.

Du Bois, W. E. B. 1973a. The field and function of the Negro college. In *The education of black people: Ten critiques, 1906–1960*, ed. Herbert Aptheker, 95. Amherst: University of Massachusetts Press.

Du Bois, W. E. B. 1973b. The future and function of the private Negro college. In *The education of black people: Ten critiques, 1906–1960*, ed. Herbert Aptheker, 144. Amherst: University of Massachusetts Press.

Du Bois, W. E. B. 1973c. The Hampton idea. In *The education of black people: Ten critiques, 1906–1960*, ed. Herbert Aptheker, 14–15. Amherst: University of Massachusetts Press.

Du Bois, W. E. B. 1995. The talented tenth memorial address. In *W. E. B. Du Bois: A reader*, ed. D. L. Lewis, 348–53. New York: Henry Holt.

Franklin, J. H., and A. Moss, Jr. 2000. *From slavery to freedom: A history of African Americans*, 8th ed. New York: McGraw Hill.

Lewis, D. L. 1995. Introduction. In W. E. B. Du Bois's *Black reconstruction in America, 1860–1880*, vii–xvii. New York: Atheneum.

Logan, R. W. 1997. *The betrayal of the Negro: From Rutherford B. Hayes to Woodrow Wilson.* New York: De Capo Press.

Myrdal, G. 1944. *An American dilemma: The Negro problem and modern democracy, Vol. 1.* New York: Harper & Row.

National Association for the Advancement of Colored People. 1919. *Thirty years of lynching in the United States, 1889–1919.* New York: NAACP.

Stewart, J. B. 1984. The legacy of W. E. B. Du Bois for contemporary Black studies. *Journal of Negro Education* 53(3): 296–321.

Trotter, J. W., Jr. 2001. *The African American experience.* Boston: Houghton Mifflin.

Washington, B. T. 1980. The Atlanta Exposition address, 1895. In *Afro-American history: Primary sources*, ed. T. R. Frazier, 194. Belmont, Calif.: Wadsworth Publishing.

Yancy, D. C. 1978. William Edward Burghardt Du Bois' Atlanta years: The human side—A study based upon oral sources. *Journal of Negro History* 63(1): 59–67.

Chapter 8

Hilda Taba: A Lifetime Devoted to Promoting Thinking

by Mark Isham

On 6 July 1967, the curriculum field lost one of its pioneers. At the time of her death, Hilda Taba (b. 7 December 1902) was engaged in two projects that represented the culmination of her life's work and thought. She was developing in-service education and staff-development models for implementing curriculum change based on teaching strategies she developed to promote thinking in children and more than three decades of work in curriculum. She also had contracted with Addison-Wesley Publishing Company to produce an elementary-level social studies textbook series, based on her work with teachers primarily in the Contra Costa County (California) school system, and a training manual to help teachers apply essential principles and processes of curriculum development. Taba—an intellectually tenacious, persistent, and energetic thinker—was one of the best and brightest minds in the field of curriculum. Throughout her life, she developed and maintained a deep and abiding respect for those, especially teachers, with whom she worked.

Throughout her career, with her words and actions, Taba mentored teachers in democratic values and thinking. Her life, thought, and work illustrate her commitment to and leadership in advancing principles of democratic living through the enhancement of teachers' and children's thinking. Her accomplishments influenced curriculum, teaching, and learning. One of her most influential achievements is her model of curriculum, which evolved over the course of her professional life. Another comprises the strategies she developed and employed for promoting teachers' and children's thinking. A third aspect encompasses her methods of leading teachers and school personnel to affect positive educational reform—specifically, changes in curriculum and teaching.

Background, Schooling, and Large-Scale Projects

Hilda Taba was born in December 1902 in Estonia. Her father was a school teacher and an administrator. Her mother worked to maintain the family farm, which served as partial compensation for the father's teaching. Her parents encouraged their children to become educated, and all of their four daughters and five sons attended college (Naylor 1980). Bernard-Powers (1999) provided insight into Taba's early years and forces that influenced her character development. She graduated from the University of Tartu with a bachelor of arts degree in 1926, having majored in English and philosophy. She received a master of arts degree in education and psychology from Bryn Mawr College in Pennsylvania in 1927. During her year of graduate study, she traveled widely in the

United States and visited several progressive schools, which sparked her interest in the Dalton Plan. Taba (1934) recalled that Boyd Bode's (1927) *Modern Educational Theories* attracted her to the basic philosophy of progressive education. She matriculated at Teachers College, Columbia University, in 1927 with a declared major in Educational Administration (Monroe 1927). Her emerging educational thought was influenced by distinguished educators and psychologists of the time. Prominent individuals such as E. L. Thorndike, Jesse Newlon, Harold O. Rugg, H. Paul Monroe, and Hollis Caswell were on the faculty at Teachers College at the time. Several graduate students, many of whom were destined to become leading educational scholars and leaders in curriculum over the next half-century, including William O. Stanley and B. O. Smith, also probably influenced her thinking. Though William Heard Kilpatrick was her major professor and advisor, John Dewey was her intellectual mentor. Her doctor of philosophy degree was conferred in 1929 (Cattell and Ross 1948).

Taba's (1932) dissertation was published under the title *The Dynamics of Education*. It reiterated and elaborated Dewey's (1902) position in *The Child and the Curriculum*. Her dissertation presented, in seven chapters, several principles that pertained to a dynamic study of human behavior. The chapter titles give an indication of her emerging thought: "Principles of Becoming," "Purposive Behaviour," "Purposive Behaviour and Learning," "Aims of Education," and "Curriculum Thinking." The ideas she developed in the final chapter provide insight into her later curriculum work. Taba (1932, 238) maintained that the primary aim of curriculum was to stimulate the development of flexible, creative thinking and that materials needed to be developed "in the form of significant problems with their subject matter as experimental data for creative thinking in the solving of these problems." From this dynamic perspective, Taba (1932, 249–50) asserted:

> *Curriculum thinking should not attempt to provide exact charts for educational experiences, not give any rigid prescriptions as to the materials to be used in connection with educational activities. Instead it should try to provide principles and materials to think with in a creative manner in dealing with educational practice. The value of curriculum planning does not so much lie in its ability to provide exact maps to be followed, as it does in furnishing those guiding the learning process with a broad and critical outlook, sensitivity to possibilities that lie in each evolving situation, and ability to see the relations that the particular experience has with as many possible general principles and implications involved in every single experience.*

Taba saw the major task confronting curriculum thinkers within the progressive camp as one of refining standards and principles, which she intended to mean ways of thinking, necessary for the guidance of self-directed learning activities. Like Dewey before her, Taba (1934) argued that many proponents of child-centered schools had overemphasized the child's immediate interests to the neglect of content and had narrowly conceived experience by dealing with it apart from context or environment. Many progressive educators focused only on the immediate; on the learner's immediate interests, immediate enjoyment, on factual information, and failed to develop interrelationships of meanings and ideas. By centering on immediate interests of learners and on discrete factual information derived from personal experience, the learner's attention became focused on the factual rather than the conceptual. Child-centered curricula that provided experiences as ends in themselves failed to provide experiences that served to integrate knowledge and personality and failed to provide learners with opportunities for the development of vital ideas and conceptual understandings. Taba (1932, 257) concluded her dissertation with the argument that curriculum planning ought to provide "fundamental abstractions and generalizations" that could be built as tools for further learning and as a means for "seeing and creating fundamental relationships between facts and ideas." These functional ideas should serve as principles for selection and organization of content.

Taba was involved in some of the more significant curriculum projects of the 20th century. The first major project in which she played an instrumental part was the Eight-Year Study, a major secondary school curriculum reform project sponsored by the Progressive Education Association (PEA) and funded by the General Education Board of the Rockefeller Foundation (Aikin 1942; Giles, McCutchen, and Zechiel 1942; Smith and Tyler 1942; Chamberlin, Chamberlin, Drought, and Scott 1942; PEA 1942). The project began in 1930, when the Executive Committee of the PEA appointed the Committee on the Relation of School and College to plan and direct the project. The primary goal of the Eight-Year Study was to demonstrate that, when freed from conventional college entrance requirements, high schools would be likely to implement various progressive practices, including core and integrated curricula designs, and that such progressive practices were effective. After four years, however, the project was floundering with no clear direction. Ralph W. Tyler was hired in 1934 to help schools define their objectives in light of the goals of the study, to devise evaluation instruments that were matched to the schools' goals, and to evaluate the outcomes of the study (Hawkes 1934). Tyler spent the fall of 1934 visiting each of the participating schools to confer with principals, headmasters, and teachers to ascertain their schools' objectives in reforming their teaching methods and curricula. Tyler (1980) recalled that, during his visit to the Dalton School, he first met Taba, a teacher and Curriculum Director at Dalton, and was impressed by her "tough thinking, enthusiasm for evaluation, and her insight into the nature of the learning process." In the spring of 1935, Tyler invited Taba to become an assistant on the Evaluation Staff, an offer she accepted when the school year ended. In that position, she became one of the major consultants to social studies teachers and served with several other promising educators on the Evaluation Staff, among them Oscar Buros, Louis E. Raths, Maurice Hartung, Bruno Bettelheim, Paul Diederich, George Sheviakov, and Harold Trimble. She was the only woman in a directing role on the Evaluation Staff.

Tyler established six committees to work with schools and teachers to formulate objectives. The titles of three of the original committees indicate the extent to which thinking was emphasized: Committee on Evaluation of Abilities Involved in the Application of Principles, Committee on Evaluation of Abilities Involved in Interpreting Data, and Committee on Evaluation of Sensitivity to Significant Problems. These committees were merged into one, called the Committee on Evaluation of Social Sensitivity, which Taba directed. The work of that committee (Taba 1936) planted seeds of what would later grow into Taba's teaching strategies for promoting thinking processes and democratic attitudes and values in children.

Upon completion of the Eight-Year Study, Taba taught courses in curriculum at the University of Chicago. When given the opportunity to return to more direct experiences with classroom teachers in 1945, she accepted a position as Director of the Intergroup

Education Project in Cooperating Schools, another major curriculum-development project. The Intergroup Education Project grew out of domestic social and economic changes in the years following the Second World War. The military experiences of African Americans brought to awareness wide discrepancies between the political rhetoric of freedom and justice and the realities of racial and religious discrimination and prejudice. The influx of African Americans from Southern rural areas into Northern and Western cities in search of higher-paying jobs raised anew the question of how African and European Americans might live together.

The PEA supported intergroup and intercultural education during the Depression as a means of reducing anti-Semitism and racial tensions and of increasing tolerance between and for religious and ethnic groups. It published more articles in its journal, *Progressive Education*, than any other organization published in the United States and sponsored the Commission on Intercultural Education, which in turn supported the Service Bureau for Education in Human Relations (Goodenow 1975; 1981; Davis 1999). The proposal for the Intergroup Education Project emerged from a workshop held at Harvard University in 1944. As codirector with Charles E. Cummings, Taba organized the workshop to explore research on attitude formation and change and on behavioral patterns toward members of minority groups. Her intention was to shorten the time that research findings, particularly those pertaining to human relations and attitude formation, could be translated and applied to classroom teaching and learning. Taba (1945) planned to do this by bringing current information to teachers and enabling them to carry new ideas and techniques into their classrooms soon after developments were described in the literature. Following the workshop, Howard E. Wilson, former President of the National Council for the Social Studies and Chairman of the Education Commission of the National Conference of Christians and Jews—which, since its inception in 1928, endeavored to improve intergroup and human relations, particularly among religious groups—invited Taba to direct the Intergroup Education Project. She took a leave of absence from the University of Chicago to lead the project, which lasted from 1945 to 1951. During the six-year project, 72 schools and more than 2,500 teachers, administrators, and community leaders were involved in the development of more than 250 local projects (Taba, Brady, and Robinson 1952).

The final, longest-lasting, and most significant phase of Taba's professional career began during the spring of 1951. Evelyn Jegi Blodgett (1981), then Curriculum Director for Contra Costa County's school district, recalled attending a session of the annual meeting of the Association for Supervision and Curriculum Development in which Taba spoke of the importance of developing critical thinking in children. This presentation was instrumental in Taba's selection to work with the Contra County schools. For three years, Blodgett and the Contra Costa County supervisors had been attempting to revise the district's curriculum. They hoped, in part, to respond to vigorous attacks on "soft pedagogy," as represented by the activity curriculum and life-adjustment education. They also planned to replace what supervisors considered an aimless, anti-intellectual social studies curriculum.

The educational situation in Contra Costa County mirrored a national perception of schooling. The opening years of the decade in question ushered in vigorous attacks on the soft pedagogy. Prominent writers and educators were bemoaning the lack of intellectual rigor and declining academic standards in the nation's public schools. The perception of critics was that schools and teachers allowed children to pursue their own, rather than academic or national, interests. Students seemed to move in whatever direction they wished, with more time and resources for social activities and personal development and a "watered down" subject matter that suggested a neglect of learning. Among the major early critiques were Smith's (1949) *And Madly Teach* and Bell's (1949) *Crisis in Education*. Among the more popular criticisms that reached the public some years later were Lynd's (1953) *Quackery in the Public Schools*, Bestor's (1953) *Educational Wastelands*, Smith's (1954) *The Diminished Mind*, Flesch's (1955) *Why Johnny Can't Read*, and Bestor's (1955) *The Restoration of Learning*. Taba did not accept the assumptions underlying these various tracts, but she agreed with the call for a curriculum that would promote students' intellectual growth. Her position in support of more substantive intellectual activities remained constant throughout her career; she had voiced many of the same criticisms against the project method in her dissertation.

One specific weakness in the social studies curriculum in Contra Costa County was the lack of intellectual coherence (Durkin 1981). Consultants repeatedly offered them nothing more than they already had or, in Durkin's words, "the same old thing"—namely, more recipes for teaching, more topics to cover, and more "interesting" learning activities to excite the students. Taba, however, articulated to Blodgett a solution—a more balanced approach that gave attention to both content and the development of thinking processes. In her interview, Durkin (1981), then a curriculum coordinator for Contra Costa County, recalled Blodgett's excitement: "What we wanted was an emphasis put on process. Topics are important, but we think with ideas. The content can be substituted. It's what you teach about the content that is important, not just whether you study a store, but what idea you are trying to develop."

Taba's argument that a curriculum should be organized around significant ideas and concepts with an aim to promoting thinking in children provided a direction, an aim, for the county's curriculum-revision efforts. When Blodgett learned that Taba would become a professor of education at San Francisco State College, she invited her to speak to a group of administrators and curriculum supervisors. The administrators were favorably impressed with both her intellectual depth as well as her approach and offered her a contract to become the district's major consultant. Taba accepted the offer on condition that the district commit itself and its resources for at least three years. What evolved out of that initial agreement came to be known as the Taba Curriculum Development Project in the Social Studies; it lasted nearly 15 years (Wallen, Durkin, Fraenkel, McNaughton, and Sawin 1969). Taba offered a comprehensive, generic model of curriculum that helped explain the interrelationships among objectives, evaluation, content, learning activities, and teaching methods. Taba's leadership also produced a wealth of research on the development of children's thinking and how teachers can promote it, six teaching strategies to promote thinking and valuing, and models of in-service education and for dissemination of innovations. Indirectly, the project resulted in a popular elementary social studies textbook series as well as text materials for secondary social studies.

Principles of a Curriculum to Promote Thinking

The generally favorable reception that greeted the publication of Taba's dissertation probably influenced the General Education Board of the Rockefeller Foundation to award her a fellowship in 1933. The fellowship permitted her to pursue postdoctoral study at Syracuse University and partially funded her position as a German teacher and Curriculum Director at the Dalton School in New York City from 1933 to mid-1935 (General Education Board 1972). Helen Parkhurst (1922) founded the school for young women and encouraged their participation in all levels of decision making, including planning courses and selecting content and learning activities. She hired teachers who would move the school toward realization of internal democratic practices in part by experimenting with a variety of curriculum designs, teaching methods, and testing procedures.

Parkhurst hired Taba as a teacher and the school's Curriculum Director. In April, Taba (1933) wrote and distributed to the faculty a "Preliminary Draft of the Curriculum Reorganization for the Year 1934–1935." The essence of the plan was to develop curriculum experiences and content that would revolve around a central theme that reflected perennial problems in human life and thought. English, social sciences, art, and science would be organized around the central theme. Taba (1933) set forth three criteria for the selection of themes and content or materials:

1. The problem must be relevant to understanding the pageant of civilization, as well as significant and persistent.

2. The particular work must throw light on and give acquaintance with the basic understandings and concepts necessary for intelligent functioning of the human mind.

3. The level of understanding and interest of learners must be taken into account in selecting themes and materials necessary for them.

These criteria demonstrate Taba's early application of principles of dynamic education and indicate three important aspects of her emerging conception of curriculum content, which she refined during the 1940s and fully articulated in her work during the 1950s and '60s (Taba 1962). First, curriculum planning for promoting thinking gives special and primary consideration to key concepts. Second, curriculum development ought to proceed from the identification of significant (i.e., broadly applicable) ideas to the selection of factual materials. Third, she concluded that ideas represent valid and up-to-date knowledge and should be consistent with social realities. These criteria applied Dewey's (1902, 26) concept of a "thought-provoking" curriculum that would give attention to both the psychological demands of learning and the intellectual demands, or logic, of subject matter.

Based on her work on the Eight-Year Study, Taba realized that neither teaching strategies nor innovative curriculum designs alone would have much impact on the development of thinking in students. The first and foremost decision that should guide the organization of content involved the selection of "focusing ideas" (Taba, Jennings, Brady, Robinson, and Dolton 1949, 36) that a teaching/learning unit was designed to teach. Taba rejected the traditional conception of curriculum as topics to be covered, in favor of ideas to learn. A curriculum plan that would focus on the development of main ideas or generalizations would address several problems encountered by teachers and curriculum developers. With information expanding continuously, a means of organizing information was needed. Without a principle to guide selection and organization of content, teachers' decisions about what content to include would likely be based on personal preference rather than on the demands of the subject, characteristics of students, or demands of society. Most important, generalizations represented the kinds of relationships that needed to be emphasized in reaching worthwhile objectives and provided a guide for the selection of concepts to be developed and of factual information. Ideas and concepts would give meaning to facts; facts would serve as samples to be selected as they best represented or illustrated the ideas and to the extent that they provided necessary contrast and comparative detail to enable students to detect differences and to draw reasonable conclusions. During the Intergroup Education Project, focusing ideas served also to coordinate the curriculum-development activities of the participating schools. Ideas could be similar from school to school, whereas specific content could vary from school to school, and even from teacher to teacher within a school, depending on teachers' areas of expertise, student characteristics, and local histories and conditions.

Ways of Working with Teachers to Enhance Their Thinking

Many of Taba's ways of working with teachers also originated during the Eight-Year Study. Soon after visiting several participating schools, Tyler realized that teachers needed extended periods of release time to work together to share ideas, support one another's decisions, and meet with scholars in the subject areas and experts in curriculum development and evaluation. To meet those needs, Tyler and Taba established in-service programs that called for teachers to be released from teaching responsibilities one Friday per month either to work on curriculum or with consultants (Reid 1980). Taba and others members of the Evaluation Staff established effective patterns of working with teachers. One pattern was informal. Constance Reid (1980) recalled that Taba and other members of the Evaluation Staff would converse with teachers after observing their lessons to help them clarify their instructional goals and intentions before asking them to consider changes to their curriculum or teaching. Taba used these conversations to help teachers define and clarify problems they confronted and, through her questioning, helped them to explore alternative actions they could take to address their problems. Out of those conversations emerged ideas for change. As Reid (1980) reported, such an approach was particularly effective, because teachers came to sense deeper respect from Taba and other consultants and greater involvement in and ownership of the entire process of curriculum development. Taba maintained this way of working with teachers in subsequent projects, including the Contra Costa County project decades later. As Mary Durkin (1981) recalled, Taba often acted as "a trouble-shooter. She would ask teachers, 'What do you see the problem to be?' or 'How do you see the problems [of teaching] in the social studies?' She took voluminous notes and quickly got to the heart of the matter."

A more formal way of working with teachers, introduced during the Eight-Year Study and expanded during the Intergroup Education Project, was the summer workshop (Tyler 1941). With Tyler, Taba designed several workshops to provide opportunities for school personnel to develop plans and materials collaboratively, apply educational and psychological theories to practice, learn to think differently about content and teaching methods, and receive assistance from outside consultants in human development, curriculum, evaluation, and content. Participants worked in small groups to facilitate the exploration of issues and the sharing of ideas and to enhance mutual support and collegiality. Many teachers who attended the workshops paid their own tuition and travel and lodging expenses.

A central contribution of summer workshops was that they could help renew teachers' attitudes and enthusiasm for change with which they were experimenting. Taba argued that teachers who were attempting to make changes needed opportunities to meet and work with leaders in various disciplines, including the social sciences, educational psychology, and curriculum and teaching, as well as with other teachers. Workshops also afforded teachers extended periods of time to explore various approaches to addressing curriculum and teaching problems with others. Finally, in bringing professionals together for extended periods of time, workshops provided a sense of collegiality and a support system for participating teachers who, throughout the school year, would feel isolated from others involved in the project. Teachers could come together to share concerns, problems, and confusions while finding sympathy, understanding, and encouragement.

One aspect of these summer workshops that has not received sufficient attention in the literature on the history of curriculum practices was the entertainment and social element that accompanied the academically oriented workshop sessions. The workshops that Taba conducted, even into the 1960s, afforded participants opportunities to socialize and relax. In the evenings, card playing, dancing, and singing were commonplace (Brady 1981). Consultants often joined in the fun. During the Eight-Year Study, for example, teachers wrote and acted in skits that mocked the consultants' mannerisms and idiosyncrasies and one another's work styles (Tyler 1941). Brady recalled that, during the Intergroup Education Project workshops, Taba set up an arts and crafts room where teachers could retire from the intellectual pressures of small-group planning, reading, and lectures and engage in more personal forms of expression. Coupled with this relatively formal arrangement for relaxation, Taba encouraged social activities, such as dances, parties, and weekend picnics, many of which she hosted (Brady 1996). Taba and the Intergroup Education staff members participated fully in these social activities.

Another formal mechanism she used during the Eight-Year Study and replicated during later projects was the "cooperative interschool committee" (PEA 1936), composed of teachers interested in formulating and clarifying objectives related to social sensitivity (Taba 1936). She would meet regularly with these committees and, through nonthreatening questioning, discussions, and active listening, and refraining from imposing her own views, she helped teachers clarify their goals and objectives. Taba worked with teachers, either individually or in small committees, in designing, developing, and field-testing evaluation instruments. Throughout her career, Taba used school-based committees composed of interested teachers, administrators, and staff members to explore problems, plan courses of actions, and develop resources.

Another effective way of working with teachers, which has again gained popularity as a means of empowering teachers and enhancing their thinking, was the action research project (Corey 1953; Taba and Noel 1957). Small-scale classroom- and community-based research directed teachers' attention to their concerns, values, and students and utilized human-relations techniques to explore the nature and extent of social and interpersonal conflicts, attitudes, and feelings. When a school was accepted for inclusion in the Intergroup Education Project, for example, Taba and her staff members gave "orientation talks" to describe the aims of the project and to stimulate interest and ideas from teachers and administrators. Taba soon realized that, due to the general ineffectiveness of these presentations, most teachers preferred to attack intergroup problems indirectly and impersonally from more general political and institutional perspectives or in the community apart from school. Few teachers expressed any desire to explore new teaching methods or new ways of selecting or organizing learning experiences. Based upon assessment reports on participating schools and communities, Taba identified an urgent need to broaden teachers' understanding of cultural differences, social science concepts, and recent research on prejudice and authoritarianism. One facet of action research that became commonplace was an effort to help teachers develop better understandings of cultural differences between themselves and their students and among their students, differences that became apparent both prior to and concurrent with the development of units of teaching and learning.

Taba convinced administrators to permit and arrange informal meetings with teachers to enable them to explore problems and issues they confronted. Trained in group relations and group processes, Taba and her staff helped teachers identify and clarify underlying, unspoken feelings, conflicts, and concerns, which indicated real problems that could become the basis for curriculum change. Taba argued forcefully that teachers are more likely to change their ways of teaching when they have collected, analyzed, and interpreted information about their pupils. Furthermore, gathering and analyzing information pertinent to one's situation and generalizing from that information enables teachers to see relationships among their own research findings, instructional problems, and conditions. What Taba emphasized through action research was the principle that "learning that changes behavior substantially is more likely to result when a person himself tries to improve a situation that makes a difference to him" (Corey 1953, 9).

A major role of the consultants quickly became that of assisting teachers to move in one of two directions. One strategy was to pose questions that suggested to teachers further lines of inquiry into the characteristics of their pupils, teaching, learning, or the selection of materials. Another strategy was to lead teachers to data that would create some dissonance between their original beliefs and behavior they observed in their pupils. As Taba et al. (1952, 153) noted:

> The data had to be pertinent to expressed concerns and had to answer the immediate questions raised. [The data] also had to raise questions that would lead teachers into further inquiry and thus prepare for redefinition of the problems. Furthermore, they had to challenge or shock the teachers into extending their ideas and changing their attitudes and orientation. . . . The data were useful only insofar as they precipitated discussion, brought forth new interpretations, and suggested changes in classroom procedures or in the school structure that permitted teachers to test a new hypothesis or develop a new insight.

Consultants would use these data to challenge teachers to take a fresh look at children's needs within the context of intergroup education.

The action research studies conducted during the first two years of the project were instrumental in helping teachers better understand their students' characteristics. Some of the research even led teachers to deeper insight into their own attitudes and values and to deeper understanding of cultural differences between themselves and their students as well. European-American teachers for the most part, but African-American teachers as well, became aware of some of their own stereotypical attitudes and beliefs and of discriminatory practices within their classrooms, schools, and communities. Many teachers became more sensitive to conflicts that existed among groups within their schools and communities. The use of published research also enabled many teachers to broaden their conception of the nature of conflict to include more than actual physical confrontations between members of racial, ethnic, religious, or socioeconomic groups. Taba's recognition of covert interpersonal conflicts as appropriate content for inclusion in intergroup education foreshadowed by nearly two decades the intense concern for and interest in human-relations training that flourished during the late-1960s and early-1970s as a means of bridging gaps between racial and ethnic groups.

Promoting Thinking in Children

Taba's long-term affiliation with the Contra Costa County schools gave her opportunities to conduct a series of research studies into the nature and development of children's thinking. Her research built upon previous research, particularly Piaget's (1926; 1928; 1929) work on intellectual development, Wertheimer's (1945) explorations of teaching methods to promote productive thinking, and Bruner's (1960; Bruner, Goodnow, and Austin 1956) research on the nature and development of thinking processes. The two sponsored-research projects (Taba, Levine, and Elzey 1964; Taba 1966) she directed led to the identification of main processes of thinking, which she termed "cognitive tasks," and a conceptualization of strategies for teaching thinking. The research also supported her hypothesis that specific, guided practice in cognitive skills would promote thinking. Further research and development by Taba and her colleagues in Contra Costa County produced six teaching strategies (Wallen et al. 1969), three of which promote attainment of objectives in the cognitive domain and three of which promote attainment of objectives in the affective domain. The three strategies, or tasks, that promote attainment of objectives in the cognitive domain are labeled "concept formation," "interpretation of data," and "application of principles." The three strategies that address objectives in the affective domain are called "exploring feelings," "interpersonal problem solving," and "analysis of values." The six strategies share several qualities. Each successive step was designed to evoke a basic mental operation. Each subsequent step was designed to elicit a more complex thought process. Each strategy proceeds in a certain order. The steps within each strategy lift students' thinking to a higher level of abstraction and generality. Finally, each successive step provokes students to greater degrees of inference, intuition, and divergent thinking. The strategies themselves are developmental. The "application of principles" strategy, for example, builds upon, restructures, and extends ideas generated during the interpretation of data strategy, which builds upon the "concept formation" strategy. Each subsequent strategy is intellectually more complex and more demanding than the previous task. The strategies and the hierarchy ensure that learners have both sufficient time to acquire a sufficient amount of data with which to think and sufficient opportunities to stretch their ways of thinking (Taba 1967).

Leadership and Influence

Among the numerous characteristics associated with leadership are communication style, enthusiasm, a dynamic approach, charismatic appeal, and the ability to persuade. Taba possessed them all and more. Ultimately, leaders act. Leaders determine focus, direction, and aims; remove obstacles; develop in their followers a sense of ownership; and stimulate self-directed action. Davis (1982) asserted correctly that the most important, perhaps the sole, criterion of leadership is the direction in which the leader points. Pointing the direction places emphasis on the process of leadership, not on the ultimate goal or objective, a principle that helps explain Taba's influence as a leader. Taba's aim was, ultimately, to develop curriculum in the minds of teachers—to lead them to reconceptualize their role as teacher, their understanding of children, and the function and structure of knowledge in promoting intellectual growth in pupils. The elements of Taba's thought that constitute her legacy are the principles and processes of curriculum development that she pioneered, which include summer workshops, action research, and experimentation, and her teaching strategies. These processes have been the focus of this chapter and demonstrate her democratic mind-set, energetic spirit, comprehensive awareness, and acute intelligence. Together, these factors help explain her influence. Taba pointed toward new frontiers in the conceptualization of the use of content as well. Years before many mainstream curriculum writers and thinkers began addressing the need to organize curriculum around key concepts, ideas, and modes of inquiry, Taba had been experimenting with such organizational patterns. The balance she sought between content and process remains one of the strengths of her curriculum model.

Another, more recent view of leadership (Belasco and Stayer 1994) emphasized four tasks in leading: determining focus and direction, removing obstacles, developing ownership, and stimulating self-directed action. These four tasks frame a summary of Taba's leadership. Taba's ways of working with teachers and school administrators, whether through formal workshops and in-service education programs, individual conferences, or directing action research projects, helped teachers determine and clarify for themselves what they aimed to accomplish and chart their own courses. Her ways of working helped teachers remove major obstacles that could have prevented successful change. These obstacles included those found in school systems, school and community structures, and conventional practices as well as those found within—the preconceptions, prejudices, mental attitudes, and motivations that are often more limiting than external constraints. She also helped transfer ownership of problems and possibilities to those ultimately responsible for implementation. As teachers accepted ownership, they energized themselves and their colleagues and became self-sufficient.

Bernard-Powers (1999) and testaments from Taba's colleagues, Mary Durkin (1981), Evelyn Jegi Blodgett (1981), and Kim Ellis (1981)—teachers who participated in Taba's workshops in Contra Costa County—affirm Taba's constant emphasis on the development of individuality and how she treasured it in the teachers with whom she worked and in school children. She fostered individuality in students as well as in teachers through the development of intellectual and attitudinal dimensions of personality and thought. Furthermore, she strove to protect the worth of each individual in her treatment of her colleagues and of students through her guidance to teachers when leading discussions. She respected both teachers and students enough to trust them and to cultivate their differences. Finally, Taba set high expectations for herself and those with whom she worked. Her projects were massive in scope and high in aspiration. She elevated her own, teachers', and students' thinking and substantiated the professional lives of the teachers with whom she worked. She pointed them in worthy new directions, and they in turn led their students and colleagues to new intellectual heights.

Her ways of working with teachers and school administrators led them to think differently about their roles, their students, and content. Her work and her words helped to point teachers in new directions and enabled them to travel with a different view as well. The success of her curriculum-development efforts and teaching strategies established both her authority among educators worldwide and her prestige among her colleagues. The leadership she exhibited explains her influence during her lifetime. The power, flexibility, and applicability of her ideas define her influence since her untimely death.

References

Aikin, W. M. 1942. *The story of the Eight-Year Study, with conclusions & recommendations*. New York: Harper.

Belasco, J. A., and R. C. Stayer. 1994. *Flight of the buffalo: Soaring to excellence, learning to let employees lead*. New York: Warner Books.

Bell, B. I. 1949. *Crisis in education: A challenge to American complacency*. New York: Whittlesey House.

Bestor, A. 1953. *Educational wastelands: The retreat from learning in our public schools*. Urbana: University of Illinois Press.

Bestor, A. 1955. *The restoration of learning: A program for redeeming the unfulfilled promise of American education*. New York: Knopf.

Bernard-Powers, J. 1999. Composing her life: Hilda Taba and social studies history. In *Bending their future to their will: Civic women, social education, and democracy*, ed. M. S. Crocco and O. L. Davis Jr., 185–206. Lanham, Md.: Rowman & Littlefield.

Blodgett, E. J. 1981. Oral history interview with the author, 17 April. Austin: University of Texas at Austin, Oral History of Education Collection.

Bode, B. H. 1927. *Modern educational theories*. New York: Macmillan.

Brady, E. H. 1981. Oral history interview with the author, 14 April. Austin: University of Texas at Austin, Oral History of Education Collection.

Brady, E. H. 1996. Hilda Taba: The congruity of professing and doing. In *Teachers and mentors: Profiles of distinguished twentieth-century professors of education*, ed. C. Kridel, R. V. Bullough Jr., and P. Shaker, 59–79. New York: Garland.

Bruner, J. S. 1960. *The process of education*. Cambridge, Mass.: Harvard University Press.

Bruner, J. S., J. J. Goodnow, and G. A. Austin. 1956. *A study of thinking*. New York: Wiley.

Cattell J., and T. T. Ross. 1948. *Leaders in education*. Lancaster, Pa.: Science Press.

Chamberlain, C. D., E. Chamberlain, N. Drought, and W. Scott. 1942. *Did they succeed in college? The follow-up study of the graduates of the thirty schools*. New York: Harper.

Corey, S. M. 1953. *Action research to improve school practice*. New York: Bureau of Publications, Teachers College, Columbia University.

Davis, O. L., Jr. 1982. Pointing the right direction: Toward the invention of our futures. Speech delivered to the 33d Biennial Convocation of Kappa Delta Pi, April.

Davis, O. L., Jr. 1999. Rachel Davis DuBois: Intercultural education pioneer. In *Bending their future to their will: Civic women, social education, and democracy*, ed. M. S. Crocco and O. L. Davis Jr., 169–84. Lanham, Md.: Rowman & Littlefield.

Dewey, J. 1902. *The child and the curriculum*. Chicago: University of Chicago Press.

Durkin, M. 1981. Oral history interview with the author, 16 April. Austin: University of Texas at Austin, Oral History of Education Collection.

Ellis, K. 1981. Oral history interview with the author, 19 April. Austin: University of Texas at Austin, Oral History of Education Collection.

Flesch, R. 1955. *Why Johnny can't read, and what you can do about it*. New York: Harper.

General Education Board. 1972. *Directory of fellows*. New York: General Education Board.

Giles, H., S. McCutchen, and A. Zechiel. 1942. *Exploring the curriculum: The work of the thirty schools from the viewpoint of the curriculum consultants*. New York: Harper.

Goodenow, R. K. 1975. The progressive educator, race, and ethnicity in the depression years: An overview. *History of Education Quarterly* 15(4): 365–94.

Goodenow, R. K. 1981. The Southern progressive educator on race and pluralism: The case of William Heard Kilpatrick. *History of Education Quarterly* 21(Summer): 147–70.

Hawkes, H. E. 1934. Letter to the General Education Board, 13 June. Sleepy Hollow, N.Y.: Archives of the General Education Board, Rockefeller Archives Center, Box 282, Folder 2946.

Lynd, A. 1953. *Quackery in the public schools*. Boston: Little, Brown and Co.

Monroe, P. 1927. Letter to Hilda Taba, spring 1927. Taba Papers, San Francisco State University.

Naylor, N. A. 1980. Hilda Taba. In *Notable American women: The modern period—A biographical dictionary*, ed. B. Sicherman and C. H. Green, 670–72. Cambridge, Mass.: Belknap Press of Harvard University Press.

Parkhurst, H. 1922. *Education on the Dalton plan*. New York: E. P. Dutton.

Piaget, J. 1926. *Language and thought of the child*. New York: Harcourt, Brace and Co.

Piaget, J. 1928. *Judgment and reasoning of the child*. New York: Harcourt, Brace and Co.

Piaget, J. 1929. *The child's conception of the world*. New York: Harcourt, Brace and Co.

Progressive Education Association. 1936. A proposal for the continuance of the evaluation program of the Committee on Records and Reports of the Commission on the Relation of School and College. Sleepy Hollow, N.Y.: Archives of the General Education Board, Rockefeller Archives Center, Box 282, Folder 2946, 1–6.

Progressive Education Association. 1942. *Thirty schools tell their story*. New York: Harper.

Reid, C. 1980. Oral history interview with O. L. Davis Jr., spring 1980. Austin: University of Texas at Austin, Oral History of Education Collection.

Smith, E., and R. W. Tyler, eds. 1942. *Appraising and recording student progress*. New York: Harper.

Smith, M. 1949. *And madly teach: A layman looks at public school education*. Chicago: H. Regnery.

Smith, M. 1954. *The diminished mind: A study of planned mediocrity in our public schools*. Chicago: H. Regnery.

Taba, H. 1932. *The dynamics of education*. New York: Harcourt, Brace.

Taba, H. 1933. Preliminary draft of the curriculum reorganization for the year 1934–1935. Unpublished manuscript. San Francisco: San Francisco State University, Taba Papers.

Taba, H. 1934. Progressive education—What now? *Progressive Education* 11: 162–68.

Taba, H. 1936. Social sensitivity. Unpublished manuscript. Columbus, Ohio: Progressive Education Association.

Taba, H. 1945. The contribution of workshops to intergroup education. *Harvard Educational Review* 15: 122–28.

Taba, H. 1962. *Curriculum development: Theory and practice*. New York: Harcourt, Brace & World.

Taba, H. 1966. *Teaching strategies and cognitive functioning in elementary school children*. San Francisco: San Francisco State College, Cooperative Research Project No. 12404.

Taba, H. 1967. *Teacher's handbook for elementary social studies*. Palo Alto, Calif.: Addison-Wesley.

Taba, H., E. H. Brady, and J. T. Robinson. 1952. *Intergroup education in public schools: Experimental programs sponsored by the Project in Intergroup Education in Cooperating Schools—Theory, practice, and in-service education*. Washington, D.C.: American Council on Education.

Taba, H., H. H. Jennings, E. H. Brady, J. T. Robinson, and F. Dolton. 1949. *Curriculum in intergroup relations: Case studies in instruction for secondary schools*. Washington, D.C.: American Council on Education.

Taba, H., S. Levine, and F. F. Elzey. 1964. *Thinking in elementary school children*. San Francisco: San Francisco State College, Cooperative Research Project No. 1574.

Taba, H., and E. Noel. 1957. *Action research: A case study*. Washington, D.C.: Association for Supervision and Curriculum Development.

Tyler, R. W. 1941.Workshops at the University of Chicago. *Bulletin of the National Association of Secondary School Principals* 15.

Tyler, R. W. 1980. Oral history interview with the author, 20 February. Austin: University of Texas at Austin, Oral History of Education Collection.

Wallen, N. E., M. C. Durkin, J. R. Fraenkel, A. H. McNaughton, and E. I. Sawin. 1969. *The Taba curriculum development project in social studies: Final report*. Washington, D.C.: U.S. Department of Health, Education, and Welfare, Office of Education, Bureau of Research Project No. 5-1314.

Wertheimer, M. 1945. *Productive thinking*. New York: Harper.

Chapter 9

Myra and Me

by David M. Sadker

Myra Pollack Sadker (1943–95) was passionate about education. During her train-ing as an educator, she saw a fundamental injustice in society; in pointing out that ineq-uity, she taught us all a valuable lesson.

The Early Years

Did you ever visit Maine in the summer? Whether you travel the coasts or the lakes, it doesn't much matter; it is all quite beautiful. The rocky coasts were always Myra's favorite—and, over the years, they became mine as well. Walking along the ocean and discovering a "pound" where the lobster rolls were fresh and cheap was Myra's favorite summer day. In her younger days, however, when she was growing up in Augusta, Maine, summer trips to the ocean were rare, and the winter months seemed endless. Back in the 1940s and '50s, when Myra was attending Farrington Elementary School and Cony High, Augusta was mostly cold, dark, and quite isolated. As one of the few Jewish families, and even fewer poor Jewish families, the Pollacks were pretty much out of the mainstream of social events.

Both of Myra's parents worked outside and inside the home, a family effort that was a bit unusual for the time, but perhaps less unusual among poor families like Myra's. Myra's dad, Lou, worked as a linotypist for the *Kennebec Journal*, a daily newspaper that reflected the strongly conservative nature of the small community. The paper was a brief (often just 8 pages) daily compilation of national wire service stories, local events, and the conservative musings of several syndicated columnists.

Lou would spend most of his day reading, cleaning, shopping, and preparing din-ner—which may have made him an early role model of male domestic possibilities. As Lou was getting ready to serve dinner, Shirley, Myra's mom, would be finishing her secretarial job for the Maine Commissioner of Industry. Widely respected for the quality of her work, Shirley had won awards for her typing and dictation skills. In the early evening darkness of 5 to 6 p.m., Shirley would drive home through the snow banks, in temperatures that generally hovered near—and often dropped below—zero degrees Fahrenheit. Dinner happened quickly. Then Shirley would attack the dishes and pick up the evening shift at home as Lou went off to his job setting the type for the morning edition.

Two children, Myra and her younger brother Murray, watched those parental ships passing in the night. The culture of the 1950s pinned the family's hopes on the son, and Murray was all about "great expectations." In the Pollack family, Shirley did more than her share in financing the family; she was the furnace of family expectations. For a Jewish boy, the road out of poverty went straight through medical school—and by the time Murray was in high school, Shirley had his medical future in her sights. Though Shirley loved Myra no less than Murray, she held less ambitious vocational goals for her daughter—also a reflection of the times. Myra loved to read, and so (her mother thought) she would be perfect for teaching. Teaching was as appropriate a career for a girl as medicine was for a boy, and Shirley knew that for both of her children the route out of their cold and isolated Maine existence was through the schoolhouse door. For Myra, the inequities inherent in these gender-driven career differences planted the early seeds of discontent that, a decade later, would emerge as one of—if not *the*—first books describing the sexism confronting girls in school and society.

Shirley's unflagging energy and precious dollars provided the means to make a happier and more prosperous future for the family a reality. As happy endings go, for Murray (and, vicariously, for Shirley), there was one. Shirley took great pride as Murray became a doctor. For several decades, he practiced at Washington, D.C.'s Children's Hospital. As director of the Intensive Care Unit, he focused on children in serious danger.

Myra was a different story, for Shirley's gender-influenced dream never quite took root. Though Shirley saw Myra in a classroom, Myra saw herself on a stage. In high school, Myra won awards and some notoriety as a public speaker. If Myra's perfect day was one spent at the shore, her perfect entertainment was a stage show. Sometimes, Myra would dash off to see Maine summer stock productions, and, on a few special occasions, she would get to Broadway. To Myra, theatre was magic, and a life on a stage seemed like the ideal choice. Those who would later see her teach, of course, got to see a bit of the theatre—and the career that never was. "How impractical" was Shirley's response to a stage career. *Practicality*, after all, was a second religion in the Pollack home. So they reached a compromise between acting and teaching, between Broadway and a classroom. They agreed on speech pathology. As you might have detected, compromises generally tilted in Shirley's direction.

At Boston University, Myra tried speech pathology. Bored to tears, she switched her major to English, where she would be closer to the words if not the stage. Four years later, she earned a degree in English, graduating magna cum laude, and was ready to earn a living. Now Shirley's admonition seemed to haunt her. As an English major, Myra saw the same few options that her mother had predicted. She decided to become a teacher, and she enrolled in the Harvard Master of Arts in Teaching program. That is how I was lucky enough to meet Myra.

From Harvard to Pattaya

In June 1964, when Myra and I first met, I was pretty much her opposite. I grew up in the South Bronx, attended the New York City public schools, and had just graduated from liberal (some would say radical), highly competitive (some would argue cut-throat), politically active, City College. I was assertive, quite verbal, and sure of myself (let's face it, cocky). I exuded urban, male parochialism and entitlement, making up in noise what I lacked in experience. Myra noticed my clamor and even found it "interesting"—or at least different from her quiet, rural, "mind-your-own-business" background. I noticed her beauty first and her thoughtful comments later—typical guy stuff.

Yet we also had a lot in common. We developed our own game, which involved countless hours debating which of us would win the title of "growing up poorer." Sometimes we moved from economics to religion, comparing religious upbringings. I was raised in an orthodox Bronx neighborhood, while Myra learned about Judaism on pilgrimages to Portland (where there were enough Jews to create a community) and at Augusta's once-a-year religious service (attracting virtually all of the 30–40 Jews in the area). As we looked back at our life experiences, we also looked ahead at our new careers. We were doing our teaching internships at that time, and this paid student teaching often was the focus of our professional lives and our personal conversations. We explored lesson plan ideas, new ways to "hook" kids, and methods for handling discipline problems, and, of course, we spent endless hours grading papers. We often graded sitting side by side, with few words spoken for hours on end (kind of like the parallel play of preschoolers). Before long, we moved from grading to dating. We tried to figure out what would happen at the end of our year at Harvard. My plans were beyond negotiation; I was expected to report for duty as a newly minted army lieutenant. Then Myra and I figured it out. Myra would have an unanticipated introduction to military life. On 4 July 1965, we were married and went together to Fort Lee, Virginia.

As I was learning about the intricacies of military protocol and Southern culture, Myra was applying for teaching positions near Fort Lee, including one with the English Department of Virginia State College, a historically black institution. To our delight, she was hired. In 1965, few whites were applying to teach in predominantly black colleges. She was one of only two European-American faculty members, and she taught writing to an entirely African-American student population. At Virginia State, Myra personally witnessed the impact of racial segregation. Her students were typically the first generation to make it to college, earnest in their efforts and hard working. Unfortunately, their academic preparation was horrid, and their writing skills were at middle school level. Failing college writing, a course Myra taught, was as common as passing. Myra was directed on the grading conventions at Virginia State, and she learned how to grade student papers using red and blue pencils. Mechanical, spelling, or grammatical errors were underlined in red or blue, based on the gravity of the error, and points were deducted accordingly. Myra was told that the typical student took seven and a half years to graduate from Virginia State. The constant stream of failing grades took their toll on both teachers and students. For me, segregated education had been a sad chapter in U.S. history; for Myra, its impact was always in the faces of her students at Virginia State, struggling to catch up on lost learning. The dejection of Myra's students was contagious, and Myra was not looking forward to her second year of red and blue pencils and broken hearts. As it turned out, the army prompted us to change our plans; I received new orders. The war in Vietnam was growing, and I was assigned as a communications officer to a B-52 base in Thailand. It did not sound good. Married for less than a year, we were suddenly facing a 10,000-mile separation—and we feared to imagine what else.

With me stationed abroad, Myra decided that returning to Maine made some sense, and she applied for a position with one of President Johnson's Great Society programs: the Job Corps in Poland Spring, Maine (well before the town became a Mecca for the bottled-water craze). Working primarily with Hispanic, African-American, and Native-American girls, Myra was once again teaching fundamental literary skills to youngsters who were academically in trouble. These young women, often with children of their own, were living in poverty. Myra had returned home, living with her parents in Augusta and driving for an hour to get to the Job Corps at Poland Spring. She loved the students, but, as the Maine winter approached, we were not sure who was at greater risk, me at the B-52 base or Myra trailing the snow plows. We resolved to get Myra out of Maine and into Thailand. We hatched a plan.

We decided to create a school in Pattaya, a town not far from the B-52 base, and I set about recruiting students. Luckily, some marine corps and construction workers' families living in Pattaya were ready to pay $25 a month for a teacher. Before long, I had a core of parents ready to start their own neighborhood school on the Gulf of Siam. Established as a private school with an "American-type" curriculum, some classes were taught at a local army facility while others were taught on our not-shaded-enough sundeck. Our school was an amazing combination of "home school" and charter school decades before those terms were in vogue. Classes were sometimes held next to a watering hole used by roaming water buffalo and visited by the occasional king cobra. Not unlike early U.S. teachers, Myra learned how to be school principal, classroom teacher, and building custodian—all at the same low salary. She also learned that, when students did not receive the "A" grades that parents expected, the adults simply pulled their children out of our school. The student body shrunk, but Myra's school never gave in to community pressure. The weather also was problematic: perfect for a few months, and unbelievably hot for the rest of the year. A small fan was no match for Southeast Asian heat. Nonetheless, we were together. We had our own school, and all of Asia was just beyond our door. Unfortunately, we did not have enough money to go much beyond our door. Half a year later, we returned to more conventional teaching positions in Massachusetts, but Thailand always remained a special memory for us.

By the fall of 1967, we both were back in Massachusetts. Myra was teaching English at Winchester Junior High, and I was teaching history at Brookline High. Living in Somerville, we were close to Harvard, where we thought we would return to get our doctorates. Instead, we wound up on the other side of the state—and in the middle of a revolution.

The UMass Revolution

We knew that we would be applying to doctoral programs after a year or two more of teaching, and we were thinking of the Boston area. While interviewing at Harvard, we heard about the excitement surrounding the new Dean at the University of Massachusetts in Amherst. He was coming from Stanford with a coterie of faculty members and students, as well as some revolutionary ideas about education. I was interested in the revolution; Myra was interested in pursuing English. I applied for the educational doctoral program, while Myra won a graduate fellowship to the English Ph.D. program. We thought that we were set. Wrong again.

I had stumbled upon the academic version of Disneyland. I was enjoying the exhilarating experiment at Dwight Allen's School of Education. Within a week, I was boarding a plane for the Rockies—setting off to invent an "ideal" school of education. Sure, it was naïve. Kettering Foundation funded the adventure west, giving school of education faculty, students, and staff scenic views to spark our souls and conjure up our Brave New World. While I contemplated the sunset, Myra stayed behind in Amherst, living the uncomplicated life of a student in the modest environs of Colonial Village Apartments. One morning, as I went horseback riding in the Rockies, Myra set off for her class in "Middle English" back in Amherst. The signs of a seismic shift were all around us, but it wasn't until I arrived home that we would feel the shock wave.

Myra's course in Middle English made an imprint that has endured three decades. Her literature professor best described Myra's objective in that course: "To speak Middle English so well that Chaucer, up in heaven, will smile down at us." At a time when educators were emphasizing behavioral objectives, this one was over the line! A week later, I returned from the Rockies, immersed in a stream of endless possibilities. Myra was less enthralled with her work, finding that Middle English had few fans. In fact, much to the dismay of the registrar, she soon made an unprecedented move, transferring from the English Ph.D. program to the far less prestigious Ed.D. program. She also abandoned her English fellowship, a major financial sacrifice for a couple trying to see how far the G.I. Bill could carry them. Myra had decided that she really didn't care whether Chaucer smiled or not.

How lucky we were that she made that change, but no one was luckier than the nation's schoolgirls. By the time she completed her degree, Myra was set on a path that would make her a champion for the educational rights of girls and a national voice speaking for so many silent girls. In the beginning, though, it was Myra who needed to find her voice.

To understand Myra's transformation, you need to know a little about the "UMass Revolution." For those of you who missed it, the UMass Revolution in the 1960s and '70s is difficult to explain in the context of today's more conservative environment. Picture a school at which sorting out professors from students was sometimes challenging, parliamentary procedure was replaced by Quaker-style meetings, and five students who chose a topic they wanted to investigate would get a professor assigned to help them do just that. Picture a place so exciting that a reporter for the *Saturday Review* would come to do a story and stay for a degree. Bill Cosby found it as compelling as show business; he decided to enroll. It was an exhilarating community, and the difference between schooling and education could not have been clearer. "'No' is not the answer," and "'Yes' is the right answer" were two of the catch phrases that captured the feeling of experimentation and change. Both phrases were immediately made into buttons, announcing to the world the school's willingness to explore new ideas. The buttons also were daily reminders that, in *this* school, the old ways were suspect.

Of course, beyond the buttons and liberating ideas, not all was wonderful. There were abuses and failures; some students and faculty members took advantage of the school's openness. Nonetheless, for Myra and me, after Harvard, the military, and teaching in the Boston suburbs, the transition from harsh reality to UMass's experiment in idealism was a welcome change. UMass was one exciting place to learn, a description too rare in today's schools of education.

Part of the excitement was the school's commitment to educational equity, evidenced by the significant numbers of students of color in the doctoral program. Multicultural and race issues were a major focus of the curriculum, shaping much of the new school's goals. Yet, as our sensitivity to race bias grew, Myra and I became increasingly uncomfortable with a growing reality. Gender bias had become an integral part of the most *avant garde* school in the nation.

Sexism Finds Us

When Myra and I coauthored articles and proposals, faculty members and students would refer to our coauthored work as "David's" article and "David's" proposals. Myra protested, "But I wrote it too!" A faculty member responded, "Of course, when we say 'David,' we mean 'Myra' too!" In class, a similar pattern developed, as males (including me) dominated class discussion. Female voices, if not silent, were quieter, less frequent, less influential. As Myra took her turn as editor of the school newspaper (another UMass norm was rotating editorships), she wrote an editorial entitled "The Only Socially Acceptable Form of Discrimination." She discussed how it felt to be female and invisible in a doctoral program. As chance (or was it fate?) would have it, that editorial was read by Lou Fischer, a professor who also edited a series of issues-oriented books for Harper and Row. "Would you be interested in writing a book about what happens to girls in school?" he asked. And so it began.

A one-page editorial, printed in a mimeographed school of education newspaper, with a circulation of about 150, guided our professional lives for the next 25 years. The question "What happens to girls in school?" became the focus of our research and writing. How strange that, for us, the formal curriculum became far less influential than the informal one. Though certainly useful and necessary, in the final analysis, the courses we studied—the long list of books we read, the worry over the next test, those long nights finishing term papers (before the advent of the word processor), and the enduring double trauma of completing two very different dissertations—did not shape our professional focus. All that sweat, effort, and worry led both of us to our degrees; much of our professional contribution, however, came down to figuring out whether our UMass experiences were personal—or prevalent. Was sexism a factor in the nation's schools?

Defining a Field

In *Sexism in School and Society* (Frazier and Sadker 1973), Myra's first book, she helped define a field. Few studies had been done about sexism, and the majority of those focused on males. Let's face it—many people did not know what *sexism* meant. It may have been coined around 1970 at the Women's Studies program at Cornell University, along with another phrase, *sexual harassment*. Before then, there were no terms to identify bias based on gender. In fact, when Betty Friedan (1963) wrote *The Feminine Mystique*, she referred to gender bias as "the problem that has no name." Not surprisingly, the library revealed precious few articles on the topic. Myra took what was available, pulled together the few studies, and began observing schools, reading school texts, and interviewing educators and students. She saw that, from the pages of textbooks to career counseling, girls were being channeled into second-rate careers and limited futures. Administration and leadership of teaching (the "women's" profession) was in the hands of men, with 80 percent of the elementary teachers being female while 80 percent of the principals were male. At high school and in the superintendent's office, males occupied more than 90 percent of the leadership positions. It was not at all unusual to discover public school athletic budgets providing 10 times more funds for male sports than female sports. Back then, even the Ivy League colleges were closed to women. Myra found that girls were doing their work and getting high report card grades, but they were often not finding success in careers. It was a terrible trade off. Girls were trading in their futures for teacher and parental approval, along with terrific report card grades. Some of today's writers refer to this as the *ability-achievement gap* (Reskin and Padavic 1994, 81–99).

In the 1970s, the idea that females were in any way paying a price because of their gender was a fairly new and threatening concept. Myra soon learned that hostile audiences awaited her, particularly among the male leadership. At a national school principals' conference in Detroit, Myra was an invited guest at a "Meet the Authors" lecture series. It was early in the 1970s, and Myra was thrilled at the prospect of sharing these new and exciting ideas with educational leaders. She called me later that night to tell me the good news—and the bad. The room was packed with hundreds of principals, attracted, Myra thought, by her topic. In fact, her photo in the program, and the idea that she would be speaking about sex attracted them. When she explained the difference between sex education and sex bias (not an insignificant distinction), the room all but emptied. The "backlash" was to arrive officially two decades later, but the force of resistance was there from the start.

Myra's book, published in 1973, was one of the first to delineate what sex bias looks like in schools and classrooms. Society's sexist assumptions were everywhere: Education was more important for boys; girls who were "overeducated" would face lifelong problems; and gender-differentiated career paths were natural and preordained. Straying from these assumptions sparked questions about one's political leanings and sexual orientation. Myra showed personal courage in detailing these issues and professional courage in challenging accepted practices. In *Sexism in School and Society*, Myra introduced new concepts and words, popularizing phrases like: "sexism in school" and "gender bias in curriculum and instruction." She also challenged old ideas and proposed new ways to look at classroom life.

With little research to guide her, Myra began to synthesize the few studies regarding sexism that were available. While Nancy Frazier, her coauthor, focused on society, Myra wrote the chapters concerning schools. There was little there, and Myra needed to conceptualize the field, pull together what was known, and begin to identify what needed to be learned. All this came together in *Sexism in School and Society*.

At the very time that Myra was researching and writing, a new law was also being formulated. Title IX, as it came to be called, would begin to balance the educational scales. This section of the 1972 Education Amendments Act specifically prohibited many forms of sex discrimination in education. As the opening section of Title IX stated, "No person in the United States shall, on the basis of sex, be excluded from participation in, be denied the benefits of, or be subjected to discrimination under any education program or activity receiving federal financial assistance."

Every public school and most of the nation's colleges and universities were covered under Title IX, which prohibited sex discrimination in school admissions, counseling and guidance, competitive athletics, student rules and regulations, and access to programs and courses, including vocational education and physical education. Title IX also applied to sex discrimination in employment practices, including interviewing and recruitment, hiring and promotion, compensation, job assignments, and fringe benefits. Myra's book had addressed those very issues, and more. Now the power of the federal government resonated with Myra's insights.

A Hidden Civil Rights Struggle

In her research for *Sexism in School and Society*, and later for *Failing at Fairness: How America's Schools Cheat Girls* (Sadker and Sadker 1994), Myra uncovered more than current examples of bias. She also illuminated a hidden civil rights struggle to win educational rights for half the nation's citizens. As we wrote in *Failing at Fairness* (1994, 15–31):

> *For almost two centuries girls were barred from America's schools. Although a woman gave the first plot of ground for a free school in New England, female children were not allowed to attend the school. In 1687, the town council of Farmington, Connecticut, voted money for a school "where all children shall learn to read and write English." However, the council quickly qualified this statement by explaining that "all children" meant "all males." In fact, the education of America's girls was so limited that fewer than a third of the women in colonial America could even sign their names. For centuries women fought to open the schoolhouse door.*
>
> *By the end of the Civil War, a number of colleges and universities, especially tax-supported ones, were desperate for dollars. Institutions of higher learning experienced a serious student shortage due to Civil War casualties, and women became the source of much-needed tuition dollars. Female funding did not buy on-campus equality. Women often faced separate courses and hostility from male students and professors. At state universities, male students would stamp their feet in protest when a woman entered a classroom.*
>
> *In* Sex in Education *(1873), Dr. Edward Clarke, a member of Harvard's medical faculty, argued that women attending high school and college were at risk because the blood destined for the development and health of their ovaries would be redirected to their brains. The stress of study was no laughing matter. Too much education would leave women with "monstrous brains and puny bodies . . . flowing thought and constipated bowels." Clarke recommended that females be provided with a less demanding education, easier courses, no competition, and "rest" periods so that their reproductive organs could develop. He maintained that allowing girls to attend places such as Harvard would pose a serious health threat to the women themselves, with sterility and hysteria potential outcomes.*
>
> *This "invisible" civil rights struggle has continued into the 21st century. It was not until the 1970s and '80s that Ivy League colleges admitted women—and not until the 1990s that the last state-supported military colleges decided, under court order, to open their doors. Yet access is not equality; it is simply the first step to equality. Even when women gain admittance to military or Ivy League colleges, they often find themselves experiencing different kinds of education. At the turn of the century, opponents to Title IX and gender equity were lobbying Congress and the public to turn back the gender equity clock and to recognize different social roles for females and males.*

Gender Bias in College Texts

With the help of several federal grants, Myra and I (1979) investigated teacher education textbooks, only to discover that sex bias was rarely mentioned, receiving less than one percent of content coverage. Based on the 24 books analyzed for *Beyond Pictures and Pronouns*, tomorrow's teachers were more likely to repeat sexist practices than remedy them. Our findings indicated:

- Of the 24 textbooks, 23 gave less than one-percent coverage to the issue of gender bias.
- One-third did not mention the issue of sexism at all.

- Not a single text provided future teachers with curricular resources and instructional strategies to counter the impact of sexism.
- Among issues often omitted were the role and contributions of women, Title IX, and gender differences in academic performance.

Much of the advice given to teachers we believed to be unwise; some of it actually promoted gender bias and stereotypes. These excerpts are drawn from teacher education textbooks and were cited in *Beyond Pictures and Pronouns* (1979):

> *For example, it has been found that boys will not read "girl books," whereas girls will read "boy books." Therefore the ration of boy books should be about two to one in the classroom library collection* (Rubin 1975, 191).

> *Teachers could make use of many parents of the children in their rooms. Some fathers could help the third-grade boys make birdhouses easier than the teacher could; some mothers could teach sixth-grade girls how to knit; many mothers would be glad to drive a carload of children to the airport, to the museum, or to the public library* (Zintz 1975).

> *Following are kernel sentences recommended for teachers to use in transformational grammar activities:*
> > *John works.*
> > *Julio gardens.*
> > *Mary teaches.*
> > *Ramon farms.*
> > *Enrique drives a truck.*
> > *Mr. Jones practices law.*
> > *Marianna cooks.*
> > *Mrs. Chacon makes dresses* (Zintz 1975).

> *"A thirty-three-year-old girl . . .* (Heddens 1974).

> *If all the boys in a high school class routinely get distracted when a curvaceous and provocative coed undulates into the room to pick up attendance slips, tape the attendance slips to the outside of the door* (Biehler 1978).

> *Women with higher levels of educational training work for intellectual reasons and notions of self-fulfillment* (Johnson et al. 1976).

> *Parenthetically, if it were not for automation all women over twenty years of age in the U.S. would have to be telephone operators to handle all the phone calls made each day* (Johnson et al. 1976).

As a result of our analysis, we developed a series of "guidelines" to be used in writing teacher education textbooks. Our guidelines were intended for authors and publishers committed to eliminating gender and race bias in these books. The guidelines called for more research and coverage of the contributions made by women and nonmajority groups, a description of the educational barriers these groups face, direct coverage of sexism in schools and ways to overcome such bias, and avoidance of sexist language and stereotypes. We believed that such an effort would be useful, and several authors and editors informed us that they were in fact using the information.

As an aside, in the fall of 2000, I revisited this issue with my graduate assistant, Karen Zittleman (Zittleman and Sadker 2002). Much to our dismay, we found that the problem of gender bias in teacher education textbooks that Myra and I uncovered in the late 1970s is anything but solved. In the two decades since our original study, there has been an improvement in some teacher education textbooks, continuing bias in other texts, and even a "backlash" against women and girls' concerns in still others. Though some of these textbooks, all published in 2000 or 2001, especially introductory ones, now include a description of gender bias, most provide only superficial treatment. For example, Title IX, the law prohibiting gender discrimination in educational programs, is typically described only in terms of athletics. Its impact in other areas is omitted. The impact of Title IX in terms of teacher employment protections, health benefits for education staff and students, the rights boys are given under the law, the creation of equitable admission and scholarship practices, and the elimination of sex-segregated programs and courses are rarely mentioned. Also forgotten is the disturbing evidence that Title IX protections are often ignored by schools. Administrators and teachers frequently line up students by gender, focus more energy and resources on male sports, and informally advise students to pursue traditional careers.

Rewriting the Books

As a result of our original study in the late 1970s and our interest in teacher education, we began to write teacher education books of our own. We hoped our books would remedy this oversight. The Non-Sexist Teacher Education Project was a program developed under one of our grants funded by the Women's Educational Equity Act Program, the same small federal agency that supported the textbook study. The teacher education material that we developed in this project eventually became a book, *Sex Equity Handbook for Schools* (Sadker and Sadker 1982). In 1980, we had published our first introductory teacher education textbook, today carrying the title *Teachers, Schools, and Society* (Sadker and Sadker 2003), about to be revised for its seventh edition.

Most of our effort in the 1980s and '90s focused on classroom interaction. We discovered that, from grade school to graduate school, boys received more instructor attention. Teachers praised, punished, and helped boys more. Boys became the focus of a more intense educational environment in the classroom. When teachers did not invite responses from boys, boys were more likely to call out. When a boy called out, a teacher's most frequent response was to accept his comments. When girls called out, which happened considerably less often, teachers were most likely to correct the behavior, reminding the girls that, in this class, students should raise their hands to speak. We also found that about half of the classrooms in our study were gender segregated. Sometimes the teacher was responsible for this segregation through seating or grouping assignments, but more often it was done by the students through quiet, informal decisions to sit near friends or at least same-sex peers. Gender-segregated areas characterized classrooms, and this gender gap contributed to different levels of gender participation in the classroom. Teachers, as if drawn by a magnet, would spend more time and effort in the male areas of the room. The hidden curriculum was teaching powerful lessons about which gender was entitled and which was to be treated to a second-class education. Myra and I were uncovering the light and the shadows in the nation's classrooms—an intense spotlight often focused on boys and a more shadowy world for females.

Though this differential instructional treatment reflected an important gender gap, grades and tests pointed to yet another problem. Girls received better report card grades, but boys did better on critical tests. Why the gap? Girls, we believed, were being rewarded with higher report card grades in part for their more effective social skills, as well as their more docile, less challenging behavior. Though girls were receiving higher grades in class, boys were doing better on high-stakes tests such as the SAT and the GRE. Even on the SAT II, an achievement-oriented test for which one would expect girls to score particularly well, boys outperformed girls. Perhaps the more intense classroom instruction was reaping rewards for boys related to stronger self-esteem and a greater willingness for risk taking on exams. Boys were more likely to be at center stage, for arguably good and bad reasons, while girls were more likely to be quietly learning, or not learning, on the sidelines. After two decades of work, we had our answer to the UMass question. Myra's invisibility at graduate school was not personal; it was prevalent.

The Backlash

As the evidence and research mounted, so did the political backlash. In the book *Backlash,* Susan Faludi (1991) documented the negative impact on women resulting from the conservative political gains of the 1980s and early '90s. Most of the educational programs designed to assist girls and women now are gone. Title IX itself is threatened. A "glass wall" still keeps women from the most lucrative careers and keeps men from entering traditionally "female" jobs. In certain areas, such as engineering, physics, chemistry, and computer science, few women can be found. In nursing, teaching, library science, and social work, few men can be found. Even in careers for which tremendous progress has been made, such as medicine and law, a second generation of bias persists. In both professions, women find themselves channeled into the least prestigious, least profitable areas.

Against this background, *Failing at Fairness: How America's Schools Cheat Girls* (Sadker and Sadker 1994) was born. It began when we were asked by the American Association of University Women to draft a chapter on classroom interaction for its publication on *How Schools Shortchange Girls* (1992). This chapter caught the imagination of the media. As the impact of the AAUW report and *Failing at Fairness* grew, so did the backlash.

By the mid-1990s, the right wing was on the offensive. With claims that European-American males were really the victims of affirmative action and gender-equity programs, a cadre of ultra-conservative ideologues denounced and attempted to discredit the work of educators like Myra and me. Though most of these critics lacked even rudimentary research credentials and were clearly funded by right-wing organizations, the media provided a public forum, adding a formidable barrier to gender-equity efforts.

Backlash critics claimed that the "natural" differences between the genders were being overlooked. With support from far-right foundations such as Carthage and Olin, backlash critics painted a destructive win-lose scenario. They claimed that females were thriving and the real victims of sexism were males. They argued that the problems boys confronted were due, in large part, to the feminist movement, female teachers, and efforts to level the educational playing field. Gender equity programs were seen as responsible for the problems boys encountered in reading and special education, though in fact, these problems preceded the feminist movement. Rejecting the idea that sexism is a two-edged sword that hurts both males and females, the backlash critics attacked the motives and integrity of educators working in the area of gender research.

The critics' arguments found a receptive audience in the press. Popular magazines, such as *The Atlantic*, found the contrarian arguments of the backlash crowd an appealing readership draw, and without fact-checking, ran a cover story claiming that because of feminist efforts, boys were now at risk and "girls ruled" in school. Politically conservative publications, such as *The Weekly Standard*, were attracted to the backlash ideology and ran stories with a similar theme and, as often as not, similar factual errors. For example, I soon found myself spending endless hours defending the research Myra and I had done and explaining that I was not declaring a "war on boys." As one example, from 1995 well into the next century, backlash critics stated that Myra and I had never written a final report on our research. To this charge, I responded that the report had been around for more than a decade and could be retrieved in thousands of libraries; I even gave the ERIC call number. Yet, to my dismay, the charge recycled in seemingly endless press stories about "the missing report." Evidently, none of the reporters actually went to the library to see whether the report existed. The groundless backlash attack was effective in several ways, because few reporters thought to ask the backlash critics themselves whether they had research reports to support their charges. Later, several of them admitted that they had never done a report, or even undertaken a single peer-reviewed study. For some reason, however, those facts rarely found their way into print. The experience taught us just how political educational research can be.

Deborah Tannen (1999) wrote in *The Argument Culture* that the press was all too ready to air heated debates, profit from a heated argument, and buy into the attractive premise that there are "two sides to every argument." She suggested that this is simplistic: sometimes there are many sides, and sometimes only one. The "Men against Women, Battle of the Sexes" approach pulled in large media audiences, and the backlash gained a national stage. "Feminism" became a word that even college women shunned. Indeed, "feminism," a word that had been a banner for equity, became synonymous with inequity, intolerance, and male hating. The backlash fed into many of the popular misconceptions and fears of the women's movement. The efforts to promote gender equity suffered a serious setback.

The Struggle Continues

When Myra first began her work, her premise was quite simple: Research the issue, publicize the findings, and encourage improvement. We were all so naïve back then. The backlash has taught us that those who promote change and try to replace entitlement with equity will themselves become targets of attack.

If Myra were still with us, she would be leading through teaching, trying to make classrooms fairer places for both girls and boys, and fighting the political forces sounding a retreat. She would also be asking us to do the same, to lead through teaching. And she, like her mother, would be very practical about this struggle.

So how can we be practical? How can we promote fairer classrooms for all of our students? Here are some suggestions that Myra and I developed over the years, designed to ensure that all students, the noisy and the quiet, benefit from life in the classroom. These suggestions are adapted from *Teachers, Schools, and Society* (Sadker and Sadker 2003). They are intended to demonstrate the connection between effective and equitable teaching, a connection that Myra always underscored in her work. These skills also reflect some of the teaching strategies that Myra used in her own classes. Of course, she always shared and described these strategies with her students.

Classroom Organization

Segregation. Avoid segregated seating patterns or activities. Not too long ago, and even in many of today's classrooms, teachers overtly segregate: "Let's have a spelling bee—boys against the girls!" At other times, students segregate themselves. Gender, race, or ethnic groups that are isolated alter the dynamics of the classroom and create barriers to effective communication among students as well as obstacles to equitable teaching. If necessary, move students around on a regular basis to create a more integrated class. Knowledgeable teachers know that, at times, children need to be in clusters rooted in a common language, gender, or other criteria. Yet, if a class has only two or three students of a certain group, separating them may increase their sense of isolation. Diversity, intentionality, and good judgment are critical ingredients in organizing students.

Mobility. Studies show that students who sit in the front row and middle seats (sometimes called the "terrific T") receive the majority of the teacher's attention. In essence, the closer the teacher gets to students, the more likely they are to participate. When the teacher moves around the room, different students become involved. By the way, students are mobile, too. Consider changing their seats on a regular basis to disperse classroom participation more equally.

Cooperative education. Collaboration, rather than individual competition, is a preferred learning style for many individuals, and a social norm for some groups, including African Americans, Native Americans, and females. When cooperation is less valued than competition, research suggests that inequities emerge, especially when students choose their own partnerships. For instance, in cooperative-learning groups, girls tend to assist both other girls and boys, while boys are more likely to help only other boys. Boys get help from everyone in the group, but girls must make do with less support. In addition, some students (usually boys) may dominate the group, while others (often girls) are quiet. A good practice is for teachers to monitor student groups, intervening to stop these inequitable patterns.

Displays. Images as well as words can convey powerful messages; therefore, bulletin boards and visual displays often act as teachers, delivering strong—and often unintended—lessons. Are women and other often-underrepresented groups evident in such displays? Are more resources needed to supplement materials and create a more equitable classroom climate? In a very real sense, the phrase "If the walls could speak . . ." is true. Look around. What messages are classroom walls sending students?

Cultural Cues

Eye contact. Teachers sometimes assume that children's nonverbal messages are identical to their own. Yet many factors can change the meaning of "eye" messages. A teacher's respectfully stated request to "Look at me when I am talking to you" anticipates that a student will feel comfortable with the request. In fact, many Asian-American, Pacific-Islander, and Native-American children lower their eyes as a sign of respect. For other children, lowering the eyes is a sign of submission or shame rather than respect. Even silent eyes speak many languages.

Touching and personal space. Our personal cultural history contributes to how "touchy" we are and how we reach out to and touch others. Many Southeast Asians feel that it is spiritually improper to be touched on the head. A similar touch on an African-American child's head may be perceived as demeaning rather than kind. Getting close or even "right up in someone's face" can be perceived as threatening at times or caring at other times. Some teachers, worried that any touch may be misconstrued as sexual harassment, avoid touching students at all. Yet we know that touch, as a support to learning can be a powerful and positive force.

Teacher-family relationships. Students, depending on their heritage, view teachers with varied degrees of attachment. Hispanics may include the teacher as an extension of family, with high expectations for contact and closeness. Asian Americans may seem more formal, or even distant, evidencing respect for adults and the teacher's role. Parents from certain cultural groups may see the teacher's job as independent of parental influence; therefore, conferences or phone calls may appear unwanted or awkward. Wealthy parents may relate to teachers as subordinates, seeing them as part of a hardworking staff that serves their children's interests. Teachers should cultivate and expand relationship skills for relating effectively with diverse student families and cultures.

Interaction Strategies

Calling on and questioning students. Do not rely on the "quickest hand in the West," which is usually attached to a male. Relying on the first hand raised will skew the pattern of classroom participation. Be aware that some students will feel intimidated anytime they are called on. For whatever reason—a lack of English-language skill, a personal power strategy to shun the teacher's control, or even a sign of respect—some students work to escape teacher contact. Asking a teacher for help can suggest a lack of understanding and may well be avoided by Asian-American and Native-American children.

Developing alternate strategies for student participation can be a useful approach—for example, writing each student's name on a card and using the cards to select students. Setting the expectation for full participation will enable teachers to call on students even if they don't raise their hands. Instead of a few students "carrying" the class, all students will be pulled into the learning process.

Wait time 1. Wait time can be a big help in promoting equitable participation. Teachers who use 3–5 seconds before calling on a student allow more time to choose deliberately and thoughtfully which student gets to participate. The extra wait time also allows teachers more time to develop an answer. Research suggests that many females, students of color, and—in particular—limited-English speakers benefit from this strategy.

Wait time 2. More wait time *after* a student speaks is also important. Research shows that boys get more precise feedback than girls do. Waiting longer gives the teacher the opportunity to think about the strengths and weaknesses of each student's answer, be more specific in reacting, and provide all students with more specific feedback.

Myra's Lessons

By the way, these tips are not meant to be secret. Explaining to students why teachers work to include all students in class discussions is an important lesson for them now—and it will serve them well later in adult life. Students must learn how important it is for all of them to participate effectively in school and beyond.

These are the lessons Myra would teach, and, in many ways, they seem as relevant today as ever before. Some feminists believe that we are currently in the midst of a national case of "girl-fatigue." There is a sense that women have tired of waging the uphill effort to win equality. At times like this, we really miss Myra's insights, energy, and intellect. As Myra often said, gender bias harms all of us—boys and girls, men and women alike. If we are to move forward, as citizens and as teachers, Myra's goals must become *our* goals. Gender bias continues to haunt curricular materials, typify staffing patterns, and impact teaching behaviors. These biased lessons that characterize too many classrooms continue to shape our adult behaviors, at home and at work. All we need to do is look around to see many of the gender differences that were born in classrooms and have taken root in our adult lives. Given the powerful and continuing history of sexism in our schools, as well as the current political challenges educators face, we must rededicate ourselves to ensuring that schools become places of equal educational opportunity for all students.

That effort was at the heart of Myra's work. She has opened the classroom door for gender equity; it is up to us to keep that door open.

References

American Association of University Women. 1992. *How schools shortchange girls: A study of major findings on girls and education*. Washington, D.C.: AAUW Educational Foundation.

Biehler, R. F. 1978. *Psychology applied to teaching*, 3d ed. Boston: Houghton Mifflin.

Clarke, E. H. 1873. *Sex in education: Or, A fair chance for the girls*. Boston: J. R. Osgood & Co.

Faludi, S. 1991. *Backlash: The undeclared war against American women*. New York: Crown.

Frazier, N., and M. P. Sadker. 1973. *Sexism in school and society*. New York: Harper & Row.

Friedan, B. 1963. *The feminine mystique*. New York: Norton.

Heddens, J. W. 1974. *Today's mathematics: A guide to concepts and methods in elementary school mathematics*. Palo Alto, Calif.: Science Research Associates.

Johnson, J. A., et al. 1976. *Introduction to the foundations of American education*, 3d ed. Boston: Allyn and Bacon.

Rubin, D. 1975. *Teaching elementary language arts*. New York: Holt, Rinehart and Winston.

Reskin, B., and I. Padavic. 1994. *Women and men at work*. Thousand Oaks, Calif.: Pine Forge Press.

Sadker, M. P., and D. M. Sadker. 1979. *Beyond pictures and pronouns: Sexism in teacher education textbooks*. Washington, D.C.: U.S. Department of Health, Education, and Welfare, Women's Educational Equity Act Program.

Sadker, M. P., and D. M. Sadker. 1982. *Sex equity handbook for schools*. New York: Longman.

Sadker, M. P., and D. M. Sadker. 1994. *Failing at fairness: How America's schools cheat girls*. New York: C. Scribner's Sons.

Sadker, M. P., and D. M. Sadker. 2003. *Teachers, schools, and society*, 6th ed. New York: McGraw-Hill.

Tannen, D. 1999. *The argument culture: Stopping America's war of words*. New York: Ballantine Books.

Zintz, M. V. 1975. *The reading process: The teacher and the learner*, 2d ed. Dubuque, Iowa: W. C. Brown Co.

Zittleman, K., and D. Sadker. 2002. Gender bias in teacher education texts: New (and old) lessons. *Journal of Teacher Education* 53(March–April): 168–79.

Teaching as Ethical Action
by William Ayers

Images of teaching abound. In scholarly literature, we are observed and interviewed, our behavior sometimes dissected, then measured, and set against student outcomes. We are a problem or we are a vehicle for change, but we are without doubt data. Teaching as science and art.

In political debate, we are depicted variously as serious professionals worthy of the community's praise if not its bounty or as underskilled and unmotivated placeholders, grown lazy in the sinecure of government employment. We are purveyors of curriculum, the stuff of classrooms, and right there lies a whole field of contention. Some focus on our dispositions and habits of thinking, others question our expertise and our proficiency; all seem giddily engaged in a conflict over our bleeding bodies. Teaching as work.

In popular culture, we are knaves and heroes, gods and monsters. The enduring image, from *Blackboard Jungle* to *Stand and Deliver*, is the solitary teacher-hero fighting valiantly to save the good juvenile delinquents from the sewers of their circumstances. Teaching as salvation and drama.

Teaching is, of course, drama, it is work, and it is both art and science. Still, none of these images holds much sustainable interest. None is wide enough nor deep enough, none vital enough to capture the reality of teaching as I know it and as I've known it for decades. But more than this, none of these images of teaching goes directly to the heart of the experience—to the intellectual demand, to the ethical purpose or moral meaning, to the larger spirit that can animate the enterprise. What they lack, even the benign and the liberal, is a sense of teaching as a relentlessly moral endeavor—teaching as ethical action.

Pursuing the Full Measure of Humanity

W. E. B. Du Bois, Hilda Taba, and Myra Sadker remind us of the heart of teaching. Each tried to make sense of the world as he or she found it, each faced reality with eyes wide open, and each insisted on struggling toward a fairer, fuller, more just and humane future for all people. Each kept faith with a particularly precious ideal—one that is simple to say but excruciatingly difficult to enact. That ideal is the belief that education, at its best, is an enterprise geared toward humanization. That's it. Education, at its foundational core, encourages our humanity; it allows each of us to become more fully and self-consciously human; it embraces as principle and overarching purpose the aspiration that people pursue the full measure of their humanity, that human life lurches toward enlightenment and liberation. In Paulo Freire's cosmology, this precious, humanistic ideal is an expression of our true vocation, which he calls the task of humanization.

Simple to say, but alive with tension, conflict, and contradiction. For identifying humanization as a goal immediately suggests an opposing recognition: dehumanization as both possibility and practice. It is these quarreling twins, finally, that make holding on to the ideal difficult, grinding, often contentious and sometimes courageous work. This is true in every epoch; it is a fresh challenge faced by each generation, the particulars and details of resistance and affirmation, absorption, accommodation, and contention, strategy and tactics, worked out each time anew. Of course, there is a particular intensity to the challenge when the humanistic ideal suffers a steady and sustained attack, a withering barrage, as now.

Inducting the Young into the World of the Ethical

Recognizing this ideal, noting that it is in dispute, and aware of what, finally, is at stake, we are thrust into the world of the ethical.

Education involves inducting the young into a world, a social order. For this reason alone, educators must keep their eyes wide open. What is the existing social order? How do we warrant, defend, or justify the world as it is? What alternatives are possible?

Classroom teachers—while they may be guided by some universal code or abstract form—soon realize that classroom ethics is a down-to-earth, rough-and-tumble, practical affair worked out on the ground by ordinary people. Universals may help (love your neighbor; don't lie or steal), and nourishing a moral imagination (how does the other person feel?) is surely a good idea. But neither of these is sufficient to settle every possible issue for all time. "Theory is gray," Goethe said, "and green the golden tree of life." Moral decision-making always involves fundamental choices; that is, choices in which no system or rule or guru can deliver the answer, none can be made into the court of last resort. Because we are free, our moral reasoning and our ethical decisions are lonely, often intuitive, filled with despair, and, finally, courage.

These three portraits remind us that education is always *for* something, and *against* something else. Education is never neutral. At the deepest, most fundamental level, education stands either for freedom and liberation, for enlightenment and empowerment, or for subjugation in one of its seemingly endless forms—sugar-coated domestication, brutal suppression, subservience, dependence, capitulation.

This is not difficult to see in the extreme. Under totalitarianism, the curriculum is mostly propaganda, the educational experience in large part indoctrination. A hallmark of propaganda is that it is in the service of orthodoxy, always top-down, never answerable. It is designed to manipulate and control, to induce a dull nod of acquiescence if not approval rather than a critical or considered response; it is to be consumed rather than engaged. Propaganda, as George Orwell argued, "is designed to make lies sound truthful and murder respectable."

Schools in these settings necessarily teach lessons in obedience and conformity, in rule-following, in power and hierarchy. The goal is compliant citizens rather than free thinkers or moral people. This doesn't mean necessarily producing people who lack skills or energy (both Nazi Germany and Soviet Russia turned out brilliant doctors and scientists), but it does mean a system twisted toward mystification, obsessed with control.

The Downward Spiral: Reducing Human Beings to Things

In *After*, her dystopic novel focused on the fallout at a high school in western Massachusetts following a tragic school shooting 50 miles away, Francine Prose draws a chilling portrait of a particular kind of teacher at work. The newly hired "grief and crisis counselor," Dr. Henry Willner, is charged with helping the school "get back on track." The teenaged narrator points out that the shooting happened elsewhere, that the school wasn't particularly off-track as far as he could see. The counselor is also to "work in the trenches with high school kids in crisis." I myself worry about the pervasiveness of the trenches metaphor, but here it is.

Dr. Willner wraps himself in the posture of compassion and concern, and he speaks the modern language of therapy and safety in a steady stream. At the assembly where he is first introduced to the school, he urges students to share their feelings in the interest of "healing and recovery," "working through grief and fear," and "becoming better people." Funny thing, notes the narrator, there doesn't seem to be a lot of grief and fear; but whatever. In this context, Dr. Willner announces, "it is a virtual certainty that some of the privileges that we have all enjoyed may have to be taken away."

On this ominous note the downward spiral begins, first on the familiar terrain of hastily installed metal detectors, random drug testing, and zero tolerance policies, all leading to increasing suspensions and expulsions. New rules are instituted, they change every day, and punishments are severe. More draconian measures inch inexorably forward, and the school begins to resemble a prison. Parents are seduced and wooed, step by step, mesmerized by a steady stream of frightening e-mails from Dr. Willner or coerced and cowed into compliance through face-to-face meetings in his office.

The worst is that Henry Willner is not the stranger we might wish him to be. Willner may be a caricature or a type, but he is not from outer space. There are Willners everywhere, and there may even be a taste of Willner in each of us. This, in the end, is what makes him both fascinating and useful. He is the fully realized authoritarian teacher, and he shows us schooling as it has been and could be, and in some places, as it is today. Human beings are reduced to things, and "thingification" turns everyone into an object for use. Nothing has value in itself or for itself. Here is the classroom as slave galley—the task of the teacher is simply to beat the drum.

Choosing a Life of Resistance and Activism

From the perspective of a democratic society, in the spirit of teaching for life in a democracy, the authoritarian approach is simply wrong; that is, it is immoral. A functioning, vital democracy requires, in the first place, active thinking citizens. It needs participation, some tolerance and acceptance of difference, some spirit of mutuality—a sense that we are all in this boat together, and we'd better start rowing. In a democracy, ordinary people are expected to make the big decisions that affect their lives, and education is designed to empower and enable. Education is characterized, fundamentally, by dialogue—the act of naming, of speaking, with the possibility of being heard and of changing others, combined with the act of attending, of listening, with the possibility of being changed, of renaming, of achieving something new.

W. E. B. Du Bois, Hilda Taba, and Myra Sadker show us democratic educators in action. Powered by hope, nourished by love, each chose a life of resistance and activism on behalf of an expansive, generous view of human possibilities.

Editors and Contributors

Editors

Sherry L. Field, Professor of Social Science Education at The University of Texas at Austin, instructs elementary social studies methodology at the undergraduate and graduate levels and is Director of Practicum Experiences for elementary preservice teachers. She is editor of *Social Studies and the Young Learner* (National Council for the Social Studies). She serves as Vice President on Kappa Delta Pi's Executive Council and has held leadership roles in the Society for the Study of Curriculum History, the National Council for the Social Studies, and the American Education Research Association. Her awards include Outstanding Social Studies Educator Award from the Georgia Council for the Social Studies and Carl Glickman Faculty Fellow Award from the University of Georgia. She has published numerous books, chapters, and journal articles.

Michael J. Berson is Associate Professor of social science education at the University of South Florida in Tampa and coordinator of the doctoral program in social studies education. He instructs elementary social studies methodology at the undergraduate and graduate levels and courses on technology in the social studies. An active member of Kappa Delta Pi, he has held leadership positions in the College and University Faculty Assembly of the National Council for the Social Studies and the Society for Information Technology & Teacher Education. He has published extensively in books and journals, and has presented his research on global child advocacy and technology in social studies education worldwide. He has received the Association of Educational Publishers Distinguished Achievement Award in the Learned Article category.

Contributors

Michael P. Wolfe is Executive Director of Kappa Delta Pi, International Honor Society in Education. He is a former university professor and administrator in teacher education and has authored numerous journal articles and books. His research interests include school reform, creating a positive school climate, enhancing self-concept, and teacher-induction practices. He has coauthored books such as *Life Cycle of the Career Teacher, The Mission of the Scholar,* and *Critical Incidents in School Administration.*

J. Wesley Null, a former public school social studies and science teacher in New Mexico and Texas, completed his doctoral degree at The University of Texas at Austin, where he studied the history of education and curriculum. He now serves as an Assistant Professor in the School of Education at Baylor University in Waco, Texas, where he teaches interdisciplinary courses in the University's core curriculum as well as Educational Studies and Curriculum in the School of Education.

Lynn Matthew Burlbaw received his doctoral degree from the University of Texas at Austin and teaches at Texas A&M University. His teaching interests are social studies education, history of education, and curriculum development. His research interests are education history, history of schools in Texas during the Depression, teacher education in the turn of the 19th–20th century, and social studies learning. He has been published in *Social Studies, Social Education,* and *Journal of Curriculum and Supervision.*

Daniel W. Stuckart is a Ph.D. candidate at the University of South Florida and a history teacher at Robinson High School in Tampa, Florida. His research interests include the integration of computer technologies with history, specifically the effects of computer-enhanced historical documents on student thinking. He is coauthor of "Promise and Practice of Computer Technologies in the Social Studies: A Critical Analysis" (in *Critical Issues in Social Studies Research for the 21st Century* 2001).

Rose A. Rudnitski, Associate Professor of education at SUNY New Paltz, earned her doctorate in curriculum and teaching at Teachers College, Columbia University. She served on NCTE and AERA committees dealing with intolerance and human rights, and has written on addressing intolerance in the classroom, as well as on Leta Hollingworth and Patti Smith Hill. She was a Hackman Fellow at the New York State Archives, where she studied public education of American Indians.

Elizabeth Anne Yeager is Associate Professor of social studies education and secondary education coordinator at the University of Florida in Gainesville. She earned her doctoral degree in curriculum and instruction from The University of Texas at Austin. For her dissertation on Alice Miel, she received the Outstanding Dissertation Award from AERA's Division B, ASCD, and the Society for the Study of Curriculum History. She currently serves as editor of *Theory and Research in Social Education.*

Derrick P. Alridge is Associate Professor of social foundations of education at the University of Georgia. His work has been widely published in journals such as *Educational Theory, The Journal of Negro Education,* and *The Journal of African American History* (formerly *The Journal of Negro History*). He currently is writing *The Educational Thought of W. E. B. Du Bois: An Intellectual History* for Teachers College Press.

Mark Isham grew up in Albert Lea, Minnesota, and he received his bachelor's degree from Bemidji State College and his doctoral degree from the University of Texas at Austin. He currently teaches education foundations and secondary education courses at Eastern New Mexico University. His major professor and mentor at the University of Texas, O. L. Davis, Jr., kindled his interest in the life and work of Hilda Taba.

David M. Sadker is a Professor at The American University in Washington, D.C. He and his late wife Myra Sadker achieved a national reputation for their work in confronting gender bias. They received American Educational Research Association awards for the best review of research (1991) and professional service (1995), and the Eleanor Roosevelt Award from the American Association of University Women (1995). The Sadkers coauthored five books, including *Teachers, Schools, and Society* (2003).

Kappa Delta Pi Laureates

O. L. Davis, Jr. is the Catherine Mae Parker Centennial Professor of Curriculum and Instruction, The University of Texas at Austin. He is a major figure in the growth of curriculum and the history of education as areas of research. His research interests include social studies education, curriculum history, and oral history. Dr. Davis's leadership in the field of curriculum led the American Educational Research Association to bestow on him its Lifetime Achievement Award in 1996. A former President of Kappa Delta Pi (1980–1982), he is also a member of that Society's Laureate Chapter (inducted in 1994).

Bettye M. Caldwell, Professor of Education at the University of Arkansas at Little Rock and Director of the Center for Early Development and Education, has worked in the development of early childhood programs in the United States and around the world for many years. Her work played a major part in the creation of Head Start, and she has been at the forefront of research on the influence of the home environment on child development. Dr. Caldwell was inducted into the Laureate Chapter of Kappa Delta Pi in 1978.

William Ayers, Distinguished Professor of Education and Senior University Scholar at the University of Illinois at Chicago, is a school reform activist. His interests focus on the political and cultural contexts of schooling, the challenges young people face in the modern world, and the meaning and ethical purposes of teachers, students, and families. He is the founder of the Center for Youth and Society and founder and codirector of the Small Schools Workshop, both projects to improve the state of learning for urban youth. Dr. Ayers was inducted into the Laureate Chapter of Kappa Delta Pi in 2000.

EXPERIENCE AND EDUCATION:
The 60th Anniversary Edition

"John Dewey has had a truly extraordinary impact upon educational and philosophical thinking, and this volume stands among the three or four most important books published in this century. That Kappa Delta Pi has chosen to issue a beautiful, enriched anniversary edition is wonderful news for all educators. Readers should rush to their telephones to obtain copies for themselves and as gifts that will be much appreciated.

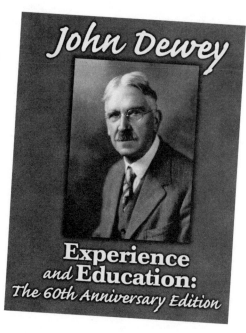

"The book was only eight years old when I first read it, and its brilliant message has guided and inspired me for more than a half century. Seeing this elegant new production of it has been a special experience for me. The new volume includes four exceptional commentaries by Maxine Greene, Philip W. Jackson, Linda Darling-Hammond, and O. L. Davis Jr. It deserves extensive use in university courses, graduate seminars, and educational assemblies."

—Robert H. Anderson
Professor and Dean Emeritus, College of Education, Texas Tech University
President, Pedamorphosis, Inc.
Counselor, Kappa Delta Pi Laureate Chapter

To order your copy call **1-800-284-3167** *or order online at www.kdp.org.*

Cloth $26 (order # 520) • Paper $18 (order # 521)

(KDP Member Prices $20 and $12)

Prices do not include shipping and handling; quantity discounts are available.

TLBT03AD-DEW

Life Cycle of the Career Teacher

Kappa Delta Pi has assembled a team of dedicated educators to study the nature of teaching as individuals progress through the phases of the profession—and enlisted the help of one of the finest publishers in the field, Corwin Press, to help spread the word. Authors examine novice, apprentice, professional, expert, distinguished, and emeritus phases, analyzing developments in skill, vision, and collaboration. They also discuss risks of withdrawal and means of professional growth for each phase.

Contributors include:

Michael Berson
Jane Bray
Rick Breault
Ruth Campopiano
Mary Clement
Ray Dagenais
Billie J. Enz
Pamela Kramer
Denise LePage
John Maddaus

Vincent McGrath
Diane Murphy
Suzanne Pasch
George Pawlas
Patricia Phelps
Betty Steffy
Kathy Weber
Michael Wolfe
Polly Wolfe

Nonmembers should order directly from Corwin Press, 1-805-499-9734 or *www.corwinpress.com*. List price is $22.95 plus shipping and handling.

KDP members can call us at 1-800-284-3167 or visit KDP Online at *www.kdp.org* to order this great resource for just $15 plus shipping and handling.

Quantity discounts apply. KDP order code 531.

Life Cycle of the Career Teacher will shape educational thinking and professional development for years to come. Order your copy now!